THE SPIRITUAL MEDICINE OF TIBET

THE
SPIRITUAL
MEDICINE
of TIBET

Heal Your Spirit, Heal Yourself

Dr Pema Dorjee with Janet Jones and Terence Moore

Foreword by His Holiness the Dalai Lama

WATKINS PUBLISHING
LONDON

This edition published in the UK 2005 by
Watkins Publishing, Sixth Floor, Castle House, 75-76 Wells Street,
London W1T 3QH
Distributed in USA and Canada by Publishers Group West

1 3 5 7 9 10 8 6 4 2

Designed and typeset by Jerry Goldie

Printed and bound in Great Britain

Library of Congress Cataloging in Publication data available

ISBN 1 84293 164 4

www.watkinspublishing.com

Contents

Part One:
Encounters with Extraordinary Physicians of Tibet

Part Two:
The Basic Concepts of Tibetan Buddhist Medicine

List of Plates

The publisher would like to thank the following people, museums, and photographic libraries for permission to reproduce their material. Every care has been taken to trace copyright holders. However, if we have omitted anyone we apologize and will, if informed, make corrections to any future edition.

All photographs by Lynette Howells except the following:

Dr Pema Dorjee and Dr Tenzin Choedrak – Photograph by Men-Tsee-Khang
Dr Pema Dorjee and Guru Professor Barshi Phuntsok Wangyal – Photograph by Men-Tsee-Khang
Dr Yeshi Dhonden – Photograph by Men-Tsee-Khang
Dr Yeshi Dhonden taking a pulse – Photograph by Men-Tsee-Khang

His Holiness the Dalai Lama with Dr Pema Dorjee – Photograph reproduced with the permission of the Office of His Holiness the Dalai Lama.

Dedication

To Janet,
whose flame of inspiration
created this book and carried it
to its completion.

Acknowledgements

Dr Pema Dorjee:

My heartfelt prostrations go to the feet of His Holiness the Dalai Lama, Tenzin Gyatso.

I also wish to thank all my teachers for their guidance, support, training and oral instructions, in particular Professor Barshi Phuntsok Wangyal and Dr Yeshi Dhonden. My thanks also go to my wife, Dr Yeshi Khando, for her support and inspiration in all my writing, and to my daughters, who are also medical students, Tenzin Yangkyi and Tenzin Choeying for reading through and helping with the basic language of this manuscript.

Thanks are due also to Dr Jampa Sonam (Lhawang la), Mr Gyatso Tsering, former Director of the Tibetan Library in Dharamsala; Mr Thinley Woser, former Secretary of Men-Tsee-Khang; Mr Thupten Wangyal, my brother-in-law; Jaya Mashewari (my Indian sister who greatly assists in the promotion of Tibetan Medicine); Mr Tashi Ghanpa; Mr Tsering Phuntsok and Mrs Chuni Tsomo. My brothers and sisters have been a source of great encouragement and inspiration in all my writing.

I also wish to thank my two co-authors, Janet Jones and Terence Moore, together with the participation of Lynette Howells, for without their efforts, it would not have been possible to materialise this book.

Janet Jones & Terence Moore:

Our deepest gratitude flows to Mrs Irina Tweedie, whose Infinite Love, Absolute Truth and Uncompromising Luminosity constantly led us to find that in us which resonated with the very highest principles of human experience.

We would like to thank His Holiness the Fourteenth Dalai Lama, for his tireless work in preserving the cultural heritage of Tibet, for increasingly disseminating the message of Tibetan Buddhism and for ensuring the creation and ongoing development of Men-Tsee-Khang – the Tibetan Medical and Astrological Institute.

We wish to thank Dr Tenzin Choedrak and the Venerable Doctor Trogawa Rinpoche, Dr Pema Dorjee and Dr Tsewang Tamdin for the various consultations and lectures we have been privileged to attend.

We wish to give special thanks to all those who helped with this book, in particular Michael Mann for having the vision to recommend it for publishing and Florence Hamilton for her most supportive work as editor.

Finally, we wish to thank Lynette Howells for her unceasing love, support, dedication and contribution to the writing, photography and overall approach to the book.

THE DALAI LAMA

FOREWORD

Tibetan medicine is one of the greatest legacies of Tibetan Buddhist civilization. It is a system that can contribute substantially to maintaining a healthy mind and a healthy body. Like the traditional systems of our neighbours India and China, Tibetan medicine views health as a question of balance. A variety of circumstances such as diet, lifestyle, seasonal and mental conditions can disturb this natural balance, which gives rise to different kinds of disorders.

This refined medical knowledge, combined with an understanding of the inner workings of the mind derived from the practice of Buddhism, makes this a complex system uniquely bringing together physical, mental and spiritual approaches to health. As an integrated system of health care Tibetan medicine has served the Tibetan people well for more than a thousand years and I believe can still provide much benefit to humanity at large. The difficulty we face in bringing this about is one of communication, for, like other scientific systems, Tibetan medicine must be understood in its own terms, as well as in the context of objective investigation.

This book presents an introduction to the subject from two distinct points of view. In the first part, Janet Jones, a psychotherapist and herself a medical professional, recounts her own and other people's vivid personal experience of Tibetan medicine and two of its recent preeminent practitioners, Dr. Tenzin Chodrak and Ven. Dr. Trogawa Rinpoche. The latter part of the book consists of a more technical explanation of Tibetan medical principles by Dr. Pema Dorjee, a well-qualified Tibetan physician, who, having trained in exile, combines deep understanding and practice of our traditions with an appreciation of the modern world and an ability to express himself in English. Terence Moore has encouraged and collaborated with them both. I feel confident that these combined talents have produced a book that will be both attractive and helpful to students of Tibetan medicine, while also providing an opportunity for general readers to better appreciate this valuable but sometimes overlooked aspect of the Tibetan cultural heritage.

March 26, 2005

Introduction

*I*N A WORLD which is constantly in a state of flux, where mankind struggles to maintain some kind of balance in the face of increasing change, dramatic upheaval, global conflict, environmental catastrophe and developing illnesses, Tibetan medicine has emerged upon the world stage as an ancient medical system dedicated to offering hope and health to humanity. For 2,500 years this profound, Buddhist medical system was developed on the roof of the world within the protected land of snows, Tibet, maintaining its pristine condition as a pure gem of healing. Through the teachings of Lord Buddha, revelations from the heavens, and the absolute dedication of masterly physicians across millennia, this multifaceted crystal was formed to perfection as a pure spiritual science with the aim of healing all sentient beings.

With the invasion of Tibet in 1950 by China, the pearls of our immensely rich cultural heritage were rudely prised from their position of protection and cast out into the world at large. Narrowly escaping complete destruction at the hands of the ignorant, the jewels of Tibet were drawn back together upon the pure thread of compassion by His Holiness the Dalai Lama, whose indomitable spirit tirelessly worked to establish Tibet in Exile within the tiny hill station of Dharamsala in Northern India. As Tibetans fleeing from our native land which had been crushed under the feet of brute oppression, those of us who were fortunate enough to escape began to regroup around His Holiness as our spiritual and political leader.

Yet the measure of man is what he manages to achieve when his back is to the wall. His Holiness inspired us to rise to the occasion of imminent demise and use it as a spiritual springboard to even higher attainments. Our own ancient texts had already predicted the invasion of Tibet, the near annihilation of our culture and the forcing of the relatively few escapees into the wider world. These same prophecies also predicted that the jewels of our Eastern culture would, through these difficult and dangerous circumstances, emerge at last triumphantly into the West for the edification and evolution of mankind.

Within a relatively short space of time we have succeeded not only in preserving our 2,500-year-old culture in its original form but have increasingly disseminated the Tibetan Buddhist teachings across the wider world. As Tibetan physicians, our constant aim is to serve the Buddha of Compassion through an essentially selfless dedication to the alleviation of suffering wherever and in whomever it may manifest. In a very real sense, when we were forced to leave our homeland, we became the spiritual nomads of the modern world. Imbued with a powerful sense of karma, believing that all our experiences are subject to the simple laws of cause and effect, we have accepted our circumstances with inner determination through the maintenance of the all-important peace of mind.

With His Holiness at the helm, Men-Tsee-Khang, the Tibetan Medical and Astrological Institute of His Holiness the Dalai Lama continues to steer a guided path across the often troubled waters of modern times. As Tibetan doctors we are called to various parts of the globe, as the world at large becomes increasingly aware of the remarkable success rate of our medical tradition. Indeed, our ancient system of medicine has much to offer and we enthusiastically enter into dialogue with physicians from all other traditions, including Western medicine, believing that the way forward for mankind can only be through a process of sharing, integration and mutual understanding.

As a Tibetan doctor practising for over thirty years, I consider myself extremely fortunate to have received invitations to practise medicine, lecture and attend medical conferences in various parts of the world, including India, France, Spain, Bulgaria, Israel, Norway, the Netherlands, Germany, the United States of America and the United Kingdom. In 1998 I was invited to offer consultations and give a lecture on Tibetan medicine in northwest London at the Kailash Centre of Oriental Medicine. On 13th October I delivered the lecture, entitled 'Stress, Anxiety and Depression' to an enthusiastic audience of Westerners. The lecture aimed to 'ground' one of the three fundamental 'energies' in the body, according to Tibetan medicine, in the modern Western world with its current concerns around the increase of stress, anxiety and depression.

The lecture was warmly received and afterwards many of the audience came forward to ask questions, discuss particular aspects of the lecture or request a medical consultation. The two co-authors of this book, Janet Jones and Terence Moore, together with Lynette Howells were amongst those who approached me. Janet, who is a psychotherapist, told me that she was particularly inspired to hear such a completely different approach to healing ailments which she had inevitably encountered within her practice, and which at that time were clearly the predominant complaints of the majority of her patients. Accordingly, she referred many of her patients and friends to me for medical consultations. Happily, the consultations proved to be extremely successful, and many patients experienced quite dramatic, almost immediate changes in their condition.

Janet, Terence and Lynette also discussed with me the formulation and particular presentation of a transcribed version of the lecture for the public, which was worked upon over the remainder of the year and officially launched on the occasion of His Holiness the Dalai Lama's visit to London in 1999. This concise and inspirational booklet, which aimed to open the mind to a new way of looking at our modern stresses and strains, was a great success. Indeed, at its launch in the Wembley Conference Centre the response was quite astonishing, as visitors from all over the world were almost magnetically drawn to it, and actually stopped to read it there and then. It was a deliberately lightweight document, yet such was the interest shown, that several hundred copies were distributed in a short space of time. Clearly it resonated with many people, and young students in particular were attracted. Since then it has been distributed in various parts of the world, often in tandem with my own visits to offer medical consultations.

As the new millennium drew near, Janet Jones approached me with a proposal and initial draft of a much deeper exposition of Tibetan medicine, which she had been motivated to produce following the level of interest activated by the first publication. Janet had been inspired by Tibetan medicine for many years and had received direct experience of its miraculous effects in Switzerland during a spiritual festival called the Rainbow Festival, held in Interlaken in July 1985. However, increasingly over the years she had discovered that whenever she told people about her experiences of Tibetan Medicine, and how successful it was in healing many of the diseases which Western medicine struggles to treat, it was not at all easy to give people a reference point from which to understand such a profoundly different approach to healing. Janet had a growing desire to somehow find a way of inspiring ordinary people to sample this wonderful system of medicine, as it seemed so clear to her that the modern world was crying out for some relief, which Tibetan medicine could offer.

I agreed to work with Janet and Terence on the book, and over the next four years it began to take shape. During this time I returned to London on three more occasions to offer consultations and deliver three subsequent lectures on different aspects of Tibetan medicine. Each of my visits naturally offered further opportunities for detailed collaboration on the book, until in 2004 it reached a publishable stage.

Heal Your Spirit, Heal Yourself – The Spiritual Medicine of Tibet is therefore a product of research and writing mainly over a period of five years. It is a spiritually-based book on Tibetan medicine, arising out of a desire for the wisdom of the ancient Tibetan medical system to be brought to the Western mind, and integrated as a system of immense subtlety and precision, where the work of the medical practitioner is inextricably embedded within an ancient and profound spiritual tradition.

The book deliberately combines Western insights into, and experiences of Tibetan medicine with my own Tibetan medical knowledge, training and experience. It falls into two clear parts. Within Part One, Janet Jones takes the reader on a journey of direct experiences by Westerners of two remarkable and renowned Tibetan doctors – Dr Tenzin Choedrak and the Venerable Dr Trogawa Rinpoche. Whilst recounting experiences of lectures and consultations with these doctors, this section imparts much precise information on the history, philosophy, nature and healing qualities of Tibetan medicine, whilst drawing out comparisons with Western traditions. Particular emphasis is given within this section, and indeed the book as a whole, to the spiritual aspect of the Tibetan medical system, which is naturally steeped in Tibetan Buddhism, and aims to heal spiritual, mental, physical and emotional diseases, with very positive results.

The reader is transported initially to a conference in Switzerland, called the Rainbow Festival, which draws together various spiritual traditions, and where Janet and Terence had their first encounter with Dr Tenzin Choedrak. At the time of this festival, Dr Choedrak had only recently emerged from twenty years of torture and suffering in Tibet at the hands of the Chinese, to be reinstated in India as the personal physician to the Dalai Lama. After recounting the transformative experience and powerful impact of this doctor's lecture and consultation, the reader is also given the experience of the closing of the conference by His Holiness the Dalai Lama.

Returning to London, Janet attended a lecture by the Venerable Dr Trogawa Rinpoche, who brought to the London Wellcome Institute a lecture on the Tibetan understanding of the process of death and rebirth. The Rinpoche is among the most highly respected practitioners of Tibetan medicine and one of the few living Masters fully trained in the Chagpori lineage, known for its unique tradition of combining medicine and spirituality. Part One concludes with a description of a Medicine Buddha Empowerment Ceremony.

Part Two is my own precise and informative introduction to the basic concepts of Tibetan medicine. This section is naturally a more textual description of the workings of the Tibetan medical system, whilst assisting the Western reader with insights and gateways to understanding, where necessary. Each chapter ends with a practical exercise or guidance from which the reader can benefit. I have also included case studies to show how people have been helped. With the aim of bringing Tibetan medicine into the Western arena, both parts of the book contain some cross-fertilization of ideas, concepts and shared knowledge. Thus Part One, whilst focusing on the experiential side of Tibetan medicine, contains much precise medical information, whilst Part Two introduces some Western insights and comparisons in order to assist the reader towards an understanding of the detailed textual information. With regard to the use of language throughout the book, italicized terms indicate not only Tibetan words, but also Sanskrit. This is because Buddhism was originally taken to Tibet from India, so much of the teachings and terminology are given in Sanskrit to maintain connection with the tradition. Teachings may also be given with parts of the mantras in Sanskrit, parts in Tibetan.

Tibetan medicine is a spiritual medical system based on the fundamental laws of the universe. As such it essentially reflects the workings of nature which apply to everything and everyone across the planet. At its very heart is the essential need for balance, harmony and a natural process of exchange, of giving and receiving. This Buddhist system and pure science which stresses the indivisible interdependence of mind, body and vitality has been transmitted to numerous inspired Tibetan physicians by various means. Some of the knowledge was received through the direct teachings of Buddha, the Supreme Healer. This was supplemented by extraordinary revelations to enlightened individuals by particular deities through the medium of visions, dreams and meditations. Exchanges with doctors from neighbouring countries further enriched the tradition which steadily developed into a most comprehensive, profound, holistic approach to the human condition.

On a very simple level, Tibetan medicine has always been perfectly attuned to the natural rise and fall of primordial daily existence, respecting the need for balance between the opposites. For if we only ever experienced sunlight, then the heat of the sun would cause our bodies to burn. This is the solar power given for the purpose of warming the body, which needs its opposite, the lunar power at night-time to increase the cold energy in the body and cool us down. The cyclical nature of the seasons similarly play their part in a round of elements and energies, one season developing into the other through heat, cold, wet, etc., all having a powerful effect upon our bodies. Indeed, the macrocosm will always affect the microcosm and as Tibetan physicians we are trained to look at the body in the context of the immediate environment when approaching a precise diagnosis of a manifesting disease.

Today, we are unfortunately experiencing immense disruption in the seasonal changes across the whole of the earth with catastrophic results, as floods, famines, environmental eruptions and disruptions of various kinds appear to beset us. These radical changes within the climate result in immense suffering as humanity wonders what is actually causing the problem. Modern environmental science has pointed towards the answer, exposing the very real effects of our personal actions by warning of the dangers of pollution and the subsequent reduction in the ozone layer. What this forces us to accept is that we are intricately bound up with the forces of nature to the extent that any abuse of ourselves is an abuse of nature and we will certainly reap what we have sown.

So rather than bewail the seasons and cataclysmic events which affect our lives, we might do well to rise to a more enlightened view of the modern world, as that which is not simply thrust upon us as something we must suffer but rather an experience we chose to enter and within which we all share a tremendous responsibility. We are each a microcosm within a macrocosm, and must accept that our modern approach to life has brought tremendous imbalance to our planet. This imbalance in nature is now causing real problems, including the onset of new diseases directly linked to our abuse of the environment.

So we should pay careful attention to the modern problems of deforestation, pollution, and extraction from mines. Nature has given everything for us. If we spoil these gifts, we will suffer. For instance, a person may have a lot of sandalwood, which is an extremely efficacious herb, but seeing that everyone else is selling charcoal, and making money, he burns the sandalwood to make charcoal, so that he too can sell it. Today we are witnessing a scarcity of healing herbs and minerals, due to such abuse of nature.

The earth is in fact being gradually plundered of its vital essences such as oil through deforestation, water and air through pollution and minerals through excessive mining, so much so that we are now immersed in a form of global suicide which must at all costs be halted. Modern science has in many ways advanced to an extraordinary degree, yet we still persist in a basic form of ignorance which lies at the root of our suffering and results in comprehensive blindness. Our task is to reach deep into our inner truth, our inner being and realize our inherent better nature. For within us all there is a marvellous structure and form, exquisite and perfect, presenting unparalleled constancy and integrity, capable of maintaining a balance of internal order as part of the universal plan.

The Tibetan medical system offers us an opportunity to more fully understand our blinkered human condition, by pointing to three root causes of not only our own illnesses, but also the current global disease. These three 'poisons', as termed in Tibetan medicine, are desire, hatred or anger, and closed-mindedness, and are directly linked to the three fundamental energies or vital forces in the body, translated as wind, bile and phlegm. In essence, Tibetan medicine identifies the imbalance of these energies and seeks to restore balance through dietary and behavioural advice, together with medicines and various therapies.

However, at the apex of the human condition, with the power to move each one of us in completely the wrong direction is, of course, the mind. The Tibetan Buddhist system continually points to the mind as the single most potent destroyer and calls upon us to make some attempt to still or at least curtail its often virulent and fickle nature, or suffer the consequences. In this sense, humanity truly needs to be saved from its own ambition and greed, its need to expand and control, its need for power at the expense of others, whilst needlessly poisoning and destroying the environment and thereby itself.

Each one of us can help to reverse this worsening situation by simply beginning with ourselves. For we are closer to the earth than we realize, even closer than to our own jugular vein and thereby have real potential to spread goodness, a sense of caring, compassion and the need for harmony and balance to others and to the wider environment. We do not exist in isolation but remain interdependent and inextricably connected with all other forms of life across the earth, the planets, the solar system, the limitless universe. Through diligent work upon the need for balance in our own body system we can become a positive force for the good of mankind.

It is the fervent, shared hope of the three co-authors that this book may in some small way serve humanity at this difficult time and offer a gateway to understanding the ancient spiritual healing system of Tibet, not only as a means of healing oneself, but more importantly as a way to truly help to heal the wounded heart of the world.

Dr Pema Dorjee

Part One

Encounters with Extraordinary Physicians of Tibet

1

The Rainbow Festival

*T*HE RAINBOW HAS ALWAYS been such a hopeful image for my soul. Whenever life seems bleak and rain-filled skies compound this feeling, the brilliance of a sudden rainbow, arched across the heavens like a bridge to other worlds, restores my spirit.

I remember one occasion when, seeking solace in retreat, two of my dearest friends and I ventured out of London deep into the countryside to find a different kind of life. Yet the weather seemed to conspire against us. The rain came pouring down and the house where we had hoped to spend time in retreat grew cold and wet as water came oozing through the walls.

We realized the move was not to be, and promptly took our sodden, sad belongings to the van parked behind the house, intending to drive back to London immediately. As we stepped out into the autumn afternoon, a glorious double-rainbow spread across the dark horizon, like a chord of exquisite harmony which gave us instantly a warmth, a light within our hearts, and tears sprang into our eyes. We stood together silently like three saluting sentinels in gratitude for this restoring vision of a future waiting for us somewhere as yet undiscovered.

So when my spiritual teacher told me one year later, in the summer of 1985, that she'd been invited to give lectures at a conference called the Rainbow Festival, instinctively my inner being leapt for joy. This festival in Interlaken, Switzerland, uniquely sought to bring together spiritual traditions from around the world. These ancient streams or paths to God, to Buddha, to the Absolute were meeting under one roof in a conference. Like a cosmic wheel of many spokes, this festival drew spiritual teachers here to represent their own tradition. Native Americans, Tibetan Buddhists, Sufis, Jews, Zen Japanese – like colours of the rainbow all had been invited here to harmonize and shine a sign of hope for everyone, a rainbow stretched across the universe.

My spiritual guide, who had received a powerful training at the hands of a great Sufi Master, would journey there to represent the Sufi tradition at this festival and asked me to take on the task of arranging flights and accommodation, to include the members of her group whom she'd invited to come with her and enter into the spirit of this conference. As just one humble member of her spiritual group, I saw it as my solemn duty to prepare and organize the base camp for our great ascent of all that is most spiritual, to culminate symbolically in climbing to the very top of the Jungfrau, the highest peak in Switzerland, our chosen Everest. No-one could understand the depth of all my preparations. For I planned a celebration, journey and a great adventure, bravely going far beyond our wildest dreams into the great unknown.

It was as if my life up to this moment was a preparation for this trip, with me a player behind the scenes, the organizer of our dreams. In this endeavour, the sacred journey to the Rainbow Festival, I marvelled at the thought of heavenly energies and forces raging over just the spot where this unusual festival would soon be held, within the Alps of Switzerland, right at the foot of the Jungfrau. I felt myself a vital part, merged with the constant circulation of these powerful energies and forces making up the seven colours of the sacred rainbow. Every atom in the universe inevitably fell within the influence of one or more of these seven rays. I saw each member of the group as part of this great sacred palette, entwined together in the ever-changing kaleidoscope of life.

Just as a rainbow brightens up a darkened sky, so I believed the inner light of every member of our team glowed as a powerful star of hope in the spiritual darkness of the world. The task before us seemed to be embodied in the highlight of our trip. Our spiritual guide had emphasized that all of us must together scale the Jungfrau. Her inner prompting had produced this outer symbol of the path of peace, the path of hope.

How powerful is the mind

Meanwhile, before I had even left London, shopping with one week to go, I found myself brought to an inner standstill as I gazed upon a parking ticket rudely stuck behind the windscreen wiper of my car. Guilt and shame came flooding in, followed by acute dismay, anger and pride. Just how on earth could such a dreadful thing have happened? For filled up to the brim with an adventure yet-to-be, only seconds earlier I had been upon cloud nine and searching here and there for climbing boots, the footwear that my teacher had so strongly indicated was absolutely necessary for our climb.

My great respect for all that is unseen, the powerful world of the unconscious, which reveals itself through symbols and through signs would not allow me to ignore this rather painful, brief experience. Significantly, it had come just at the point where I was in preparation for a climb which symbolized for me the highest spiritual aspiration. My mind debated restlessly the reasons why this portent had appeared, but with a tired sigh of resignation to my fate, I rashly threw the thought of climbing boots aside, for something clearly was not quite in place. I felt I might be better buying boots in Switzerland, amongst the snowy mountains; surely there I'd find the best. I started up the car and left the scene behind, but took this omen as a warning that this journey soon to be was not quite as I envisaged. My mind was on alert and, like a cat before the mouse, I watched so carefully my every move, in order to discover where my fault lay hidden. In this way my wondrous journey to Shangri-la became plagued by obstacles as my mind was sucked into a vortex of anxiety.

How powerful is the mind. It has the power to turn us on and switch us off. The fickle populace of thoughts inside are turned within an instant by the clever words of oratory proclamations of the mind. Where can we find relief? I wondered if the force of destiny would answer me. Perhaps this Rainbow Festival contained a key, and with that thought there came a breath of peace to soothe my mind and help me leave the parking fine behind.

The week flew past and after days of packing and re-packing, whilst finalizing every tiny detail of the trip for everyone, at last I heaved my heavy bags aboard the Gatwick Airport train and found the nearest front-facing seat. I set myself to looking forwards, let the past assume its rightful place, and focused on the coming climb, the expedition, journey on a spiritual quest to gain enlightenment in Switzerland. My Holy Grail was surely there, and waiting for me somewhere in this festival; symbolically it seemed to be in essence at the top of the Jungfrau. My spiritual teacher deep within my heart and soul was guiding me, so surely I would reach the top and fly the flag. How could I fail, with her strong grip upon my ropes?

So in this state of buoyancy, I let my mind scan through the lengthy checklist I'd compiled in order to ensure the swift removal of all obstacles that blocked our path. The tickets for the flight were set, all perfectly in order, and in finding good accommodation for each member of the group, I felt I'd put the world to rights. I'd managed brilliantly to book the Bear Hotel for almost all the party at a very reasonable price. Naively, I believed that everyone must be as overwhelmed as me at facing this great feat of climbing up together with our teacher to the top of the Jungfrau. My personal summit was to create a strong base camp, a place of inner harmony, a family atmosphere where all could feel secure within the womb of our great teacher's heart.

Tibetan Doctors in Switzerland

Feeling reassured that preparations were in place, I sat back in my seat and took the conference leaflet out to see what different traditions were assembling at the festival in Switzerland. My eyes were drawn to notice that some doctors from Tibet would be there, lecturing and leading seminars on Tibetan medicine. Something lifted in my heart and brought a glow into my soul. I'd been inspired by this great healing system back in my mid-twenties, at a spiritual healing conference in 1970, where I heard about miracles and wonders at the hands of physicians from Tibet. All of this was made more valid since the story was imparted by a Western doctor, who, whilst practising in Switzerland in a children's hospital, realized she'd contracted a cancer of the oesophagus. A colleague confirmed her fears and told her she would need an operation soon, within six months, to have the cancer surgically removed. She had no choice but to agree with his alarming diagnosis and elected to undergo the operation just as soon as possible.

Yet still her mind held out and hoped to find a healing miracle. So in her quest she then approached a doctor who practised Tibetan medicine and had immigrated recently to Switzerland. War-torn Tibet had been his home, now ravaged and destroyed by China. As a refugee he had escaped and been invited with so many others to reside in Switzerland. This simple doctor felt her pulse and offered her Tibetan herbs. She returned home and took the herbs and suddenly to her surprise felt energy rush through her body finally emerging at the apex of her head. This filled her with a certainty that all her cancer had been cured. Initially, she remained within this happy state, until arriving at the end of six months' waiting for an operation, suddenly the weight of all her training forced her to admit she should not just rely upon a cure that was so magical. She again approached her colleague with a view to surgery. Amazingly, upon conducting an examination to prepare for surgery, the x-rays clearly demonstrated that the cancer in her throat had gone. Comparing with previous x-rays it was clear that she had indeed been cured by something quite miraculous. This lady with a second life was jubilant and joyful. She infected everyone with ceaseless admiration for the wonders of this marvellous system from Tibet.

This extraordinary story had remained within my heart as an oasis in the commonplaceness of the spiritual desert in the West – the rigid, scientific mind – for it had touched me deep inside and sparked a longing to discover these great secrets from the ancient, inner sanctum of Tibet. This miracle defied the laws of nature and became a star of hope for me. My life was once more full of meaning. It set me free from modern bondage and gave me balm to heal my soul and lift my health. It opened up within my heart a wondrous vista with fantastic possibilities. And from that day on I had remained completely starry-eyed.

So vivid was this memory, it filled me with expectancy. Perhaps upon this trip I might connect again with wonders from Tibet. But for the time being, I focused on my shouldered task, to see that all of us arrived without a hitch. All went to plan and we arrived in Switzerland to find ourselves within the Bear Hotel, a beautiful example of picturesque accommodation. With great relief I dared to hope that all the unforeseen and karmic forces would now spare me from my sins, and not destroy my work, my selfless hopes for everyone. But registering the party at the conference proved to be the first of several painful episodes. For just as I strode up to see my teacher, wreathed in smiles and admiration, someone stepped right in front of me and proudly claimed to take upon himself my very role as organizer of the group. I was aghast and unprepared for this perceived usurper causing so much pain within my heart.

My gift of love could never now be seen, received or recognized, for love without conditions is so often trodden on, dismissed as foolish. So stumbling on as one of God's great fools, my heart already blighted, and reminded of the omen of the parking fine in London, all I found that I could do was distribute the registration tags admitting all into the Rainbow Festival, then gracefully withdraw. I knew at least I had attempted to provide a solid start for our task.

A Journey of Failure?

I focused forwards on the climb up the mountain, on finding nourishment of heart and soul within this Rainbow conference. But first I had to follow the instructions of my teacher and acquire the perfect shoes for this great climb into the clouds. I felt that in the end I'd timed this very well, to buy the perfect boots in the very home of mountaineers. This heady wish however was my sole conspirator. Desire for absolute perfection was my Nemesis, my downfall. For I suddenly discovered that there was to be no time for any shopping sprees. The morning, bright and early was to be the time to climb. No-one had even told me of this simple change of plan 'til far too late. Oh why did I not choose to buy my shoes before I came away? I went to bed and prayed that God might grant me just one wish: "One gift of perfect climbing boots beside my bed when I awake. Or let me never wake again."

The next morning on the mountain peak my punishment was all too clear, and in my face. My teacher was furious to see not even shoes, but open sandals on my frozen feet. No desert here to welcome such hot-weather footwear for the trek. My small attempt to satisfy the cold conditions were a pair of mountain socks I'd bought upon that fateful day in London. Yet somehow they only seemed to emphasize my foolish plight. The glassy ice and Alpine snow were sure to send me slithering back down again from every step I'd try to make towards the peak. I felt I'd let my teacher down. My plea of innocence that I had hoped to buy the boots in Switzerland was soon dismissed. I had not acted on her earnest wish, her inner orders. This was unforgivable, excuses not permissible.

My journey to the top of the Jungfrau was an ordeal that left me feeling wounded. My great pain about the sandals changed to fear when I drew closer to the peak, for all too clearly my slippery soles were actually quite dangerous. This was indeed a mountain of the finest kind, but such great mountains should command equivalent respect, for in an instant they can throw a climber down. Oh why did I not heed my teacher's point so basic and profound? That we must meet each spiritual venture with our feet on solid ground, prepared with all that rightly fits the task. That we must follow every word and not fly off to dizzy heights in heady pride, to throw such good advice aside. All this I'd done unwittingly yet now I suffered pitifully. To add to all my inner pain the outer group were laughing smugly at the stain upon my purity. Yet this was nothing to compare with all my inner, deep despair at failing her, my spiritual guide.

This journey she had offered as a rainbow bridge to help the world had turned for me into a journey of naiveté, of failure and embarrassment. A growing pain of isolation took its toll, and on returning to the Bear Hotel, I sensed the damage had been done, for whilst the group excitedly prepared to go along to join the festival, I felt alone, my spirits dropped, and inwardly I knew that I'd withdrawn from each and every one.

So at an all-time low, I silently resolved to go into retreat, to leave the bustling Rainbow Festival behind and seek more time alone with nature. Nature always was my solace, my best friend, the one who never let me down. Yet dismal fate was set against my quick escape as partway through the week I met my teacher quite by accident, for I had been avoiding her, avoiding all the lectures too. Why wasn't I attending all the lectures by such great, inspiring teachers? In this way, she sternly stopped me in my tracks, annoyed that I had turned my back on everyone, reproaching me for being aloof, for not part-icipating. Demanding I attend at least one lecture every day and thus support the festival, she fixed me with a fiery glare. Shrinking rapidly inside, I had no choice but to accept her short and to-the-point proposal. So I tried to make an effort and to enter into the spirit of the festival in spite of my complete despair.

My situation now seemed even bleaker than before, because my teacher had me in her grasp, and fixed me to a festival where thousands thronged together in a search around the super-mystic-market, whereas inside I felt only emptiness, a sense of disconnection and rejection. Yet even with my painful feelings of this separation, trusting her implicitly, I knew she must be pushing me to some unforeseen destination. Sometimes it can only be the worst of situations that prepare us for a leap, a step, a spiritual transformation. So I turned to prayer. I prayed for a drop of grace to heal my broken heart and quench my spiritual thirst. I prayed to find a panacea to compensate for all my feelings of inferiority, my shame at all my senseless aspirations.

I wandered in to see if something in this festival could lift my sombre spirits. The leaflets, posters and information desks were full of choices for the day. At any time there were at least three teachers from quite different traditions who'd been timetabled to give a lecture, seminar or workshop. With thousands of participants, all mainly European, in the breaks and lunchtimes every corridor, café or congregating spot was heaving with so many ardent seekers, all debating their last spiritual experience. I mindlessly merged with the crowd that strolled around the conference corridors and let the Rainbow Festival wash over me.

Two Ordinary Men

And then it fell from heaven to earth. A miracle of miracles fell at my feet for no apparent reason than to seek me out. Suddenly I was shaken just as if the sky had fallen in upon my head. I felt my heart give such a jump and start to knock against my ribs as if someone had thrown a bolt of lightning. I jumped involuntarily, amazed to see just who had fired this force at me. And searching for the perpetrator of this swift experience I noticed two Asian gentlemen who passed me by, quite simply dressed in plain, brown sweaters and brown trousers, both appearing on the surface to be quite insignificant. As they passed, one turned and looked straight at me, with penetrating eyes that seemed to spin like whirlpools of fire.

Instinctively I knew he must be a yogi hidden in an outer simple guise. I quickly smiled as he passed on, wondering who this stranger was. How could he have such awesome power? How could such electricity have poured from him into my heart? The violent movement in my chest was proof enough that something had occurred to leave me shaken and still trembling. Yet inside I felt a sense of reverence. I had no fear, but clearly an eruption had just manifested deep within my being causing temporary loss of balance. Inner shock had robbed me of my clarity and by the time I recovered some composure, this great yogi from the East was gone, lost in the crowd. And all I could remember was his spinning eyes that sent a powerful laser beam of light deep into my heart.

An act of grace had filled me with a wonder, awe and reverence. I felt as though I had been changed, set apart. It was as if an inner force sent from another world had crossed all barriers of time and space and manifested powerfully within my heart, transporting me onto another level. My heart was touched by something rich and rare. As I saw him disappear into the humming crowds around, I knew I had to let him go, let destiny, which was clearly operating powerfully, take its course, and hope our paths were soon to cross again.

I staggered in an altered state into the nearest café and sat down to try and take in what had just occurred. I felt the world had turned. Something had changed. What had he done? Where was he from? I fell into an inner reverie and would have sat for hours in meditation on this dazzling phenomenon, but suddenly my dream was shattered by the shout and sight of someone rushing through the café calling out to me. As he grew closer and my mind restored to some kind of normality, I recognized my friend Terry.

'I've just seen the Dalai Lama! He was there in front of me sitting in the audience. The Dalai Lama, Dalai Lama – really I have seen the

Dalai Lama! It was in this morning's lecture all about Tibetan medicine and he chose to sit in front of me. It must be a most auspicious sign. He felt my gaze upon him, turned and gave me quite a glance. The power that emanated from his look was so amazing! I've been blessed by the Dalai Lama!'

As you might imagine this was just the thing to cause a stir in this, the café spiritual. Already he had drawn a crowd who enviously looked upon this chosen soul. They hung upon his every word, which wasn't hard, for Terry never whispered any esoteric secret. No, an Aries born and bred he couldn't whisper if he tried when fiery passion took a hold of him. He had to shout it out like John the Baptist, spitting fire as if to smite the very devil with a ringing sword of truth. "The time has come for us to act!" he cried aloud, and thumped his fist upon the table, spilling coffee in an instant on the floor. I couldn't fathom all he said, for his miraculous experience and utter transformation seemed a little on the wild side. In particular, I didn't really think he'd seen the Dalai Lama sitting in the audience, for this was not at all Tibetan etiquette. Security alone would have demanded that His Holiness be separated by a wall of personal protection. So I had my doubts about it, but couldn't knock his fiery blast. At least he's living dangerously, I thought with just a little trepidation, for the café crowds were wildly pressing in upon us to see who'd caused the pandemonium.

I dragged him from the scene to save him from himself. He was in danger of becoming yet another Christ reborn, a man of mission with a flock of mystic lemmings in his tow. At first, I feared that he'd been caught up in spiritual glamour, like a butterfly alighting here and there in a desperate attempt to escape the painful traces of reality at any cost. But then I came to feel that, real or not, this phantom Dalai Lama in the lecture on Tibetan medicine was a symbol sent across my lonely path. It was a symbol to rekindle spiritual fire, for his experience had managed to elicit such a passionate involvement from the depths within this man, and far beyond his reasoning mind.

Terry was on fire. A driving force had activated his faith and sent him soaring to the peak of spiritual aspirations. Spinning there, just like a dynamo he couldn't fail to energize, uplift and to inspire. To me his very real experience seemed strangely synchronistic after my unusual happening. It felt as if the light was breaking through our personal shadow lands. For rebirth can commence whenever man is at his weakest; in the depths of winter solstice, spiritual healing is at hand.

On the Trail

It was the healing aspect of Tibetan medicine that had drawn him to the lecture, for he'd always had an interest in the ancient healing systems. He had told me many times about holistic healing concepts, and the fact that human bodies have two aspects; firstly the body, dense and physical and secondly the web of woven energy upon which map the structure of the body is then built. Trained as an acupuncturist, he had also studied various arts and sciences – massage, reflexology, Oriental herbal medicine, dietary therapies and healing through the mind. The ancient world of Taoist thought and various concepts of traditional Chinese medicine were familiar to me simply due to many lengthy discourses we'd had upon the nature of this medicine from the Eastern world. On such occasions he'd inspired me, talking well into the night, his cabinets all filled with several hundreds of particularly potent-smelling herbs (so much so that just a briefly opened door would send you reeling to the floor!).

I felt that destiny had thrown us both together at this festival, so I joined him in his heady inspiration and his search for spiritual healing. Risking all, I followed Terry on his trail, for with a pin he'd let his intuition guide him to choose the workshop we would visit next. It was a workshop by the Native Americans.

'They're the noblest souls of all,' he then declared. 'I've been so drawn to them and captivated even as a child. It's clear I must have distant links with Indian Chiefs – perhaps it's something from a life I've had before!' he spouted out in rather passé New Age lingo. As we stepped across the point of no return, I wisely chose to sit towards the back, encouraging Terry to take a seat up front, as he was now already well into his stride and growing eagle feathers by the very minute.

Our leap into the atmosphere of healers from the Native American race was actually an inspiration. For their offering was genuine. They cared for all humanity. An ancient chief was sitting there in all his Native finery, whilst by his side his son was much more Westernized – smoking cigarettes and drinking coke. So even visually they were an interesting paradox, and on beginning, it was clear that both were humorous and wise. They joked about the modern food fads, goading the audience out of its complacency. The son presented quite a story, for he'd suffered in the gory war in Vietnam. His designated route to healing was to smoke his cigarettes and drink his coke. A medicine man had given him this prescription to cure approaching cancer.

They talked in tongues it seemed to me and, through their down-to-earth responses, helped us all gain some perspective. When they asked if anyone had questions, unsurprisingly I saw that Terry was already waving his hand madly in the air. His question was extraordinary, but largely unintelligible. He rambled on about the mystic power of Native string games and the need to take the deeper meaning of these games to children near his home. The ancient chief immediately recognized calamity within the heart and mind and soul of Terry, clearly on a roll. His answer was quite brief. He said: "Just give the children all the tools and you will find that they'll teach you!" Although the reference indicated Terry's need to come back down to earth by being with the souls of children in their innocence, this chief had also seen within the question, signs of illness in us all. He promptly asked us to join hands and gently sway to left and right as he began a song of healing, sending such a power of love across the audience that soon the atmosphere around us all was calmed.

The workshop closed and we emerged into the sunset light to walk along the wooded path that led back to the hotel. My mood was growing lighter and more positive. Instinctively, I knew the man with spinning eyes had shifted something in my inner being, by the force of his most penetrating glance, for it was after this that Terry had appeared with his extraordinary tale of seeing the Dalai Lama. Something from Tibet had sought me out. To me, the Dalai Lama and all that he represented offered modern day humanity an answer to its spiritual impoverishment. Tibetan medicine, I had heard, essentially focused on the Medicine Buddha as a powerful emanation of pure healing. The physicians, through meditation and devotion, sought at all times to identify themselves with this great spiritual King of Aquamarine Light, the highest symbol of compassion. Through this focus they could generate enormous healing power. To me this was a most important sign, for I had always felt compassion of the highest kind was like a stream that flows deep underground beneath the surface of the great religions and was the only route to healing. Knowing this was something that I simply had to follow further, I went to bed that night deciding in the morning I must seek Terry out.

Coming down to breakfast, it was Terry who found me, for he was still full of his experience in the lecture on Tibetan medicine. 'Janet, you must come along. Another doctor's lecturing this morning,' he insisted. And without a further word, he grabbed my hand and led me out to seek Tibet, to seek again the Dalai Lama. He was very sure we'd see the Dalai Lama yet again! We bustled out together, striding off into the clear, cool morning, drinking in the crystal air of Switzerland. My heart was lifting high, for something new was in the air. A breath of life in all its glory was now flowing through my being whilst an elusive feeling, tender like the touch of one small feather to the fringes of my heart, was leading me along to find Tibetan medicine.

Terry told me as we travelled that the lecture would be given by a great physician from Tibet, called Dr Tenzin Choedrak. Although I had not heard of him, I couldn't help but feel that something in his name was so familiar. My heart was beating, beating fast. Our walk became a jog, a run, like children we excitedly danced on along the path that wound through the countryside. My eyes were drawn to the Jungfrau, that mountain dominating all. That source of such pain within my heart somehow was looking down on me, and beckoning me back again to restore my soul. And as we drew closer to the festival, this mountain seemed to rise up like a god to tower over me, a powerful affirmation that at last I had returned to place my feet again upon the best climb of my life. That inner climb to set me free was there just for the treading. My gait grew lighter with each step. I'd found again my vision from the past, those great Tibetan doctors emanating miracles to all who had been blessed to cross their path. I'd found beneath the briars and the thorns that had so painfully grown over me, that ancient gateway to a secret garden I'd once loved. The source of inner healing was before me in Tibetan medicine.

At last we reached the entrance to the conference hall and rushed inside to find the lecture room. With seconds left to spare, we found our seats. I felt entranced. A pregnant atmosphere surrounded us. We waited for the doctor to emerge. As he appeared before our eyes we dropped our jaws in perfect synchronicity. And with a gasp I turned to say to Terry, 'It's the man with spinning eyes!' He turned to me and with a laugh admitted, 'Yes, this is the man that I thought was the Dalai Lama!' Mistakenly he'd lifted this great doctor up onto a spiritual pedestal, whilst I was simultaneously quite shocked to find he was the very man whose eyes were whirlpools of pure fire, the one who filled me full of light and electricity.

As we sat back in wonder and fascination, our hearts instinctively bowed low before this man who seemed to channel such an energy, a force, an unstoppable power, the miracles and wonders of Tibetan medicine flowing through his pores. His very being was an emanation of this sacred system. We were mesmerized, completely held in awe of this physician who sat smiling before us, humbly poised, about to speak.

Chapter 2

The Blue-Faced God: the Medicine Buddha

So THERE HE SAT, this embodiment of ancient knowledge: a mild and quiet man who would have passed almost unnoticed, such was his humility and unaffected sincerity. He had no need of fanfare, outer display, standing ovation – no need to seek the world's acclaim. This father of Tibetan medicine simply opened up his mind and heart before us all. He channelled such a mighty force of healing for he was indeed a true Grand Master in his field, and we were blessed to be before him, as he transmitted the ancient spiritual teachings of Tibetan medicine.

He became for me the point of calm within the centre of the storm and was so completely still, just like the central seat, the golden orb, the Mecca of the deeper world is absolutely silent. The peace within him was palpable. It was as if the world outside this room revolved initially quite peacefully, yet if we were to move away much further from this centre and begin to leave his powerful inner focus for our outer worldly thoughts and needs, we'd soon become unbalanced. For it seemed to me that typically our actions in the world were like a battle flung across the earth, a cyclone sent to shake the very birds out of the trees. Yet if we really tried to make a change and struggle back to push aside our deep desires, our anger and our ignorance, we stood a chance of finding once again that central balance, oh so still, that archetypal emperor who in this Eastern doctor sat amidst us all in stillness so supreme. And there the peace would soon return. Indeed this peace would never go away unless we left it for the shadows. For me this doctor represented something waiting here for all of us.

Dr Choedrak's Teachings

This man of peace, so clearly sent to heal the storm around him, was the jewel I had longed for when I came to Switzerland. For peace and deepest stillness filled our hearts. We sat and bathed in healing rays that shone effortlessly for all who'd made a choice to be within that conference room and sit before this gem of healing. It was as if he held the hub of all and everything within his heart, inviting us to come and sit with him and stop the dashing whirl of running in the wrong direction. He exuded such tranquillity and inner freedom, connected deeply to his ancient sacred voices. The very air seemed magnetized as words of sweetness fell from his lips. His healing emanations offered up the only antidote for all life's troubling complexities. For there within this great Tibetan healing system lay a potent medicine for our modern rush-around-and-buy-it-quick materialism. Contentment and acceptance sprang from inner ancient wells of healing waters, deeper than we could imagine, stillness from another world. His very presence soothed our bodies like a healing balm, and calmed the currents agitated by our turbulent minds.

He held out the fruits of his knowledge and invited us to leave our rigid grip on frozen minds and sip upon the wonders of his medicine. He presented a vision of salvation and vividly reminded me of all I'd heard before about the wonders of this system. Memories of my encounter with the doctor long ago, who clearly had been so inspired and healed of cancer by a lama doctor, floated up again into my mind. Until this day, this quite amazing tale of healing at the highest level had remained a precious story. Yet before me now this man, gazing with extraordinary eyes, was all too real and I became enchanted by every word he said. He was living, breathing evidence that doctors with the power to truly heal our depths are still emerging from Tibet. These extraordinary fugitives had suffered dreadfully since the Chinese invasion of their country in 1950. Yet, against all odds, they had fought to smuggle out the ancient key they had inherited from heaven, the key to open up the Medicine Buddha's garden, a precious land of healing, now preserved and offered to the world outside the walls of torn Tibet.

This Himalayan alchemist who sat before us was a survivor, one of very few physicians left alive to hold the secrets of the tantric medical wisdom which had been transmitted to him from that hidden paradise of Shangri-la. This humble doctor was inherently a legacy of Tibetan medicine, embodying the spirit of the great Tibetan culture. He was a living icon of his system, a skilled exponent of the teachings, of the original Four Tantras, the heart-essence text of medicine from Tibet. These profound teachings had been developed and elaborated into a philosophy of life.

He drew me deep into the wonders of his system. The entrance to this fascinating labyrinth was carved out in his language, and as he began to speak, a translator by his side interpreted the meaning to the audience in English. This Tibetan tongue resonated deeply with my being, almost like a memory. The sounds resounded in my heart, awakening an opening, a gateway to another level. It was as if the very words that he emitted were suffused with rays of healing rising from the deep substratum of a language born of universal mantras. The audience collectively was being dipped into the healing waters of Tibet directly through its ancient language. Coming up for air to hear translation, our minds were then presented with various facets of this medical system. The overall effect was quite hypnotic. As if under the spell of anaesthesia the audience slowed to a standstill. Some were experiencing meditation far beyond the grasping mind.

Yet what my mind could hold, whilst in my heart I meditated, somehow pieced together like the fragments of a lost, forgotten jigsaw. I encountered a vast repository brimming with the wisdom of an intensely spiritual medicine raised in a cultural history over 2,500 years old. I felt myself submerged within an ancient, timeless orb where emphasis was placed on meditation and heightened sensitivity for every action that we make, for all the thoughts that fill our minds. Such an attitude to life and care for every sentient being was the basis for enlightenment, and ultimately sought to raise humanity up to a higher level. He said that suffering and illness were related quintessentially to all the inner movements of our mind and senses, which had the power to block the life force flowing through a tapestry of channels in the body. The currents of our personal seas were typically determined by our deeply ingrained habits, tossing us upon the waves of our self-created chaos. This spiritually-focused doctor injected me with hope for all humanity, if we could find complete contentment and acceptance through the medium of Tibetan medicine. He opened up a world of healing where the history, myths, and archetypes were woven altogether and above it all the great divine was working through its instruments, the devoted doctors, sages and healers.

A Lesson in History

In his lecture Dr Choedrak took us back several thousand years, when sufferings first arose and corresponding medicines and their sciences were first developed in Tibet. He told us how a pre-existing system based on native natural medicine and shamanic practices had gradually been developed and refined across the centuries. A primary impression came from India, where a certain famous doctor, Bhindi

Kaji, brought two healing systems into Tibet, one a system which had been taught by the Buddhas, and the other was believed to have dropped down to earth from heaven. Such occurrences were totally accepted as a part of Tibetan medical history, which was impregnated with a retinue of sages, gurus, gods and various manifestations of Lord Buddha. The history was full of mystery and wonder, as if any attempt to pin it all down into a fixed, entombed existence would destroy its very essence. He admitted that the teachings could not be completely understood by reading them, for there were hidden meanings, covered meanings, and some passages placed out of order by design. As he took us into this ancient, enigmatic system, I allowed myself to drop my Western mind which seeks to analyse, to calculate and penetrate with microscopes to certify the chemistry. I was recognizing more and more how very privileged we were to sit with this Tibetan Master, who was part of an ancient oral tradition.

The system was informed and influenced by countries bordering on Tibet. The medical techniques of the tantric practitioners found in India were profound initial influences and, over time, Tibetan doctors collected information from the flowering nations of the East, including India, China, Mongolia, Nepal and Iran which had all brought doctors to Tibet for exchanges on the development of a healing science of the highest quality. The best minds of Tibet, a precious lineage of lamas, yogis, doctors and great saints had tirelessly collaborated on this cornucopia, and contributed to it ceaselessly throughout Tibetan history. Over time, the practice of medicine had become inextricably entwined with magic, religion and mysticism as the various monasteries of medicine developed as great centres of research.

The fundamental text for this ancient healing system was called 'The Secret Quintessential Instructions on the Eight Branches of the Ambrosia Essence Tantra'. These sacred tantras, briefly called the 'rGyu-shi' in Tibetan, were originally transmitted by the Buddha Shakyamuni in his sacred form, Vaidurya, known as the Medicine Buddha, or Sangye Menla. It was said that the occasion of the teachings was conducted by the Lord Buddha in the realm of Tanatuk, a mountain plateau he created which was 'pleasing when looked upon', and there he manifested as the Medicine Buddha, blue-faced god of healing. Before an array of sages, gods, ascetics, Buddhists and non-Buddhists, he went into deep meditation. Different coloured healing rays then issued from his chest, and as a method to address the waiting audience, an emanation of the Medicine Buddha's mind appeared within the sky. This was a sage called Rigpai Yeshi, who announced that all who wanted to receive the fruits of health, long life and happiness and who truly desired to meditate and finally attain nirvana, a state of blessedness, should learn the science of medicine.

At this point more healing rays of light came pouring from the Medicine Buddha's tongue to bring a second emanation of the Medicine Buddha's speech, another sage called Yilay Kye. This sage responded to the words of Rigpai Yeshi, saying that everyone would like to receive the marvellous fruits he had described, and pleaded with the sage to tell them how this science of medicine could be learned. Here a dialogue ensued between the sages, with more questions and more answers. In this way the secret teachings of the rGyu-shi were revealed. Every member of the audience heard the teachings in accordance with their own particular religion and level of understanding, and proceeded to transcribe the teachings into medical treatises. The legendary Jivaka, personal doctor to the Buddha, was among those who received the teachings, which were passed down through a lineage of Buddhist physician saints to the present day. According to Tibetan legend, the rGyu-shi in its perfect form was inscribed in lapis lazuli ink on sheets of pure gold and stored within a divine realm.

A major contributor to the rGyu-shi came within the eighth century, with the best physician of the time, Yuthog Yonten Gonpo the Elder. Later, during the twelfth century, the Younger Yuthog Gonpo refined the teachings even further. He took what was best in all known medicine, collecting texts which went back over centuries, and in this way enriched the rGyu-shi. It is his version which forms the basis of the modern text. In the seventeenth century, Desi Sangye Gyatso wrote another famous text of great importance. He produced a list of illnesses, and of the 1,600 he described, there were a set of 18 illnesses he said would manifest in the future according to changes in the environment. Desi Rinpoche had drawings made to illustrate the system in a set of medical paintings.

A Picture of the Medicine Buddha

As this history unfolded, I could feel that Dr Tenzin Choedrak was the living emanation of the rGyu-shi, for as he spoke about the system, every element he touched upon responded almost physically within me. The very impact of his presence was very powerful and many others, it seemed to me, were similarly affected.

He said the practice of Tibetan physicians was to merge with the Medicine Buddha, through sacred, secret rites, chanting, prayer, meditation and visualization of this blue Buddha seated in his healing paradise. This pure realm, a Buddha-field, a sacred place beyond the earthly plane of illusion was a palace of healing, completely in keeping with the inherent nature of the Buddha himself, who was in fact known during his lifetime as the Great Physician. As the doctor continued to reveal this hidden land, speaking in reverential tones, his words seemed to unveil a *thangka*, sacred painting of Tibet, created with dedication and absolute perfection in order to transport the viewer in meditation onto another plane of being. I envisioned the emergence of a tapestry of colours, purest colours ground from rarest minerals, raised out of the earth into the light and painted so exquisitely onto canvas.

This geometrically perfect mandala drew all eyes into its very centre, where within a crystal palace the supreme healer, known as the King of Aquamarine Light was seated, cross-legged in full lotus meditative posture upon a throne carved out of lapis lazuli. His radiant body, painted in the deepest blue of azurite, emanated rays of healing light, enshrined within a halo of gold leaf. In his left hand he held a bowl containing the essence of ambrosia, which conquers death and eliminates illness, whilst his right hand was outstretched in an open gesture of giving, holding a sprig of the myrobalan tree, known to have great healing power. Surrounding him was a retinue of gods, sages, ascetics and saints. Beyond the palace with its particular structure of five walls, eight steps and four gates was an incredible array of healing agents: plants, minerals and beautiful creatures stretching in all four directions.

The doctor informed us that once merged with this potent, precious scene within the mind, a Tibetan doctor would envisage healing rays emerging from the heart of the Medicine Buddha. This healing power could then be sent to every sentient being, whether focused on particular individuals, or in general to help to heal the world. This approach demonstrated to me how a powerful inner focus could influence one's surrounding environment; when fixed in meditation, gazing inwardly upon the Medicine Buddha, the wondrous, visioned splendour of this sacred image would impress itself upon the mind. Ever deepening impressions would pervade the practitioner's inner universe, impregnating him with this potent archetype, until his consciousness had merged totally with the deity, creating a corresponding healing 'presence' within the outer world. To complete this visualization each practitioner eventually allowed the inner screening of the tapestry of wonder to diffuse and melt into the body before going into meditation.

He continued to explain that each physician, whether practising or student, would pray to the Medicine Buddha without fail throughout their lives. Meditation on the medical mandala was the path for every doctor to realize a higher plane of operation on three different levels. The first of these three levels was to dedicate oneself as a medical practitioner to the sacred Medicine Buddha. The second level was one of merging, whereby one was attempting to merge with the Medicine Buddha, and identify one's surroundings with the Medicine Buddha's garden, a land of potent healing energies. At the final level one should aim to align one's body, mind and speech with the pure, serene and perfect nature of Buddha to the effect that there is a realization of oneself as the Medicine Buddha, and a realization of one's body as the medical mandala. The aim of each Tibetan doctor was therefore to become totally immersed inwardly in the Medicine Buddha, whilst outwardly continuing to function perfectly well as a doctor conducting medical consultations.

The Spiritual Roots of Medical Practice

So, here before us in the centre of the Rainbow Festival this doctor held within him a pure, untainted vision, vibrating at the highest healing level, whereby this magnificent blue being was sending his powerful healing rays deep into the heart of all who sat before him, streaming through his sacred instrument, this doctor of devotion wielding the sword of compassion. Dr Choedrak was envisioning the Medicine Buddha for us all, which through him had manifested in this simple conference room. We were effectively transformed and sitting in his sacred gardens, enchanted with the sweet and healing scents of medicinal trees, incense and perfumes. At last I understood how this magnificent mandala, full of wondrous healing wealth with the patron deity of medicine from Tibet at its centre, revealed the true power behind their medical system.

To me, this philosophy of medicine from the East had unequivocally revealed that spirituality was the driving force behind all healing, to which treatment (however complex, knowledgeable and highly skilled) would always ultimately be secondary. Spiritual support lay as an all-embracing power at the foundation of all ancient cultures. These cultures were linked so inextricably with this divine power, that every fragment of their existence was totally aligned with spirituality. Physicians from these cultures encouraged spiritual practice for their patients as an essential aid to healing. The place where they received their patients would essentially be like a perfect inner sanctum, where all thoughts and actions were purified through focus on the Medicine Buddha. Every interaction with a patient entering this hallowed, healing space would correspondingly be infused with the Buddhist ethics of selflessness and compassion.

This great system had retained a powerful link with Buddhist practice and belief. There was no separation here between the spiritual and the rational. Philosophy and metaphysics had been completely integrated. With no division from the deeper stratum and essential core of this enlightened system, it tapped into the very root of ancient healing. There within its core was inner balance on all levels, whether physical, emotional, mental or spiritual, equilibrium in everything, a universal harmony, peace and deep contentment as the key to perfect health. The central vision of this system was historically derived from the visions of ancient seers, who in their mystic meditations had perceived the fundamental principles of life.

I also now understood how the former story of the healing of a cancer had profoundly elevated my being and restored my inner balance. Dr Choedrak talked of the importance of our inner luminosity, a brightness and a glow about a person stemming from a super-essence that primarily resided within the heart, but was also distributed throughout the body. This spirit was a crucial key to healing and could be severely depleted through worry and depression. Long ago when I had heard about that miracle, the wonder of it had clearly fed my inner spirit, inner essence, and restored my sense of hope. I realized that in one second a positive word in someone's ear had the potential to reverse a downward spiral towards illness. For by giving love and showing compassion, the energetic 'field' around a person, so vulnerable to thoughts and feelings, could be positively affected. Conversely, anyone carrying unhappiness, anxiety and stress could only have a negative impact and this, the doctor said, was particularly important where the relationship between the doctor and the patient was concerned.

Clearly, this relationship was crucial to the process of healing. If the doctor had not cultivated peace and contentment within himself, essential in order to establish a potential state of balance for the patient, then the vital healing transference initiated by the patient's doctor could so easily become a recipe for disaster if the doctor's own imbalance was transmitted to the patient. It was easy now to see how the ability to bring about a cure and heal the sick was linked essentially to high Buddhist ethics. These simple doctors were so humble that they treated every being in the world, even creatures such as insects and the worms beneath the ground as always equal to themselves. Care and affection were held highly as the most important factors in all healing. So the doctors, recognized as truly great, were not acclaimed because of the outer trappings of fame and public renown more typical in the modern world. It was their inner qualities that were considered to be supremely important: the level of compassion in a doctor; the quality of his morals; the depth of wisdom, purity of action, thought and feeling. These were the marks of a great physician in the East, for the sum of these qualities would manifest as an obvious ability to bring about a cure.

The physician mentioned earlier, Yuthog Yonten Gonpo the Elder had been a prime example of this capacity for healing. Known as the 'Turquoise Roof Physician', he was noted chiefly for his wisdom and the depth of his compassion. He had far outstripped the bounds of any normal basic concept of the morals of a doctor. The memory of this unusual healer had been held in high esteem and had been recognized as a precious model of the medical tradition. This dedicated physician, who had lived to be 125 years old, had followed in the footsteps of the Medicine Buddha and was a brilliant practitioner, known for many examples of seemingly miraculous accomplishments in healing. Yet he was only one of many great saintly physicians, lamas, yogis and venerable doctors who had continued this tradition up to the present day, devoting all their energy, wisdom and aspiration to the development of Tibetan medicine and promotion of healing to all beings in the world.

To me, this bright new star of Tibetan Buddhist medicine was appearing even brighter by the minute like a piercing light of hope on the horizon of my mind. It was shining out in purity, protected almost entirely from polluting modern influences. The influence of Buddhism had given Tibetan medicine a protection against what Dr Carl Jung, the eminent psychologist, referred to as the 'heresy of sep- arateness', which he revealed as a dreadful alienation from the inner, deep substratum of our being. Modern man's most urgent need is to discover the reality and value of his inner and subjective world, the world of his own psyche, there to find the symbols of a richer universe. Dr Jung further underpinned this by stating that man cannot bear a life lacking in meaning. Here in Switzerland, this festival was trying to offer up a deeper meaning than the ceaseless search for mastery within the outer world. In presenting this great medicine from Tibet, the Rainbow Festival revealed for those with ears to hear and eyes to see, a very different vision of the processes of healing. To me, this elixir of life emphasized the vital truth that we are not isolated, separate individuals living our personal lives in a vacuum, but are inextricably intertwined with each other and with the universal energies. The recognition of this fact was required in order to facilitate the healing process, and Tibetan medicine offered the means by which we might approach a more all-embracing awareness of this reality.

By walking through the doorway of traditional Tibetan medicine I had been completely shocked and challenged to the very core by ancient metaphysical concepts so revolutionary to the Western mind. I felt my mental state was in line with the Renaissance, when the scientists discovered that the world was round, not flat. Over several thousand years, Tibet had remained an isolated region, where uniquely its culture advanced in a vacuum, geographically closed by snowy peaks. Thus, its customs and systems grew in solitary, mystical confinement to produce a healing system quite unequalled in the world, sophisticated and coherently developed in its particular philosophy and peerless metaphysics. Now, this extraordinary doctor from Tibet was submitting a completely different kind of world reality, or rather more precisely, a much wider view of medical reality than had been previously apparent to my Western mind. I felt he had created in his audience such a massive shift in consciousness by offering a very new perspective on the concept of disease. Deep within its very roots it was the blending of the spiritual and the rational that made Tibetan medicine so exceptional, offering up a cure for the modern Western malaise – the loss of meaning in life.

Every cell within my body felt at peace as Dr Choedrak brought the first part of his lecture to a close. My perception of the world, of every illness and disease had been transformed. This subtle transference of healing reaching to my very depths had occurred within two hours, sitting in this Master's presence. All was silent. All was calm. My mind was empty like a quiet, sylvan pool of utter stillness.

Clearly the unique quality of Tibetan medicine lay not only in its commitment to healing the human body of illness and disease, but equally, in its revelation of a path in which body, mind and spirit could be liberated from the sufferings of conditioned existence. His final words embraced the essence of the system and I understood the depth of meaning in his words, as he quoted from the Buddha, from the first of his great teachings, a simple stanza on the subject of universal suffering:

> Noble one, think of yourself as someone who is sick,
>
> Of the dharma as the remedy,
>
> Of your spiritual friend as a skilful doctor,
>
> And of diligent practice as the way to recover.

Chapter 3

The Whispering Pulse

*A*s WE SAT whilst the doctor prepared to enter the second part of his lecture, I wondered how this great Tibetan Master could hope to bridge the gaping chasm between the wonders and mysteries of his ancient, sacred culture and the rigid, scientific views of modern times. Today we focus much more on the outer, materialistic world, a very different planet, most particularly where the subject of medicine is concerned. Yet I sensed we were on the fringe of something wondrous, and a chance perhaps to change, for Western, worldly consciousness is not an all-pervading state that is set in stone. It is inevitably a product of its own particular history and geography, yet still only represents a certain part of humankind.

I realized how the sacred knowledge he offered had largely been lost to the worldly nations of the earth, and that the only way in which we could still receive the enlightened wisdom of the ancients was to turn to these extraordinary teachers from the East who were alive and embodying the Truth. Destiny had guided me to a Master such as this and provided me with the chance to merge into the stream that flowed from him. It was clear from the impact of his being that he had raised his consciousness to a very high level and that subsequently, the words he offered us were powerful living things, potent thought forms manifesting on the physical plane.

Within the ancient Tibetan language lay an endless stream of energy. In the true oral tradition, he was channelling the force behind the diction of the ancients to the hearts of those before him. He was a living example of a *menpa* (the Tibetan word for a doctor) and his powers were extraordinary. The effect of his presence pervaded every atom of my being and as he began the second half of his lecture, I drank in the sudden truth that I had completely merged with this inspired physician.

How Suffering Begins

Dr Choedrak announced that he now wished to talk to us about the process of reading the signs of a patient, specifically with regard to the art of taking the pulse. He said that a good practitioner could read the signs of every person who approached for treatment. From the foot upon the stair, to the knock upon the door, the physician would be completely attentive, absorbing everything about the coming patient, which would already be pervading the atmosphere like a fragrance. The way in which the patient entered, how he or she sat upon their seat, all these subtle but revealing external signs were inevitable reflections of the inner state of the patient. In Tibet, experienced doctors would take heed of various signs right from the moment that they left their room to travel to the clinic to receive the coming patient, for they were tuning in to the workings of the universe. All the answers lay there waiting to be found, and this naturally extended to the face-to-face exchanges with the patient. Thus, the clarity of focus on all levels, from the material to the spiritual, was a necessary requirement for successful diagnosis.

This was the measure of the doctor, his ability to read the changing colours of complexion and various patterns on the skin.

The inner brightness of the patient's vital spirit could be perceived within the sensing of the outer body's halo. The very tone in which the patient's conversation began would be a mine of information; how the voice would rise and fall; how the illness was presented; what emotions were expressed. So the state of health was like a book for those who knew the art of reading between the lines. The information, wave on wave, would always be flowing out into the atmosphere, so every doctor, if refined enough, would merge without exertion into the river of the life of every patient. Every swirl and every eddy drew him closer to the source. Every contour of the body would reveal the inner geometry through palpation. Doctors would therefore seek to bring their senses to a point of high refinement, whereby with their eyes, ears, nose and hands, they would carefully begin to diagnose each patient. Looking deep into the eyes, scanning signs upon the tongue, pressing known diagnostic points upon the body, gradually they would build up a picture of the condition of the patient. In this way they could begin to see beneath the surface, delving deeper than the presenting signs and symptoms.

This great physician then led us deep beneath the surface of ourselves to reach the fundamental cause of illness. He said that in order to acquire a complete understanding of healing, we had to understand the root of suffering, for this exploration in itself was the most important factor in any healing process. The root of all our suffering lay in the mind, which was the seat of ignorance. Ignorance created a blinkered life, where the illusion of 'I' as being separate from everyone else caused all manner of problems. Like shutters falling down across our windows on the world, this ignorance blinded us from the light of Truth, our universal interconnectedness and sense of common humanity, and fortified what Dr Choedrak referred to as the 'three mental poisons': desire, anger and closed-mindedness. From these three poisons sprang three physical energies: *rLung*, *Tripa* and *Badkan*, translated as wind, bile and phlegm.

The energy of *rLung* related to the element of wind and was responsible for the different kinds of movement within the body.

Tripa corresponded to the element of fire and was responsible for the body's heat. *Badkan*, the third energy in the body, was cool in nature, based on earth and water, representing all the fluids in the body. At a fundamental level everyone had within them these three energies, sometimes referred to as the three humours, and diagnosis would aim to discover the degree of their balance or imbalance within the patient's body, for this related directly to the state of the body's health.

Dr Choedrak said the pulsation of the blood within the body was due to the action of *rLung*. This wind blew life into us all. It rippled through the very atoms of the universe and spoke to us in tongues of living motion, for it simply could not keep still. It floated within the breeze of peace, and raged wild within the swirling, spinning cyclone of destruction. The more I heard, the more I felt this *rLung* around me and inside me like a quiet revolution in the world of my perception. It was the breathing of the leaves within the trees, the heaving swell within the ocean, the clapping hands, the nodding head. It was the air that's taken in to bring expansion to the lungs and the churning of the stomach in the process of digestion. It was the force that drove us on and on, from the first breath of a newborn baby to the last gasp of a person at the point of death.

This force within the blood produced the wave within the pulse, which a Tibetan doctor considered as the most vital source of information when seeking a precise diagnosis. Of course this was an area covered in a Western diagnosis; indeed almost every doctor in the world would take the pulse. But here again the spiritual element was powerfully present in Tibetan medicine. The Buddhist viewpoint had suffused this integrative system of medicine to the point that not a shred of the system stood outside it. Thus there was always an essentially spiritual extension to what might otherwise be perceived as a mechanical procedure of diagnosis. Apparently there was even a highly esoteric system of retreat and meditation, whereby if one cultivated a special deity of the Buddha, and recited words of power, one could, within a specific period of time, acquire the skill of reading signs within the pulse.

The Rhythm of the Pulse

This whispering pulse was like a messenger for those who had the touch, and in that touch there was an answer to the calling from within the patient's inner universe, a web of fine connections streaming on up to the skin. To touch the skin and read the pulse the slender fingers of the doctor were 'all ears', they listened in and reached down into the blood to hear the beat of heart, the beat of lungs, the beat of liver and gallbladder, the beat of spleen, the beat of stomach, the beat of kidney, bladder, large and small intestines and the reproductive organs. Every organ in the body fed the rhythm of the pulse. This melody of the blood was rich in information, for disease would manifest as an obstruction in the system and, by transmission to the pulse, produce a kind of echo, a particular sensation sliding underneath the fingers of the doctor, informing him of everything.

We were told that physicians, through the pulse, could perceive a problem before it even manifested as an illness on the outside. Through this fine medium they could reach right to the root of any problem. Even simple manifestations such as a headache might in fact be linked to very different internal conditions. Through the pulse, the precise cause could be revealed, lying beneath other more superficial manifestations. By way of example, he said that Tibetan doctors could distinguish between two completely different causes for a condition, which through an instrument of measurement typically employed within the West, would register as high blood pressure. Their approach was essentially tactile and holistic as they targeted mental, emotional, physical and spiritual obstructions in need of healing and transformation.

It was explained that a physician must develop his capacity for sensitivity to such a very high degree that even if he were only to be presented with a patient's hand, with the rest of the person concealed by a curtain, he could nevertheless arrive at a reliable diagnosis of the condition. Pulse-taking was therefore the keystone of traditional Tibetan diagnosis. Here the doctor was equipped just with himself.

He alone was the very instrument of accurate and lucid diagnosis. Using all of his fine faculties he aimed to scan the body in an instant, through palpation, tapping deeply into the human physiology, quite literally in touch with the most vital circulation of energy and blood, and thus in contact with the whole of the extraordinary inner world.

Pulse-taking was inevitably an art requiring much extensive study, first in theory and then through years and years of daily practice. Skill in reading every impulse from the various inner organs to the arteries was developed and refined across the years, as was the competence to translate every message into terms of etiology and particular pathology. Three fingers on each hand of the physician were placed lightly on the wrist above the radial artery, which acted as messenger between the doctor and the patient. Dr Choedrak said the reason for reading the pulse in this particular position was like considering a man who is trying to listen to the sound of water. Listening to the carotid artery within the neck where the rush of blood is loud, being so close to the heart, was akin to standing at the Niagara waterfall. He would be deafened by the water which is cascading in torrents. However, feeling the pulse at the ankle position, much further from the heart, would be like a man who has his ear pressed to the ground near a tiny, trickling spring. It's far too faint to really discern what's going on. So the radial artery was the perfect place to listen. Being neither too far from nor too close to the heart, here the concentration of the blood and wind within the pulse was the most appropriate for subtle diagnosis. Every characteristic pulse beat linked directly to the organs could be felt just like the wind's effect upon the surface of the water, from tiny ripples to the great, rolling waves on the sea. It was this feeling of the waves that could be felt within the pulse and through it the trained physician tuned into the vital balance of the energies, or humours in the body.

The balance or imbalance of the three energies manifested as different rhythms and sensations. For instance, if the pulse was beating strongly, yet felt 'superficial', like a balloon upon the water which when you press it down would spring immediately back up again, this was the classic sign of an elevation of the *rLung* energy within the body. If the pulse was beating thin, fast and tight this was the measure of the *Tripa* humour. Whilst a pulse that felt quite sunken, slow and weak, just like a lazy person's gait, was pointing to the signs of *Badkan* in the body. From here there were unlimited variations which could lead the practised doctor to particular conditions.

Listening to this information on the art of taking the pulse, emphasized to me the extraordinary level of refinement and sensitivity required of a Tibetan physician, who was ultimately involved in an amazing act of surrender to faith in the highest intuition born of touch. This ancient tool of diagnosis was perhaps the most perplexing part of Tibetan medicine, for it could be taken by a Master to the heights of sensitivity, where he could even use pulse palpation on a patient to inform him about the state of health of a relative or friend. This was indeed a most amazing legacy of a medical system which over a thousand years before had left behind all thought of surgical invasion of the body. At that time, for reasons of both religion and health, it was decided that surgery was fundamentally not the best proposition when aiming to heal the human condition, so they proceeded to tackle illness and disease from quite a different angle.

Correspondingly, their art of diagnosis had ascended to a very high position. Apart from pulse palpation they also investigated the urine, reading much within this fluid we expel. They added to this the signs of faeces, sputum, tongue, eyes and complexion, together with palpation of the body and questioning, in order to establish an accurate diagnosis. So if the pulse did not agree with signs and symptoms, one could look to other means to find the proper diagnosis. For although the pulse was a brilliant indicator of the state of disease, sometimes the root cause could be hidden behind a 'false' manifestation within the pulse, so a good physician had to be practised in distinguishing the true signs from the false.

Seven Amazing Pulses

Nevertheless, the pulse remained the most reliable of methods to approach a diagnosis. It was said within the teachings that the one who had attained a complete, abundant understanding of the pulse would accordingly become a good and competent physician. For those who'd sought to plumb its very depths it could reveal the panorama of disease before the doctor with an awe-inspiring clarity. There was no limit to the vision of a doctor who'd surrendered to this art. Dr Choedrak then took us deep into the mysteries of pulse-taking, with a description of the Seven Amazing Pulses.

This was a means of divination through the pulse, so esoteric that only the most enlightened doctors could approach its sacred art. Within the ancient Tibetan culture, the physician was much more than just a doctor, being also an adviser to the family in the world of spiritual matters. For the purpose of particular divination such as this, the pulse was read within a healthy member of the family. In this category of pulse-taking there were seven types of pulse known as the Seven Amazing Pulses. He explained that to go deeply into this would take too long, but for the purpose of this lecture he would refer briefly to each one.

The first of these Seven Amazing Pulses was the Pulse of the Family. It could be examined within the eldest or most senior member of the family, thus to determine the condition and fate of the family as a whole. This pulse could reveal imminent disease, distress, fearful occurrences, suffering, loss of wealth or being subject to the gossip of others. By means of an even more detailed reading, taking into account which position on the wrist the particular pulse sensation was located and in which season it was manifesting, the experienced physician could determine exactly who within the family would potentially be the object of such occurrences. If the pulse, however, displayed normal characteristics, this would be an omen of good fortune.

Secondly, the Pulse of the Guest could determine the fate of an expected friend or guest, and for this purpose, the pulse of the person to whom the guest was considered closest would be examined. If the pulse located on the wrist, in the position where one would normally discern the state of the liver, was felt to be strong, this indicated that the guest was still at his home and would remain there. If the pulse of the lung was strongest, then his journey had just begun. If the pulse of the heart was strongest, then the guest was said to be well on the way and very close to arrival. But if the pulse of the kidney was strong, this was a sign that something was wrong. This was a sign of some delay, or some kind of hazard along the way.

The next pulse, the Pulse of the Enemy, was consulted as a means of divination in ancient times by examining the commander of an army facing battle, but in general it could be used to see if one would be successful in the accomplishment of one's aims. The strength of particular pulse positions could therefore indicate success or failure in the achievement of one's aims.

The Pulse of Wealth could be found within the pulse of the head of the household. Strength in the pulse of the liver would indicate increase in friends and increase in wealth. Weakness within the pulses of both heart and spleen would indicate decrease in friends and decrease in wealth.

The Pulse of Demons, or Malefic Influences would be taken when a person was being affected in a most unusual manner and was typically confirmed by a distinct irregularity within the pulse. Treatment in this case would always be accompanied by specific spiritual practices.

The sixth pulse, known as the Reversing Pulse, was consulted to determine the state of a loved one or family member who could not be examined directly. This commonly happened in mountainous areas, where someone was too ill to travel to the doctor. The reversing pulse of a family member could not by itself reveal the exact nature of the disease, but would determine the prognosis and thus assist in prescribing the appropriate form of treatment. The pulse of the father examined in detail could help with the health of the son. The pulse of the mother could help treat the daughter, that of the husband, his wife and vice versa.

The last pulse was the Pulse of Pregnancy, and was described as moving like a caterpillar. This pulse assisted in predicting any problems within childbirth and could give an indication as to any difficulties in raising the child, its future prosperity, also indicating the sex of the child. A strong right kidney pulse indicated a son, whereas a strong left kidney pulse indicated the birth of a daughter.

Well, these seven amazing pulses left me feeling quite in awe. The act of reading signs within the pulse of a patient was to me already quite extraordinary, but reading signs of divination at a level such as this was almost incredible. I was astonished that these signs were revealing someone's destiny, the fate of someone's family, the actions of a guest, a friend or enemy, lying there within the beating of the blood. The great magnificence of the world of the unconscious as examined by Dr Carl Jung came to mind, where the sights, sounds and smells about us can act as powerful 'triggers' of inner memories and our dreams are full of signposts to the truth about ourselves. Within the unconscious lay a language born of archetypes and symbols, which if translated by an experienced interpreter could greatly assist the human condition. Similarly, Tibetan doctors had, over thousands of years, developed a system totally aligned with spirituality, refining themselves as highly sensitive instruments, capable of reading the signs of the times within each and every patient sent their way. In an attitude of selflessness, humility and surrender, they were capable of receiving and deciphering complex information from the patient's body. Like interpreters of echoes around a whispered secret gallery, these doctors were attentive in their listening, to catch the very thread of our tomorrows in their fingers.

The ability of these doctors to completely merge into their patients so deeply through the medium of palpation was truly marvellous and made me realize the inherently limiting edge of technology, which in sophistication had inevitably focused more on the powers of diagnosis through medical instruments. The foremost duty of a Tibetan doctor was to function with his brain and with his senses, thus to reach a diagnosis, then prescribe a form of treatment which would present minimum disturbance to the system. This very human, tactile, practical, immediate approach was one of many basic differences between the Western medical establishment and this amazing system from Tibet.

Healing in my Heart

The gentle words of this great doctor had borne me up into a world of spiritual splendour, where the body could be sensed so perfectly and tenderly. I felt blessed to be allowed into his presence and receive his voice of healing into my heart. As the end of his lecture was approaching, suddenly this humble doctor drew the audience physically closer to him, offering to take the pulse of anyone who might like to come and sit beside him.

In a second, queues were forming. This was a chance to touch the hem of something rare, to be the patient of this doctor from Tibet, who clearly offered all his skill and knowledge in utter selflessness. With extraordinary sensitivity the doctor placed three fingers on each pulse and in an attitude of listening and alertness he tuned into the state of health to give each person almost instantly a lucid diagnosis. His precision was amazing; it was clear upon the face of every patient that he knew them all too well. Such relief was passing through them as he gave his diagnosis and suggested they take this information to their doctor for further consultation. He translated all his knowledge into terms we could relate to; known diseases such as diabetes and arthritis were quickly identified as without any hesitation he pointed out their condition.

Yet even more than this, it seemed to me that his compassion and care for everyone who queued to see him was itself a healing balm. From the tortured look upon the faces of so many, it was obvious how painful was their personal story. Yet, as they sat there and received his rapt attention, I could see how steadily their mood became elevated, as if some heavy burden was taken from them. On one or two occasions I could see him wipe a tear out of his eye, as if he shared their pain, or even took a drop of it away through his compassion and his inner focus on the Medicine Buddha.

I sat back in awe and wonder. All too quickly it was over. He had left. I couldn't move. It had been quite amazing, incredible to witness, and I fell into reflection as to how this Eastern doctor could appear to lift the pain of a lifetime within a moment.

My friend Helen, who sat beside me, talked of travelling to India to find this marvellous doctor and secure a consultation in more detail. She was inspired by all the wonders she had witnessed in the lecture, for not only had she basked within the healing energy that poured from him, but her mind had been released from so much worry when she'd placed her hands in his to receive a diagnostic miracle through the doctor's skill in reading signs within the pulse. Before the festival she'd trailed for several months across the hospitals of London in an effort to discover what was causing her excruciating pain within her womb. In spite of many, varied tests there seemed to be no answer to her problem. Her pain was an enigma and her general practitioner had given up trying to help her, saying it was all in her mind. So she was ultimately left in a complete state of confusion as to what was going on, suffering real pain without any diagnosis or opportunity for relief being offered to her. Yet Dr Choedrak answered all her questions simply by laying his three fingers on her wrist. He said the root lay in her nervous system; this was forming pain within her womb. She was so grateful for his insight, yet his diagnosis raised for her the question as to how her nervous system could be cured.

As I watched light begin to flood into the faces of my friends, I became fired up by the prophetic nature of my previous memories of miraculous healing, together with the powerful impression left behind by this Tibetan doctor wafting out of the door with his entourage. I took up the healing challenge and decided I must become the pioneer. My heart and soul had become totally animated by this vessel of Tibetan medicine, and I was driven upon a quest for healing. My mind was set and I was soaring on the wings of self-denial, flying on towards the highest ideals. My chosen, single-pointed focus was now potently aligned with one desire, to bring a miracle of healing to my friends at this festival.

I then remembered the advice I had received when I had first heard about the miracle of the Western doctor cured of cancer. Her great blessing had been framed within a summary of the training that these doctors were required to follow, training she herself had sought. It seemed each doctor was required to follow in the sacred footsteps of the Medicine Buddha, at all times emulating his great example. This required them to be available to the sick at any time in any place across the world. The very room in which they stayed was therefore considered to be suitable for setting up a clinic. Consultations were on offer, free of charge, for they would charge solely for medicine, if prescribed. Armed with this knowledge I sought out the conference organizer, seeking to establish where this doctor was residing. Though resistant, she admitted that she knew about his lodgings and when quizzed further, was eventually persuaded to divulge the whereabouts of Dr Tenzin Choedrak.

A great joy that knew no bounds was bubbling up like an effervescent spring of enthusiasm within me, as I finally returned from the conference to the hotel. I felt as though I was swimming in a stream of living energy, which carried me along amongst the birds, the trees and flowers. Feeling young again and very much alive, my feet barely seemed to touch the ground, such was the buoyancy inside me. And when I went to bed that night I threw my windows open wide to let the beauty of the night sky and the moon above the mountains fill my room. To find this doctor in the morning was the prayer upon my lips and my fervent hope, as I envisioned myself high up in the kingdom of the lapis-bodied healer where this pure, celestial physician had invited me to sit within his realm, right in the centre of the mandala of the beautiful, blue-faced god.

Chapter 4

The Sacred Consultation

*T*HE DAWN APPROACHED and I began to surface from some distant reverie. My body felt in bliss and as my mind began to piece together reality, I felt the pull of something deep inside gently tugging at my mind. It was a dream about the doctor. I could clearly see his face, and yet the movement of the dream was still eluding me. I struggled to reflect and recall when, with a rush of flooding consciousness, a room came billowing up into my mind. It was his room, his place of work and he was seated at his desk. I sat in waiting on a small settee, expectant and attentive in humility. The atmosphere around him and pervading every corner of the room was one of golden sweetness. His assistants were occasionally moving in and out about their business; they exuded quiet ease within the presence of this father of Tibetan medicine.

Then, as if he had been called, he rose and turned to see me there. With a smile he bathed my heart with warmth and kindness, beaming love and deep compassion. He approached me and I stood to give respect to this great being who had manifested here within my dream. Without a word he then produced within his hands an ancient scroll. It was a tome of other times, a sacred, precious document. With a seriousness of purpose, ceremonially performed, he stretched forward his right hand and offered me this scroll from other worlds. I instinctively bowed low and received it with reverence in my heart.

The dream had ended here. Yet even whilst I dressed myself, preparing for the morning's expedition, the quality of this dream possessed me like a fragrance. My dream was most auspicious, coming on the morning when I hoped to gain a consultation with the doctor. It brought a lightness to my step as I skipped down into the lounge to meet Lyn, my dearest friend, for she had also touched the hem of mighty healing in the lecture by the doctor and was overjoyed to come with me to seek a consultation. After a simple breakfast of tea and toast, for we had been informed that it was best to eat lightly on the morning of a consultation, both of us sprang out into the clear, morning air.

A Chance Meeting

We had not been at the bus stop for very long before destiny immediately strode in and brought another person to seek the doctor's help. James, another member of our party, was out taking his morning walk and came right past us. He almost didn't see us until I spoke his name, for he was clearly gripped in a depression and had lost all sense of anyone around him. Compassion welled up inside me as I asked him what was wrong. My simple question of concern unleashed a torrent of emotion. In a second he was pouring out his soul right there beside us at the bus stop. He was the bearer of a secret, something terrible to tell. Just one week before he came to Switzerland, he had received results of tests which had been carried out by doctors. They had confirmed he had a cancer, which had re-emerged after many years of healthy life. The pain of this conclusion was too much for him to bear, for he felt he had not much longer to live.

Of course, he had no way of knowing of our recent experience with Dr Tenzin Choedrak and certainly no intimation that I was about to bundle him into the bus with Lyn and me to seek the doctor. I was moved inside to find how quickly my resolve to help my friends was bearing fruit. Here I'd found someone who clearly needed to meet the Eastern doctor. Higher powers had brought him to me, almost propelling him along the road to this bus stop. What extraordinary fate had brought us together, and was now about to bring him to the doctor? The Tibetans would have called it karma. In fact, these doctors claimed that the only way in which anyone could walk into their clinics was if a pre-existing karma existed between the doctor and the patient.

Karma, destiny, decree beyond the mind, the winds of change, the wheel of fortune – whatever name we might have sought to put upon it, something within the fine connections of the universe was guiding James, previously so alone in his distress, to find Dr Choedrak. Very quickly and succinctly I told him about the doctor, of his great spiritual presence, his compassion and extraordinary skill. Both Lyn and I poured something of the essence of this doctor into James' heart, inviting him to come with us and meet this physician face to face. Immediately, he responded as if a light had suddenly been switched on inside him. Brimming over with gratitude, he thanked us for giving him this golden opportunity. Our meeting at the bus stop was to prove to be a turning point in James' health affairs, for even just the timely mention of this doctor from another plane of healing had produced in him a shining sense of wonder, awe and mystery to brighten up his world which had fallen into the shadows. Even though we were careful not to raise his hopes too much, he must have sensed the awe and reverence we felt for this Tibetan doctor pouring from our hearts.

As we boarded the next bus and sat together in excitement, gazing out upon the morning panorama of the mountains, the bible story of the resurrection of Lazarus came to mind. For Lazarus had heard the powerful inner call, when he was summoned from the dead. This brush with cancer had completely turned James over, shaken him and forced him to come to terms with the lurking shadow of his own death. I prayed that James would, like Lazarus, be granted an extension to his life, for in religious terms all was in the hands of God, if he could truly open up and receive the grace and power of the spirit in his meeting with the doctor.

After a short bus journey we emerged in another part of Interlaken, soon finding the doctor's lodgings on the first floor of a nearby hotel. We formed a queue outside his room, sitting cross-legged on the floor in humility and supplication for the cup of his compassion to be offered. In the silence of the corridor, we had no way of knowing whether there would be a meeting, much less whether he would have the time to give a consultation and prescribe Tibetan healing herbs. We resigned ourselves to sit and wait, allowing providence to take its course.

Consultations begin

The minutes ticked along in silence, until suddenly the doctor's door was opened. He emerged. Was this our moment? But with a smile he passed us by; we were so near and yet so far. What now? Was everything in vain, or were we simply to return another day? No, one of several Tibetan monks who were accompanying him informed us that he'd only gone for breakfast. What relief this knowledge brought us, as the possibility of a consultation still remained. After some time, the sandalled, monkish party could be heard returning up the stairs. They sounded so happy, bringing an atmosphere of pure joy into the corridor. Their leader was still with them as they disappeared again into his simple hotel room. At last the door opened and a monk appeared, asking us who was to be the first patient. We happily agreed that James should be first, and with a look of poignancy and hope upon his face he disappeared into the room to see the doctor. We now relaxed in the knowledge that Dr Choedrak would indeed be giving consultations, so our turn would come.

After almost twenty minutes, once again the door opened, this time to reveal a completely changed man emerging. James was full of light, his face wreathed in smiles and vibrancy within. My comparison with Lazarus seemed most apt, for his energized and joyful appearance was visibly striking, as if he had truly stepped out of an entombed existence. Although we had no time for any real exchange, he thanked us profusely for bringing him along, before dancing off down the corridor into life. The monk then invited both of us to come in. They had intuited that we wished to come in together, and it seemed it didn't matter to the doctor if he saw us both at the same time.

As we stepped across the threshold I just had time to realize that something in me was in trepidation, before my eyes connected with his and immediately I began to reel inside. Once again, those spinning eyes were on my being, and completely overwhelmed, I staggered in. It was fortunate that Lyn was there to steady me for otherwise I might have fallen over. A mighty bolt of energy had exploded deep within my heart and all that I could do was gaze somewhat blankly, my mind completely blasted, as the doctor bade me sit beside him.

This physician of an ancient tradition first stood up, and with a finger raised to heaven, came closer to my eyes. He asked me to follow with my eyes the tip of his extended index finger as he seemed almost to bless me in a movement side to side and up and down. In his lecture he'd revealed that the eyes could be a mirror to the doctor of the signs of illness, but even just the quality of beauty and reverence in his movements had already stilled my mind into tranquillity. His perfect fingers, bronzed and slender, then touched lightly to the skin of my right wrist as he assumed a pregnant attitude of listening to my inner state.

The very second that he touched my skin, I knew that I was gone. I was no more. I was now merged entirely with him. Everything within my mind became blank as I sat meekly to the side of him. I lost all sense of time and was now totally unaware of where I was. In fact I couldn't quite remember why I'd come. So when the doctor asked me why I had consulted him, I stared at him dumbfounded. I'd forgotten who I was. I had forgotten all my pain. I had forgotten all my problems.

Lyn then nudged me in an effort to restore me to my senses and I managed to emerge a little from my stupor. I told him I had a problem with the energy in my upper back, where it felt as if something was trapped. The doctor seemed to look beyond me as he focused on something above my head. Then in a flash, without a word, he stood above me and struck down on both my shoulders with his fists as if to unlock this stuck energy and free it in my back. My senses slipped again into the maelstrom of his healing. Energy was rushing in a river up my spine, as if the plug of a volcano had suddenly erupted, and come streaming out of the top of my head.

What this doctor had recognized and treated within me I could not possibly comprehend. He seemed to have the ability to reach into the microcosmic world of the unseen, far beyond the reach of any microscope ever made, or ever likely to be made. For this particular inner world, this inner science did not look to the improvement of its instruments, but required the best development of man, the real observer. This doctor had become a perfect instrument; his finest senses were alert and reading signs within my being that most doctors could not ever hope to reach, for he had cultivated himself carefully through spiritual development to the very highest stage. He could penetrate much further to the very heart of nature than a host of complex instruments of measure could ever do. Yet there was really nothing supernatural about him. He behaved so very humbly like an ordinary man, and if confronted with the idea that he was performing miracles, he'd deny it, and proclaim Tibetan Medicine as a science.

Seeds of Healing

Such sainted ancients as this doctor who carried the knowledge of healing in his fingertips, were few within the world; they were passing on. Across the course of several decades, they had seen the steady ending of the ways that had existed over centuries, and witnessed the decline of relationships with nature that the cultures of the world had maintained over millennia. But here these teachers and their heirs were reaching out to me through this most powerful consultation with Dr Choedrak and the seeds of the ancient teachings were being passed on to me as precious healing substances in the form of pills, which I was offered. An interchange in Tibetan followed which I understood to be the doctor giving instructions to his gathering of monks as to what he'd diagnosed and what Tibetan healing herbs he would prescribe. The monks then promptly dived into a mass of different bags of pills within a suitcase on the floor. They seemed to rummage for an age; I thought perhaps they had run out of my prescription. But these Masters never seem to waste a second, and I realized that whilst my mind's attention was in focus on the bustle of the monks, the yogic doctor was transmitting something to me merely through his smiling eyes. Was this the ancient scroll within my dream?

Within my inner mind I seemed to hear a voice, something familiar that I'd read some years before:

> I confide only in you, Vajra Yogini,
>
> The Great Seal in the nature of immutable bliss,
>
> The heroine in a magician's dancing posture,
>
> Kindly bestow the mystical act of embracing,
>
> Comprehending from the depth (of my heart) that the numerous
>
> Pithless yet obscuring preconceptions of this life are my enemy,

I shall give the instruction on Extracting the Essence

As a favourable condition for practising the holy doctrine.

Gyalwa Gendun Gyatso –
The Second Dalai Lama (1475–1542)
From the fifth part of the instruction on *Extracting the Essence*.

This was the introduction of a very great instruction by the Second Dalai Lama on the means by which a pill to cure all ailments was prepared. The lineage of this instruction was unbroken from the mid-eleventh century when the quoted Vajra Yogini, one of the female forms of the Buddha, gave a teaching to a certain Padampa Rinpoche who lived, so it was said, for 572 years. What had struck me very forcibly when first I came across it was the emphasis on giving this instruction only to the very spiritual receptors. Once again, the words came floating back lucidly into my conscious mind, exactly as I'd read them. Within the text the Dalai Lama had identified disciples who were suitable receivers for this very secret knowledge:

Those who possess strong renunciation – who see that the whole of cyclic existence is like a fire-pit and that even the pleasures of great gods like Indra and Brahma are like dust on the souls of their shoes, who, having strong repulsion for material possessions, yearn for the attainment of the unsurpassed bliss of nirvana, the state beyond suffering, and who, having completely renounced the things of this world, love the life of seclusion – are the suitable receptacles for this instruction. Those who wish to receive the teaching because they are in need of food and clothing are but mediocre aspirants, and those who seek it merely as a cure for a serious illness are receptacles of the lowest calibre.

Gyalwa Gendun Gyatso – The Second Dalai Lama (1475–1542)

Identification of the disciples to whom the instruction may be given.

From the fifth part of the instruction on *Extracting the Essence*.

This distant memory evoked in consultation with the doctor placed the aim of Tibetan healing on the very highest plane. The doctors had realized that the path to spiritual freedom actually lay within the path of medicine and over many generations had produced a range of special herbal formulas, which not only acted as healing agents, but had the ability to protect and extend life, with the overall aim of elevating consciousness to an enlightened position. The balancing of the body's energies, producing a normalized state within a person, was clearly just the first step on the path to much higher aspirations, so the highest use of herbal preparations was for meditation purposes. They seemed to seek a different goal, a holy grail beyond the more basic understanding of health as we typically understood it in the West. They constantly aspired to another plane, far above the fundamental position of anatomy and physiology. So when Lyn and I had staggered in with our pain to seek a desperate diagnosis, hoping to ease our fearful minds, these great doctors from Tibet, in their compassion, were treating us from somewhere close to paradise. We were indeed blessed to receive this sacred consultation.

The doctor then began to voice some ancient sounds which were gently rolling like a mantra, chanting underneath the breath, yet quite distinctive and effective. My mind began to still and almost stop. It seemed the recitation of these mantric verses, where the words were potent energy, was the means by which the obscurations of my mind were steadily decreased. The pitch, tone and wavelength varied as he voiced the sacred syllables in Sanskrit. This science of sound, which seemed to me to be changing my internal chemistry almost at molecular level, was quite alchemical, a magic far beyond my wildest dreams, and I felt as though I was swimming in the currents of the universal stream.

At last, the doctor began to bring my consultation to an end, presenting me with three sets of pills. But when I was given very definite instructions on nutrition, daily routine and just how and when to take the prescribed pills, unfortunately nothing of this communication could hope to penetrate my mind. For I was in a state of nothingness, caused by the two sudden blows upon my shoulders. I wondered just what this most powerful doctor had unblocked which was now rushing like a torrent from my head, affecting my brain and eyesight.

My friend Lyn, who was attuned to me, had registered my state of mind and so assured me that she'd taken in the detailed information, so I now could move aside and let her take her place before the doctor. It was all that I could do to slide along the simple bench on which we sat, for my legs began to quiver from the profound experience I had been given. But as soon as he began to focus on my friend Lyn, I found it easier to be present and observe him as a witness, not a patient.

Blessings of a Different Kind

Lyn, who'd sat so patiently, supportive of my tendency to drift into another world without a moment's notice, now was nervous as she gingerly approached the doctor and his flock of monks who surrounded him like bees around a honey pot. The doctor looked into her eyes for just a second, flashed a smile, then began pressing on the pulse of her right wrist with his left hand, turning inwards to listen to the condition of the soul who sat before him, see her destiny, and help her on her journey. His head was gestured slightly sideways, tipping forward in an attitude of listening to the deepest inward motion of her pulse. It seemed to me that with each finger he was journeying within Lyn's body to the site of a related organ, scanning back and forth across this organ with a laser-like focus to establish if there was a problem lurking there. After listening to each of the positions on one wrist he then moved over to the left, and ventured deep inside the corresponding organs there until he had performed an examination of the whole body.

Then he asked Lyn to offer up both wrists together, and as he leaned towards her once again, I felt certain I could see a bluish tinge around him. For an instant he looked to me just like the Medicine Buddha, as if his merging with the deity allowed this great Buddha of the East to move gently through Lyn's wrists into the very finest channels, down her arms, into her chest and into her heart. It was as if the blue-faced god sat within her heart upon his lotus seat, emitting rays of healing to suffuse her body with healing nectar. Her body seemed to pulse with his blue light, as shining rays of healing penetrated every atom, every fibre of her being. As I watched, I saw a tiny tear of gratitude and love appear within the corner of my friend Lyn's eye. Then, with a quick intake of breath the doctor surfaced from the reading of her pulse, as if he'd surfaced from the deep, and was now coming up for air.

'So, what is wrong?'

The doctor broke the sacred silence with this question which he threw into her heart. Lyn was scrambling to find the perfect words to ask for help, to ask for healing, anything which could relieve her almost wretched state of being. As she had no obvious illness, she stammered out 'I'm full of fear and anger.' The monks immediately all roared with laughter, dancing about the room to hear Lyn expressing her problem so openly. They seemed to lift the atmosphere and raise her vibration all in one go. It was a joyful, over-whelming experience. Lyn, encouraged by this positive response, then blurted out 'And I am petrified of men!' Again the laughter flooded out like bubbling hot springs sent to heal her. All the monks now began gathering up pills in response to the doctor's instructions, handing each of them to her, contained in plastic bags.

The dancing, laughing, joking gestures of the marvellous monks had produced a veritable wind of energy within the room. I believed that they had responded to Lyn's fears and worries by erupting into a chorus of semi-ritualized sounds and gestures. Had I been witnessing a sacred dance of healing during which they absorbed the waste and debris of a lifetime, clearing out all the obstructions which were causing her fears? Certainly she had been given a great blessing, no less mystifying than the powerful blow the doctor gave upon my shoulders.

Tibetan Herbal Pills

We were intrigued about the pills he had prescribed for us. I'd never taken Tibetan pills before, and asked the doctor if he'd tell us more about them. As no-one else had yet appeared for a consultation, Dr Choedrak kindly agreed to talk with us about these pills formed from precious healing herbs, plants and minerals. He reminded us of the three humours he had presented in his lecture and how these could easily become unbalanced, leading to disease. Tibetan medicine understood exactly which qualities, tastes and energies affected these humours, so could apply a science whereby they could rebalance the humours by enlisting these specific qualities, tastes and energies through a range of methods, including the prescribed ingestion of herbal pills.

He said that at its simplest level the whole world, including every human being upon it had been formed from the five elements: earth, water, fire, air and space. From the combinations of these five elements, six different tastes could be identified: sweet, sour, salty, bitter, hot and astringent. Therefore the remedy or nourishment needed by our body would contain a particular combination of these same five elements and their subsequent tastes. It was for this reason that the myrobalan tree (Terminalia Chebula Retz), a sprig of which is held in the hand of the Medicine Buddha, was revered as a universal cure for all kinds of disease. For it provided all six different tastes. Further to this, Tibetan physicians understood that all substances, together with thoughts and actions, had definite qualities affecting the balance of the three humours, so through a combination of precise advice on diet and behaviour, together with pills and therapies, they could facilitate healing for every patient.

This refined science of Tibetan medicinal substances had been taught by the Buddha over 2,500 years ago and the formulas for the pills were very secret, initially transmitted orally and later inscribed on wooden printing blocks. Some formulas were quite simple, containing a few ingredients, whereas others were much more complex, with as many as a hundred or more substances within them. It seemed incredible to us that so many different substances could work together in one formula, but he explained that the subtle combination of various interacting substances was one of the main reasons that there were no side effects to taking Tibetan medicines.

The collection of herbs was an important part of study during training for aspiring Tibetan doctors and they were required to go on field trips high up in the Himalayas with an excellent physician who would teach them how to identify and classify the herbs. The wondrous Himalayas were a storehouse of these precious, efficacious healing herbs and he informed us that the hills of Arunachal Pradesh were particularly rich in herbs of quality. Dr Choedrak smiled as he recalled his treks into the Himalayas. Traditionally, they would wear their best clothes to such events, which although arduous, were happy and enjoyable experiences. At times, however, he felt a trifle uneasy when he had to pick these extraordinary friends upon the hills, the gorgeous, dancing Himalayan flowers and herbs. One of the funniest sights on those expeditions was the sight of a herd of sheep and a group of medical students both rushing towards the same herbs and flowers. Besides the sheep, the herb collectors on these sometimes dangerous trips had to endure the changing weather, which could turn within a moment in the mountains as they journeyed across deadly, deep ravines.

Such collections of the herbs were held at specific times of the year and all students were taught how to distinguish between the minerals, metals, earth, woods, twigs, roots, leaves, flowers and fruits, all of which were utilized in various medicinal remedies. Attention to location was required, as the particular qualities and tastes of various plants were affected by their position, whether they leaned towards the sunlight or were cooling in the shade. Time of harvest was particularly relevant, for this maximized the healing quality. Precision in identification was naturally vital, as was the knowledge of exactly which parts of the plants were to be used. He emphasized that the harvesting of herbs was always accompanied by great respect and reverence, and invocations to the Medicine Buddha would be made throughout the expedition.

All students were essentially involved in the full process of manufacturing medicines. Some processes were unbelievably detailed and time consuming, particularly those required for the special jewel pills, which would require a team of twenty people over a period of four months to be involved in such practices as smelting gold, silver, iron and other metals, working day and night whilst chanting prayers and meditating. One of these pills was called the 'Precious Black Pill' which actually included detoxified mercury, together with a fascinating array of minerals such as gold, silver, copper, iron, turquoise, amber, mother-of-pearl, lapis lazuli, coral, corindon, ruby, sapphire, rock crystal, diamond and conch shell. This pill was particularly effective for healing any form of poisoning in the body. His description of the detoxification of potentially poisonous substances through most exacting processes reminded me of alchemy. These physicians were true alchemists who had laboured ceaselessly across the centuries in search of golden healing secrets.

I had seen the precious pills before. They were most distinctive, being silk-wrapped, sealed in wax and individually boxed. I understood that each of them was passed on to the doctor who would chant and blow upon them whilst focusing on the Medicine Buddha, thus magnetizing them with the breath of this healing deity. It was clear from all he said that every herb and every mineral was blessed by inner prayer, right from the point of harvest up to the time of prescription. This spiritual element was essentially integrated into a practical process, and I understood that it was this element within the pills which had a very real effect, reaching deep into the patient's psyche and condition.

The doctors seemed to view the herbs almost as deities, revered for their uniquely different potencies, and sought to blend them together like a choir of ancient friends who had been gathered with such love and brought into a unique formula for healing. These herbs were carefully dried, cleansed, detoxified, weighed out into formulas, pulverized in mortars and sifted into powder form. A sacred atmosphere of chanting, ritual and prayer ran like a golden thread throughout the whole process. With the addition of liquid, the powder could be transformed into hand-rolled pills which were then dried. When the pills were hard, which usually took several days, they were polished within a hand-held tube of cloth. Within this tunnel of prayer, the pills were rolled in time to mantras just as if it were the Medicine Buddha who, with the hand of his great being, had gently fashioned them and polished them to shine within his healing garden.

The whole experience of visiting the doctor had been totally transforming and intriguing for Lyn and me. The greater part, the greatest measure of the healing had been given wordlessly and effort-lessly, bound up within the mystery of the doctor–patient relationship. This physician with his retinue of monks had emerged out of a land where the power of prayer, mantras and spiritual blessings together with a perfect, divine focus were completely accepted as being the most important aspects of healing. They had brought this tremendous faith in the power of spiritual practices into the Western arena, to the benefit of many.

Finally, Dr Choedrak brought our conversation to a close. He gently smiled and looked at each of us in turn before a gesture to the door from one of his devoted monks indicated that it was time to go. All too quickly it was over, and we left his hotel room, converted for the purpose of a consultation into a palace of austerity, where the Medicine Buddha presided over all. This Eastern doctor had received us and I knew within my heart that he had healed us. Yet it might take some time to understand just how deeply he had healed us. As we wandered on our way, we sat and paused within a shady place to look at all the pills the doctor had so kindly given us. These pills that filled the simple plastic bags were sitting in our laps and silently together we pored over the precious jewels we'd been given, these mementoes of our inner, great adventure with the doctor.

Chapter 5

Waiting for the Dalai Lama

*A*FTER THE GIFT of my consultation with Dr Choedrak, something within me felt profoundly changed. I still felt mystified as to what exactly had transpired in my meeting with him, but the blocked sensation at the top of my back had completely vanished and the energies in my body seemed to be moving much more freely. I had begun taking the three different pills he had prescribed, one before breakfast, one after lunch and the other after my evening meal. The sense of reverence which had permeated the consultation naturally extended into the act of taking the medicines and already I sensed a difference, as if a kind of inner light was growing inside me.

As the Rainbow Festival moved on towards its completion, a powerful air of expectancy grew within everyone, for His Holiness the Dalai Lama had been invited to come and give his blessing to the festival and formally bring it to a close. Finally, on the last afternoon, thousands of people began assembling for this occasion in the central auditorium, which soon became full of the sense of waiting. The atmosphere was already electric as we settled into our seats. It was

63

almost as if, on another level, the universal forces had been building towards this final event throughout the week. I remembered Terry's initial mistaken impression that Dr Choedrak was the Dalai Lama and realized how significant this illusion had been. Not only was His Holiness about to appear physically before us, he was also an extremely potent inner presence for the Tibetans as the pole star in their lives.

Men-Tsee-Khang

Recognized in Tibet as the fourteenth incarnation of the Dalai Lama, referred to as the 'Wish Fulfilling Jewel' and believed to be an emanation of the Buddha of Compassion, this living icon for the Tibetan race had been forced out of his country back in 1959. Taking the high road through the Himalayan passes, in the shadow of the sacred mountain Everest, he had left his native kingdom for a life in total exile. The Chinese had invaded and were systematically destroying every sign of Tibet's ancient cultural heritage, to the point at which most people thought Tibet, together with its precious culture, would soon be lost forever. Yet against severe and over-whelming odds, this quite unparalleled spiritual and political leader immediately began to marshal the indomitable spirit of his people; firstly establishing the Tibetan Government in Exile and secondly a programme to preserve the cultural heritage of Tibet. One of the first institutions he created as part of this extraordinary drive to save the culture was Men-Tsee-Khang – the Tibetan Medical and Astrological Institute.

His predecessor, the thirteenth Dalai Lama, founded this institute of medicine and astrology in 1915 in Lhasa, central Tibet. The purpose in starting it was primarily to offer various medicines to assure the health and intelligence of all children and in general to cast astrological charts for all Tibetans. This programme was widely practised throughout the thirteenth Dalai Lama's reign, not only in Lhasa but across the country, as official doctors and astrologers were delegated to each of the government headquarters based in fortresses in every district. Whilst the doctors would take care of all the newly born and prescribe appropriate medicines, the astrologers would cast the birth charts, and if someone appeared who had a most outstanding chart, or a very bad chart, then this information would be given to the central government. This practice gradually declined after the Dalai Lama's death in 1933, although the teaching of it still remained within the institute of medicine and astrology.

Many great doctors worked on religious texts and medical teachings across the centuries. A host of colleges and monasteries grew up with ample libraries, developed and extensively informed on Tibetan medicine. A famous doctor named Champo Tung was the official doctor to the thirteenth Dalai Lama and headed the Chagpori College of Medicine at that time, an institution very similar to modern universities with very many students. The school of medicine and astrology in Lhasa was led by another great doctor, Kenrab Norbu. The lineage of Tibetan Buddhist doctors remained unbroken in Tibet until the Chinese occupation became a serious threat to its continued existence. The devastation of the Tibetan medical system was considerable as countless monasteries and cultural institutions were reduced to rubble, including Chagpori and Men-Tsee-Khang. Precious medicines, medical *thangkas* and scriptures were destroyed as numerous doctors and lamas were either killed or imprisoned and tortured. This annihilation of Tibetan medical ideas and institutions, with the loss of many great physicians, continued throughout the Cultural Revolution. The Chinese considered all forms of religion to be poison and Tibetan medicine was considered the same, for the Buddhist link essentially ran through it just as all else in Tibetan life.

Yet a powerful resurrection began within the small, north Indian hill station of Dharamsala, just across the Himalayas from Tibet, where His Holiness resolutely and energetically worked to preserve the Tibetan culture against the wave of destruction. One of only three doctors to have escaped Tibet, Dr Yeshi Dhonden was summoned before the Dalai Lama who requested him to begin the task of rebuilding Men-Tsee-Khang in exile. With almost no funds, this intrepid and highly skilled doctor began training a group of ten students. From this small beginning, the important work of preserving this extraordinary medical system steadily grew as funds increased, students graduated and a few more doctors arrived out of Tibet to assist in this noble task. The mere handful of learned, elder doctors who had managed to escape the slaughter of thousands, worked tirelessly to re-establish their medical system under very basic circumstances. In rooms barely wide enough to stretch one's arms, the oral lineage survived under the tutelage of these master physicians and from there the workload and the manpower of the institute steadily grew alongside other cultural aspects of Tibet to a new stage of flowering.

Tibet Across the World

In a remarkably short space of time, under the powerful, protective mantle of the Dalai Lama, the people of Tibet were successful in preserving their 2,500-year cultural tradition in its original design. The appearance of Tibetan doctors and His Holiness at the Rainbow Festival was clear evidence of how they were increasingly distributing the message of Tibet across the world, so that the other nations could experience and benefit from its unique and ancient wisdom. Success in preserving the amazing possibilities that the Tibetan cultural heritage held for humanity flew in the face of history, which had witnessed the destruction and loss of so many of the great, ancient cultures. This was indeed a miracle for human life everywhere, for healing knowledge gained across millennia had narrowly escaped extinction and was being taught in present-day Tibetan medical schools.

The pole star for Tibet and all Tibetans was indeed the Dalai Lama. Like a mighty magnet he had drawn them all along to inner victory in spite of outer ruin and defeat. Even in his own country, under the oppression of Chinese rule which had sought to stamp out any memory of the Dalai Lama, the Tibetan people had held him sacred within their hearts in spite of beatings and torture. Dr Choedrak had suffered greatly, having been imprisoned for a period of over twenty years. Yet, retaining faith in the Dalai Lama and Tibetan Buddhism at all times, incredibly he survived a terrifying period of inhumane incarceration until 1980, a mere five years before this festival. At last he was released and allowed to leave for Dharamsala, where he took up his former position as personal physician to the fourteenth Dalai Lama. Perhaps the most amazing aspect of his story was the level of compassion he had retained for his captors and torturers, to the extent that he had even given them medical treatment, unreservedly offering them his great skill and knowledge. I found it almost unbelievable from both a psychological and physical point of view that he was able to operate so calmly and humbly as a doctor after such horrendous experiences. Surely this was a powerful reflection of his spiritual training and powers in meditation, helping him to control the mind under almost impossible conditions.

As the last few people took their seats and the time approached when the Dalai Lama would appear, I realized how impoverished many of us in the West were in comparison to this spiritual nation which had retained such an unshakeable focus on the Buddha of Compassion. Tibetan Buddhists were so steeped within their system of religious thought that they had completely aligned themselves with it, and an understanding of their medical system could only be reached by embracing this fact. The nature of their alignment with spirituality and with the Dalai Lama as their spiritual and temporal leader, was similar to the powerful effect of magnetic earth upon humanity. All of life and the experience of life upon the planet earth was inevitably influenced and determined by this awesome magnetic force. The Tibetans, who accepted the Dalai Lama as the most compelling and meaningful force in their lives, naturally aligned themselves with him as a powerful, magnetic pole star, leading them ever onward. Such an alignment with a potent spiritual force could not fail to form a correspondingly deep impression upon the whole nation.

The atmosphere within the room heightened steadily as I sat waiting with so many others. The fact that His Holiness had accepted the invitation to the Rainbow Festival had already confirmed a great blessing from a very high authority. Inevitably, he was the subject of many similar requests, not all of which he could possibly satisfy, so presumably his counsellors and deepest inner guidance had concluded that he should attend this festival. He had travelled all the way from his home in exile, and would soon deliver his own particular contribution to this unusual festival. His security guards were lining up on both sides of an open door quite near the left side of the stage. He would be coming in directly from the outside to give a short speech and blessing, before drawing back into the powerful protection around him and returning to Dharamsala.

Yet there was still no sight of him, even though the audience were all in their seats. As the minutes passed, from a psychological perspective I began to wonder what were the obstacles within us that needed to be cleared to allow His Holiness to come inside our hearts and feed our souls? I realized that as a Westerner, although I was deeply impressed by the strangeness of the system of Buddhist thought, I still as yet could not begin to really scratch beneath the surface and penetrate into the seemingly unfathomable vitality of Tibetan wisdom. Instead, I stood before it somewhat embarrassed, still wondering just how this great Tibetan world of thought might be embraced and truly merged into the West. Such a merging, however, risked the swallowing up of this unique, unprecedented treasure of philosophy by the all-consuming Western psyche. Either that, or worse still, when faced with the dilemma of just how to grasp the ideas of the East, rather than integrate them into our lives in a meaningful way, we might so easily stoop to offering up second-class imitations.

One of the organizers then appeared upon the stage to assure us that the Dalai Lama was on his way but could not yet enter due to the essential safety and security arrangements always required when His Holiness appeared before the public. The security guards stood impassive, yet alert in every fibre, as their eyes were on us all and took in every single movement, sweeping laser-like across the auditorium. The air felt charged as these guardians stood like a powerful ring of protection to guard His Holiness. This gentle monk was under threat because he remained such a powerful focus of worship for all Tibetans who revered him as the breath of life. He had also travelled across the world, beseeching support in his endeavour to return Tibet to his people, for his country had been subsumed into the Republic of China, losing its independence.

A Personal Message

Was it my mind, or was the light within the room becoming brighter, as we sat anticipating his arrival? Was it the shuffling of the feet of the audience, or could I hear a growing whisper on the ether, like the gasp of the collective in the audience as something very precious was approaching the stage? The atmosphere was climbing by the second as again someone announced that he would be entering very soon. We turned in unison to focus on the doorway where he was expected to enter. A very high vibration seemed to ripple through the whole audience as the bustle of his entourage of monks became visible. At last we could see him, beaming and waving to all as he steadily progressed towards the stage.

The glow that emanated from his smile seemed to touch each one of us as he quickly mounted the stairs with his assembly. He approached the microphone and looked around the room until the audience fell silent. With his hands up to his heart and palms placed together for a prayer, he briefly chanted something in Tibetan. Then he steadily allowed his dancing eyes to flit around the many people there before him. It was just as if he drank the audience in for several seconds as we waited for the gems of truth to fall from his lips. Then with a quick intake of breath he made a start, surprising all of us by making several jokes at his expense about the fact that he was late. In an instant he put us all at ease and quickly lifted us into another mood, breaking the tension with a wonderful display of easy humour. It was as if instantly he had read the state of mind within his audience, responding to their needs within a second. Although he spoke to thousands, the quality of his heart and extraordinary focus of his mind was such that I felt as though he was talking to me in private. It was as if he was delivering a personal message to every individual in the audience.

This light opening to his presentation lifted us into a place of joy. This man of the heart, who had been forced to offer up everything he loved and valued in the stark annihilation of his country and his race, began his presentation with a joke. He had been strong enough to sacrifice the world that he had known, yet had immediately set about rebuilding this world, like the phoenix which rose anew out of the ashes of the past. There was no sign of past atrocities within him, for he emanated great peace, was full of joy and grinning broadly to us all. I wondered how it was possible to cheerfully go forward into the future, having lived through such a past. Normally, this would be very hard to bear, taking years, in fact a lifetime, to begin to come to terms with such loss. He had been forced to let his world go completely, and to witness the destruction of his nation, all he loved and lived for shattered in an instant. Yet he'd used this tragedy to catalyze a resurrection. Understanding the spiritual truth that sometimes one had to lose the world in order to attain a greater wonder, he had led his people across the threshold of darkness, fear and anger, inspiring them to rise above personal pain and continue to reach towards the glory and joy of the higher spiritual life.

Immediately to his left stood his personal translator, so merged with His Holiness that they stood together as if they were one. But the Dalai Lama chose to speak to us in English, occasionally with the aid of the translator with regard to specific words or phrases. His whole presence, attitude and presentation was imbued with a profound feeling of peace, harmony, joy and equality. He was supportive of the festival, praising the aim of bringing different spiritual traditions together, for this, he believed, was the way forward, for us all to live together in true spiritual harmony. He believed that fundamentally, all major religions in the world had the same aims and sought to improve the human condition through spiritual practice. All religions preached love, promoted peace and offered a moral foundation, particularly advising control of the mind as a way of defeating selfish attitudes and their accompanying destructive emotions. He was encouraging us to set aside our minor differences, which were inevitably linked to cultural traits and different ways of understanding spiritual truths, in order to celebrate our shared goals of the promotion of goodness and eradication of suffering for all humanity.

As he stood, slightly bowed towards the audience in an attitude of true humility, I felt he had placed himself right at the very centre of the Rainbow Festival, where we all shared common sacred ground. The image that came to mind was of a cosmic wheel with an infinite number of different spokes all radiating from one centre. The Dalai Lama embodied this centre, this place where we were all equal, where we were all members of the same human family who aspired to happiness and wished to avoid suffering. He was at the heart of us all and had come to bring us together in a final blessing and prayer for humanity.

Points of Unity

Of course, this drive to seek a point of mutual understanding and coop-eration amongst the different nations and religions of the world must also have naturally permeated the Tibetan medical tradition. I had already been impressed to learn about how Tibetan doctors were increasingly coming into the West and offering their skills and knowledge to the betterment of mankind. They seemed enthusiastic to forge links with Western practitioners and promote platforms for exchange. Far from viewing their medicine as exclusive and superior, they seemed to retain respect for the different medical traditions of the world, sharing the common aim of seeking health for all human beings. Their ancient texts had predicted the onset of such modern diseases as cancer and AIDS, so clearly they had much to offer. Indeed it seemed extraordinarily synchronistic that this ancient nation had been forced out into the world at large by an invasion of their country, just at the time that these modern diseases were emerging.

His Holiness emphasized that he did not recommend one religion above another, nor did he support the need for a new world religion. It was essential to maintain the richness of the different traditions to suit the diverse spiritual needs of so many nationalities. Yet he constantly looked for the point of unity between us all and praised the festival as a fine attempt at achieving a better understanding amongst religions. If all religions could truly come together in the shared goal of the improvement of humanity, then this represented a great step forward in the pursuit of global peace and harmony.

He put everyone at their ease by emphasizing how alike we all were and how as a human being he did not see any difference between himself and us. Throwing aside such superficial differences as language, skin colour and mode of dress, we were all bound together as members of the human race, basically all wanting to improve our situation in the pursuit of happiness and avoidance of misery. For me, this was a wonderful inspiration, coming from such a loving, compassionate, pure-hearted and truly spiritual person, for he was encouraging us to aspire to the very highest within ourselves. Certainly, we all had the same capacity to either rise above our personal needs and seek to help others and do things for the greater good, or choose to go into the darkness and destruction of all we held dear.

The more he talked with us, the more I felt drawn closer to his great heart. His title, the Dalai Lama means 'Ocean of Wisdom' and it was almost as if we stood upon the shore, being bathed by the gentle, caressing waves of his compassion. He talked about the importance of connecting with the feeling of universal brotherhood and sisterhood which helped to counteract the more typical selfish and ultimately destructive approach to life. For we were, he said, essentially interconnected and interdependent, so rather than pursue our self-interest at the expense of others, we should always strive towards developing a sense of shared human responsibility.

This emanation of the Buddha of Compassion was filling *our* hearts with the essence of *his* heart. He was pouring his positive thoughts into our minds and his meditative stillness into our souls. He seemed to be saying that we must at all costs focus on the positive attributes of humanity, as if by this constant focus we would help such goodness in the world grow in spite of the darkness and difficulties we often had to face. The potency of the experience of listening to this great spiritual leader as he emphasized a positive, all-embracing attitude was heightened by the knowledge of what he had faced personally. I had often despaired and felt angry about the terrible atrocities perpetrated upon Tibet, yet had come to realize that this focus on Tibet's problem was at times more of a means by which I could release my own personal pain, anger and aggrieved feelings at how badly I felt treated by the world. In stark comparison, His Holiness had every reason to feel personal rage and anger, yet there seemed to be not a shred of it within him.

He demonstrated through his whole manner and way of being, how inner peace and calm was a potent medicine with a very real effect upon others. Increasingly the audience seemed to hang upon his every word as if he had the power to soothe their problems away. It was as though within him was an essence he could effortlessly give to us through his presence at the festival. Clearly, the Tibetan doctors aspired to do the same, for they understood how love and compassion were healing energies which could in a very real sense be poured into the patient, like wine into a glass placed before them. In this way, aside from any prescribed medicines, a consultation with a Tibetan doctor was in itself a profound healing experience.

These doctors were expected to place kindness before anything else and this was not difficult to understand, seeing their spiritual leader emanate such benevolence, living out the highest spiritual ethics by way of personal example. His message seemed clear, that it was of course difficult to rise above one's petty personality and offer up responses to the sufferings of others without neediness, demands for more attention to the pain we called our own. But if we fully realized and understood in perfect sympathy the suffering of humanity, we would gradually lose sight of our own problems and forget our personal sufferings because we would see the suffering of humanity as much greater, thus becoming permeated with the essence of compassion. We would begin to realize that that which fell upon us as our lot was, after all, a tiny fragment of a much greater tapestry.

Choosing Inner Balance

The Dalai Lama was living proof of the importance of realizing that we all had the power of choice, for no human mind could really concentrate on two completely different things at once. We could choose darkness or the light. We could be negative so easily. Why didn't we choose the positive? The Dalai Lama had given his whole attention to the most important task of rebuilding Tibet in Exile and by doing so had focused with his mind upon the positive. He therefore must have helped expel the evil around him which was ruining his country and destroying many lives. Yet he had achieved this remarkable result without directing any force towards the evil. In this way, no energy of his mind had been wasted; no vitality had been lost whilst he was focusing on rebuilding. This indomitable spirit of the positive in everything he did could only have gained in strength, so that his mind remained impervious to negative thoughts. This must have been a vital discipline especially when he was constantly faced with stories of atrocities continuing in his country.

To bless and close the Rainbow Festival, he had taken it upon himself to make a special journey to nourish us all with his love for all humanity. He said he did not harbour negative feelings such as hatred and anger for those who had caused the Tibetan race to suffer so terribly. On the contrary, he had much compassion for them, for they too were human beings searching for happiness. The words of Christ came to my mind, who asked God to forgive those who crucified him, for they did it in ignorance. Tibetans clearly understood ignorance as the root of all the problems in the world, and were committed to helping all human beings release themselves from this self-imposed prison. The Dalai Lama had been guided here this day and it was our good fortune to receive the emanations pouring forth from his great heart. I sat in awe as I watched him and wondered how he had managed to maintain such a perfect state of inner balance through the most difficult of times. It must have been due to the combination of the level of his incarnation and the training of the mind he had received right from the beginning of his childhood. Naturally, he was determined to preserve the spiritual lineage of Tibet which had produced such mental training. These ancient systems of Tibet had been developed over centuries and the Dalai Lama saw the importance of preserving them, not only for Tibet, but so the world at large could now benefit from the richness of their wonders.

Listening to him speak, I became firmly convinced that Buddhism and Tibetan medicine held the key to the disease and sickness of the mind that had inundated and devastated such noble countries as Tibet. The insights of these Tibetan minds, evolved to such a high degree, could bring the change of attitude needed as a counterpart to the destructive forces of materialism, prejudice and scepticism. Their medical and spiritual approach directed us to look inside ourselves for the resolution of our problems which typically manifested as outer calamities. The root cause was a form of inner blindness, which led to desire, anger and closed-mindedness and the never-ending passions which bound us too tightly to the outer, visible world.

The Archetype of Compassion

The Dalai Lama then talked about compassion. He said that true compassion focused on all sentient beings and wished them to be free of suffering. Such compassion should be limitless, extending to all without exception. He encouraged us to think about a friend, an enemy and someone who was neutral, like a stranger. Once our feelings towards each of these had become completely equal, we were then ready to extend our compassion to all human beings. True love was something quite different to the love for friends and relatives based on attachment and desire; this feeling of 'me' and 'mine' was subject to change. True love and compassion should embrace everyone, including our enemies. Again, the story of Dr Tenzin Choedrak's imprisonment came to mind, how when he was approached for medical help by the Chinese, he acted according to this high principle of compassion which transcended all normal limitations. These doctors were totally without prejudice and received everyone into their clinics without any feelings of personal attachment or aversion. They truly treated everyone in exactly the same way, as people who were in pain and suffering. So the question of friends or enemies never even entered their minds. Their Buddhist training had totally prepared them to meet all sentient beings as equal.

The powerful effect of several thousand years of Buddhist thought reflected in this perfect attitude was also related to the concept of karma. After all that had happened to the people of Tibet they, on the whole, persisted in viewing the evil happenings that fell upon their heads as the result of their past karma, or the simple law of cause and effect. In their view the causes of a frightening future were set in motion long ago in other lives, and therefore could not be altered. In fact, the thirteenth Dalai Lama, one year before he died, had predicted a time of great destruction even before it manifested as the Chinese invasion. So, philosophically they tried to bear the present simply as the result of actions in the past. Rather than carry such pain around as a constant weight upon the shoulders, they had followed their Buddhist system which advised its followers to first learn the lesson brought by such difficulties, but then clear them from the mind as much as possible. In this way they used their karma to develop the qualities of courage and endurance, whilst aspiring to retain a clear, calm mind at all times.

Taking this profound regard for karma and its workings a stage further, they viewed all the troubles in the world as a debt to be paid, and if it was paid with the right attitude, a new cause could be set in motion. Making the best of what looked like bad karma could set in motion forces for the good. In this way, the approach to situations and events that were full of suffering could be used to quicken progress on the spiritual path. It was becoming clearer to me how an understanding of karma lay at the root of the inner code of ethics prevalent in many from Tibet. Thus the gain we had in finding the adept Tibetan doctors and the high Tibetan lamas was an intellect imbued with pure and noble ethics, which could be used to confront the all-embracing 'I' with its tendency towards self-inflation and supreme arrogance.

I suddenly realized that when Terry thought he saw the Dalai Lama in the doctor, he had in fact been granted a glimpse of the inner potent spiritual archetype of the Buddha of Compassion. The focus on this archetype by Tibetan doctors allowed them to merge with their patients by means of a spiritual state where nothing was outside or separate from themselves. In this way they truly shared in the problems of the patient as if they were their own. This inevitably facilitated support for the patient at a very deep level. There was a world of difference between the help that one could give from a relatively superficial level and the help given from a place of true compassion. This was directly related to both the capacity for healing and also the depth of the healing achieved.

Through their visit to Switzerland, where so many different representatives of the global family had congregated together in spiritual aspiration, the Dalai Lama with his monks and doctors truly were helping to heal the world. As I looked around me, I could see that the effect of the words of His Holiness upon the audience had been profound. His smile had become their smile. His eyes had become their eyes. His radiance had become their radiance.

In conclusion, he shared with us a short prayer which he said always gave him great inspiration and determination:

> *For as long as space endures,*
>
> *And for as long as living beings remain,*
>
> *Until then may I, too, abide*
>
> *To dispel the misery of the world.*

I was lost within his smile, within his eyes, within his words, within his being, within his wonder, so much so that I forgot all sense of time. When he had finished, and was leaving with a wave to all who stood up in unison to thank him for his blessing, I could feel his impression in my heart. I was uplifted and knew that deep within me was a seed which I must feed with pure compassion for the world without conditions, or personal ambitions. His Holiness the Dalai Lama had blessed us all with the seed of pure compassion for the whole human race.

Chapter 6

Reflections on an Aeroplane

*T*HE MORNING FOLLOWING the Dalai Lama's closing of the festival I awoke into a state of bliss. This was typically the time of day I loved, emerging gently out of a sea of dreams and visions into a sublime peace, but for some time now I had been unable to reach this glorious state. Some kind of blockage in my body rhythms had seemed to be the cause and I was deeply grateful that this had been released. I packed my case, ready for the journey back to London that morning, took some breakfast and boarded the bus to the airport. The state of bliss stayed with me and I could observe myself engaging in the normal worldly processes, whilst spiritually I remained somewhere else. This sense of being in two different places at one and the same time was not a source of concern, for it always facilitated a tremendous stream of wellbeing, which like an essence seemed to pervade every cell of my body.

As I watched the last few members of our party take their seats, every person seemed to radiate an aura of great beauty. This festival had been a blessing for us all. I felt a great sense of harmony and ease of communication. The love I felt for everyone and everything was endless, like a never-ending stream which effortlessly issued from my heart to touch the hearts of all around me. After our extraordinary consultation with Dr Choedrak, Lyn and I had referred several of our party to seek him out. All who'd found him had a tale of healing wonder on their lips. James, who had initially accompanied us was a transformed man, gleefully telling everyone that he was convinced that his cancerous symptoms were disappearing (back in England this was eventually proven to be true). Helen, who had such pain within her womb, was deeply grateful, for the pills the doctor had prescribed for her were already bringing so much peace into her system. As the bus steadily began to climb up out of Interlaken, I took one last view of the magnificent snow-capped peak of the Jungfrau, which seemed to rise up in its majesty as if to salute me in a fond farewell. The opportunity to attend this festival had been afforded me by my spiritual teacher. It had been a wonderful experience and I felt an enormous sense of gratitude towards her.

At the airport, as we all queued to check in our luggage, I found myself automatically reflecting on the last week in order to reach a point of inner understanding as to the way in which my psyche had been nourished and transformed. Suddenly, I felt my spiritual teacher standing right beside me. She was so pleased to see me and immediately suggested we walk together to the gate of departure where we would await permission to board the plane. As I fell into step alongside her, I felt totally embraced and at one with her presence. We walked in silence until we came to a stop before our particular gate number. The air and everything around us seemed to hang in complete stillness as I let my vision swim into a reverie, a meditation. From deep within I felt her inner gaze upon me as she turned to break the silence.

She insisted I tell her everything about my experiences at the festival, for she could see quite clearly that all my energies had changed. I was quite stunned to hear this revelation, coming from someone whose powers of inner sight I knew to be unquestionable, so I immediately began to pour the story out of how I had met the doctor and had been given a consultation with him, when he had powerfully released the knots of energies located in my back and on my shoulders. I gave her a complete account of both the outer occurrences and my inner responses. Throughout it all, she remained completely silent with her eyes looking full upon me. As soon as I had finished, without hesitation she told me that my meeting with the doctor had been profoundly destined and that as a result of his healing actions I would be able to realize the Truth in this life.

Amazed at the depth of her perception and completely shocked by her pronouncement, I struggled to try and find the words to ask her more. But suddenly our flight was called, effectively bringing our conversation to a close. I resigned myself to this sign that I must accept her words without any further explanation, as we all began to move onto the aeroplane. Finding my seat beside a window, I allowed all she had said to sink deeply within me and relaxed into the flight home. I loved these journeys, for whether by bus, train, or aeroplane they always gave me a wonderful opportunity to be reflective. Whilst the body had no choice but to sit quite still for several hours, I could let go into my inner world and meditate upon the meaning and wonder of it all.

Thoughts on my Encounters with Tibetan Medicine

As the jet rose powerfully from the runway and began to soar into the sky, I reflected on the different styles of medicine across the world and what it was about Tibetan medicine that made it so unique. Basically, all medical systems were either those which leaned more towards suppressing disease or those, like the Tibetan system, which focused more on the art of restoring and maintaining health. Preventative medicine, in essence, aimed to ensure that illness never manifested at all. I had heard that according to the ancient Eastern traditions, patients would regularly visit their doctor for a checkup. The responsibility of each physician was to ascertain the faintest signs of the approach of a disease, and through treatment and medication, pre-empt its onset. The importance of this approach was reflected in the fact that in some traditions the doctor would only be paid if all went well, but if a disease manifested, then the doctor paid the patient for failing to prevent the approaching illness.

Every country had a different style of medicine, inevitably linked to the predilections, aspirations and traditions of the countries themselves. Geographical location was therefore of paramount importance, for every science of medicine was a product of its environment. Medical systems essentially reflected the inner attitude of the people who had founded them. This attitude to others and towards the world in general which evolved across the centuries within a social system, naturally impregnated and permeated the structure and development of medicine in that country. Thus, medical systems could not fail to embody a particular approach to life or view upon the world.

In this way, a national drive towards money and material comforts would inevitably have an effect upon the nation's system of medicine. Such systems could not hope to stay pristine and somehow clinically removed from the inner viruses of greed and selfishness. Conversely, if a medical system existed within a culture promoting the values of compassion, love, sharing and harmony whilst seeking to preserve a clean and wholesome environment, the system would inevitably be imbued with these ethics and would develop a balanced, holistic approach to health. One of the most particular differences between the Tibetan medical system and other systems, resided in the ultimate aim of restoring health. For the Tibetan doctor, spirituality and healing were so intimately linked that they could never view the body as merely a life-supporting system. They upheld the human body as a temple, as a vehicle for realizing a state of spiritual enlightenment.

The healing from such Masters as Dr Tenzin Choedrak therefore offered us the stage from which we could begin to move into a higher spiritual state, achieving emancipation from suffering. Through

achieving a healthy body, mind and spirit, with everything functioning in harmony, one could hope to bring the mind under control, for
without control of the mind, the comprehension of the ultimate
reality was far beyond one's reach. The alchemic physicians of Tibet
hoped to sustain this balanced state and promote spiritual practices
upon it, thus offering a potential springboard to higher consciousness. It was for this reason that a range of secret formulas for pills
had been developed across the centuries to assist in meditation and
to sustain the body during long fasts.

I was coming closer to understanding how a relatively brief
encounter with a Tibetan physician could have had such a profound
effect upon me. Certainly the fact that the system had been protected
for so long within the extraordinary land of Tibet was a factor to take
into account. This medical system was inextricably linked with the
unique geographical nature of Tibet, with Buddhism and the cultural
history of the Tibetan race. For over two millennia the jewels of
Tibetan medicine had remained hidden within an almost inaccessible
terrain, protected by mountains and accordingly relatively untainted
by other traditions, in particular those from the West. Yet almost
overnight, this legacy of Tibet had been quite literally and mercilessly
forced out into the world at large. Without this explosion propelling
Tibet into the West, arguably none of us would have benefited from
its wisdom.

The Prophesy of the Buddha

I had been appalled at the nature of the invasion of Tibet, yet part of
me remained in awe at the workings of higher destiny which had
driven this great tradition out of its ring of protection. Tibetan history
had demonstrated that these medical teachings were highly sacred,
revered and essentially kept hidden as they held within them potent
revelations. They had originally been transmitted from the Buddhas
and deities into the human world and further teachings had been
revealed through dreams, visions and insights in meditation. Because

of the profound nature of the teachings and the inherent power which lay within them, the timing of their exposure to the world was crucially important. In fact, there was a time in the first century when the great guru Padmasambhava ordered that the original teachings should be buried within a pillar in a monastery until the time was ripe for them to be revealed and propagated, as he said that people were not ready to receive them. When the time came to take these *terma*, or hidden treasures further, they were revealed to a person with supernatural knowledge, who was told where to find the teachings. He in turn taught them to the great twelfth-century physician, Yuthog Yonten Gonpo the Younger, whose work formed the fundamental text of the rGyu-shi, or Four Tantras.

On deep reflection, I realized that for such teachings to be hidden in this way, the power contained within them must be quite extra-ordinary. The history of their dissemination into the world revealed a completely guided process. The Buddha had prophesied that the Buddhist teachings would eventually be taken into the West, and one year before his death, the thirteenth Dalai Lama wrote a testament to the Tibetan people predicting the annihilation and destruction of their homeland and culture. With the fulfilment of this prophecy, the fourteenth Dalai Lama was forced out of his homeland, and became instrumental in spreading these teachings across the world. I was sure that the instant these ancient secrets stepped outside the sacred walls of the inner sanctum of Tibet, something profound had irre-versibly changed, as if a bright new star had suddenly appeared on the horizon.

Yet when observing people's responses to the magic of Tibetan medicine, I felt that it had been received more as a dazzling attraction than a system that could be seriously understood and integrated into the Western understanding. So in a sense this great truth had remained buried within its own ancient system, almost totally eluding the Western audience. It was as if this highly polished and exquisitely fashioned jewel of the East had somehow simply bounced off the Western intellect. The Western audience had certainly been entranced, but returned to its former ways unmoved, lacking a key to the hidden depths of this great system.

Everything within my experience of the system and its doctors had pointed to the fact that these Tibetan medical teachings were not solely theoretical medical texts for practitioners, but were in fact revelations, coming into the West at this time, imbued with the wonderful inner essence of a deeply spiritual nation. I had witnessed the hypnotic effect of Dr Choedrak's lecture upon his audience. This had not been any ordinary lecture for the mind, but a delivery affecting the body, mind and soul on many different levels, achieved primarily through subliminal means. Tibetan medicine was surely, in essence, a revelation of great truth and it was for this reason that throughout its ancient history there had clearly been times when such truth had either been totally hidden, or kept as a secret for only the high doctors and lamas, so that its power should not be abused. Now, however, I had been privileged to witness and directly partake in this revelation to humanity.

Dr Choedrak had demonstrated the brilliant aspect of Tibetan medicine: its very wholeness and oneness. The three humours, which formed the foundation of the whole system, reflected the Trinity at the heart of the universe. This Trinity was an ancient wisdom reflected in many of the ancient religions of the world such as Christianity and Hinduism. But for the first time, this Trinity was being scientifically explained in terms of the three humours. These humours were essentially rooted in the earth through the five elements and thereby tied us to the earth upon which we lived. The Tibetans' holistic approach recognized, therefore, how deeply sensitive we were to any changes in the earth and its atmosphere.

A Revelation of Personal Truth

I turned to look out across the carpet of white clouds and the clear blue air as the aircraft flew on, realizing how little attention we gave to the importance of the earth's atmosphere, which perhaps should symbolically have been understood as the amniotic fluid circulating around the embryo. When man polluted the atmosphere and increased the hole in the ozone layer, he was tearing a hole in his own protection, and thereby weakening his own immune system. This kind of insight was possible through an understanding of the Tibetan medical system, which was profoundly revealing each person's own truth through the vehicle of his or her own body, mind and spirit. The opportunity that lay within this marvellous system was to open to the truth that lay within it and therefore open to a completely and fundamentally different attitude to life.

For years I had been inspired to study the history of alchemy, sensing that inherently its secrets held the key to universal truth. Alchemy and Tibetan medicine both reflected the great truth of ancient wisdom that the universe was built on a triad of energies. In the case of mediaeval alchemy, ancient and deliberately secret revelations of how one might refine base metals into gold had lain hidden within the special language of images. Tibetan medicine clearly had strong alchemical links, and was now being revealed as a way of taking the basest parts of ourselves – our very elements – and of harmonizing and refining them to the utmost degree – for this represented an essential stage in the evolution of mankind.

I felt that we were on the edge of a revolution in healing, and Tibetan medicine was not only at the forefront of this, but was the main initiator of this global revolution. For the Highest Truth lay within this miraculous system, given by the gods for man's education, for his development, for his healing, for his refining and ultimately for his greater enlightenment. I realized that my encounter with Dr Tenzin Choedrak had allowed me to touch the hem of an exquisite Eastern system within which lay the potential for powerful transformation on a number of levels.

To me, it was a great blessing for us all that this Tibetan medical system was now rapidly expanding and developing across the world in a way previously not witnessed. Westerners were becoming interested in Tibetan medicine, and a growing number of patients were coming to depend upon Tibetan consultations and medicines. This increasing interest in the Tibetan medical system was not due to advertisements or propaganda, but simply attributable to word of mouth from those patients who had experienced its very real benefit. Added to this, several Tibetan physicians were regularly being invited to the West to give lectures on their medical system.

Clearly, this rapid expansion was no accident, just as it was no accident that the original texts had dropped down from heaven. The ancient texts had actually predicted the state of the world at this time, including the advent of eighteen modern diseases. The relatively dramatic increase in cancer and the recent identification of AIDS were considered to be two of these. These diseases were only now manifesting, and Tibetan medicine had appeared in the Western world in order to help treat them. For thousands of years, only the personally initiated had ever been allowed to go near these texts, until now. The texts themselves were also couched in a unique language and ancient Sanskrit–Tibetan script. Yet now the gates were being opened to these revelations, brought into the consciousness of modern man for the purpose of his enlightenment.

As the aircraft dropped down below the cloud level and the bustling London landscape opened up beneath me, I inwardly thanked the higher powers for enabling me to make a real connection with this unique medical system through one of its most accomplished physicians, and the spiritual leader of Tibet, His Holiness the Dalai Lama.

Chapter 7

From Death to Birth
with the Rinpoche

O<small>NE YEAR LATER</small>, in 1986, I was fortunate to meet another great Tibetan doctor. As with all of the best experiences in my life, the opportunity came my way as if by chance. I had been enthusing about Tibetan medicine one afternoon at the home of my spiritual guide in north London. Here she regularly held open house for members of her group and on this particular day, almost out of the blue, she suddenly asked me to talk about my experience in Switzerland with Dr Tenzin Choedrak. Knowing that there must be a particular reason for her initiating this, I let myself fall deeply into that precious memory once again and over the next hour gave a full account of the event, expounding on the wonders of the Tibetan medical system.

At the end of the afternoon, just as we all began to leave, someone unknown to me approached and pressed a book into my hand. She explained that she felt moved to present me with a book she'd been passionately reading over the past month and which she happened to have within her bag. She had been fascinated by my tale of healing and was curious to know if I would continue with my interest in this system from Tibet. *In Exile from the Land of Snows*, the book she'd kindly given me, was a very comprehensive and deeply moving account of Tibet and how Tibet in Exile came to be established. I was shocked to read details of Dr Choedrak's sufferings under the Chinese rule in Tibet and completely overwhelmed to touch the greatness of the human spirit manifesting within this doctor who had managed to transcend so much hatred.

Within the book, I found a leaflet left there as a bookmark. It announced the coming visit of the Venerable Dr Trogawa Rinpoche, a most revered, respected, high physician from Tibet, who had been based in Men-Tsee-Khang in Dharamsala in its early days. He had been trained within the Institute of Chagpori, though this college was destroyed by the Chinese when they invaded. In his aspiration and desire to safeguard the lineage of Chagpori he eventually re-established the Institute in Darjeeling. The Chagpori practice was held in high regard because of its unique tradition, which combined medicine and spirituality with particular success.

I felt a strong, inner compulsion to be present at the lecture of this doctor. Something was driving me to seek out anything that I could find about Tibet, its medicine and highly trained physicians. These physicians, who were unlike anything I'd ever come across, were now appearing much more regularly in the West and I felt it a duty to go out and meet them and let myself be enriched by their marvellous medical system and somehow integrate it into my being.

Dr Trogawa's Teachings

The Wellcome Institute, devoted to the history of medicine, was the venue for the lecture by the doctor. This prestigious place in London aimed to bring the diverse medical traditions of the world under its roof. Its founder, Sir Henry Wellcome, had a personal interest in the medical traditions found in Asia, and uniquely this library had already acquired Tibetan manuscripts, blockprints and medical paintings. The Rinpoche had been invited to present a lecture as part of a symposium on Tibetan medicine to an invited audience which included Western medical practitioners, together with a number from the public at large. So together with my two friends who had been present at the lecture held in Switzerland, we entered the hallowed doors of medicine to be greeted in the entrance hall by a display of wonderful Tibetan *thangkas* and ancient texts. It created quite an atmosphere and enthusiastically we went upstairs to the lecture room, going right to the very front.

As we waited, my attention was immediately alerted to a glowing feeling of complete contentment emanating from someone sitting in the audience on my right. I peered along the row to see a monk in most distinctive red and saffron robes. It was clear he was the Tibetan doctor, in meditation, still, sublime and deeply peaceful, with a man in Western clothes seated beside him, who I thought must be the translator. This highly refined and sensitive doctor felt my gaze upon him, gently turned his head and smiled. As he did so, a radiance flowed out across the room from him into my heart. Such an exquisite sweetness was enfolded in his smile and in his eyes, which were perfectly still. I felt entranced and warmed inside to see the Rinpoche in such repose before he lectured. Within the context of an audience of Westerners, some quite esteemed and qualified by Western medical standards, all rather tensely perched upon the edge of their seats, this resting doctor looked so humble, undisturbed, a simple Buddhist monk.

The afternoon of information began with Dr Terry Clifford, who gave an absorbing account of Tibetan psychiatry and mental health. Throughout her inspired delivery I kept thinking how very Eastern she was in her overall manner and general presence. I realized that she must have completely aligned herself with the Tibetans, for many great lama doctors had contributed to her research. It was like an aura that surrounded her, creating a powerful subliminal effect upon the audience.

The second presentation was by Dr Elizabeth Finckh, a German doctor who gave brief descriptions of the humours existing in the body according to Tibetan medicine, and how they would typically manifest within the human race as three different types of person. It was genuinely interesting to hear her deliver this unusual perspective, but once again, it was so obvious to me that she had been with the Tibetans; it was as if they'd left their mark upon her heart. She had been inwardly affected to such a degree that when she gave thanks to Dr Yeshi Dhonden, an eminent doctor who had been directed by the Dalai Lama to help her throughout her studies and translation of the rGyu-shi, it was as if this noble doctor came to speak to us in person, so deeply was she linked to him.

Both of these introductory lectures whetted my appetite to hear about the system first hand from Dr Trogawa Rinpoche. Excitedly I leaned towards the front to see the doctor now begin to make a move towards the podium, accompanied by his translator. Once again the quiet gentleness and warmth was in his movements, every step towards the stage was contained within an ethereal inner beauty, almost as if he floated elegantly slightly above the floor. He reached the lectern and stood silently, smiling upon the audience, and through his translator offered thanks to those who'd given him this lecture opportunity, and thanks to all the audience for coming to receive him.

Then he paused as if in prayer, with his eyes half closed and inwardly attentive to a voice that seemed to come from deep within him. Every word, all in Tibetan, was a potent incantation. I felt that he was paying homage to the Medicine Buddha, the King of Aquamarine Light, in this way allowing him to speak to us directly through his servant, through his Rinpoche. The choice of lecture seemed to me auspicious and engaging, for it was about the final journey from one's death into the processes of birth. I had always believed that nothing in this world was ever really left to chance. The movements of universal synchronicity were all too powerful, so I mused what ending of a precious cycle this represented for me and what birth or new beginning it heralded. As he began to speak, I could feel that through his carefully chosen words he was taking the whole audience into a profound meditation on our inner origins according to his system of medicine.

Death and Rebirth as a Process

The understanding of a person's death and subsequent birth was naturally informed by the Tibetan Buddhist philosophy of human life. Reincarnation therefore underpinned his presentation, for the passage from one's death towards one's next life in the world was something totally accepted by the people of Tibet. They held a view based on their learned scriptures, the visions of ancient seers, expositions verified by insight from enlightened ones in meditation and near death experiences. The Bardo Thotrol (Tibetan Book of the Dead) had presented observations of the process of one's death, the after-death state and the path of consciousness into the world of form at birth. The doctor's lecture thus assumed a measure of acceptance of this process of rebirth.

In wondering how the Western mind could accept this, I remembered a book I'd once read, a unique and mind-expanding explanation of the mystery of what happens after death. *Life Between Life* had told how two men, based in America, had stumbled across something inexplicable. One was a writer seeking evidence for rebirth and the other, a physician specializing in psychiatry, was quite expert in the technique of regression using hypnotism. Together they had presented extraordinary evidence that there was a world existing between one life and another. After thirteen years of research and a host of medical histories, these pioneers had ventured to give proof that there was a *bardo*, as Tibetans would have called it. Through regression into past lives, Dr Whitton had discovered, quite by accident, that patients had a memory of some place quite distinct which they related as existing in a space between two lives. The different stories of these patients were astonishingly consistent with each other, which gave the book its credibility.

It was highly intriguing to me that this Tibetan doctor focused on the death-to-birth experience, for all our Western conditioning was typically centred on the journey from birth to death, or the seven ages of man as Shakespeare called it. Rarely did we have the courage to consider what would happen when we died. This fear of death was very powerful in our culture, so that even on one's deathbed it was unlikely that one would focus on the coming transition, and surrounding relatives were often more preoccupied in trying to keep a person alive with their own needs. So the whole process seemed to be perceived as being a kind of wrench away from something very precious.

Yet typically Tibetans would spend their lives in preparation for death without any sense of morbidity. They knew and understood the deeper meaning of death, not as an end but as a journey just beginning. When a relative or friend was close to death, they would sit beside the deathbed and begin to take the dying person to the threshold of what they perceived to be another world, relating in an open, honest way to the distinct and unmistakable condition of death. It seemed to me that they had the capacity to be completely present and give love to a companion or relative with no avoidance of the truth.

I realized just how significant and powerful was this lecture by the Rinpoche, injected straight into the very heart of Western medicine, manifesting in the library and physicians in the audience. I prayed deeply that his message, like a seed, might find rich soil within this audience which possibly was sceptical and might become defensive at his challenging ideas. It seemed essential for our human evolution that a meeting of the West and East should occur and be accepted. I felt certain that this kind of exchange with an essentially spiritual medicine could help the rift between religion and science, which to me should never have been polarized, but should be moving closer together to embrace a more holistic and coherent perception of life.

The Rinpoche began by describing the various stages of one's death, the dissolution of the elements, the dissolving of the senses and sense elements. His channelled, clear delivery, both in his mother tongue and then in English through his translator, seemed to transport me, as if he tangibly and consciously gave me an experience of the process of the move towards unconsciousness and death.

The Stages of Death are as follows:

Dissolution of the Elements

1. The element Earth dissolves into Water.

2. The vision declines.

3. The person feels that he or she is sinking, and there is an impulse to pull oneself up.

4. The element Water dissolves into Fire. The mouth, nose and pores begin to become dry.

5. The element Fire dissolves into Air. The heat starts to concentrate in the centre of the body from the extremities.

6. The element Air dissolves into Space, that is, the consciousness space.

Dissolution of the Senses

1. The power of the eye dissolves into the ear.

2. The power of the ear dissolves into the nose.

3. The power of the nose dissolves into the tongue or taste.

4. The power of the taste dissolves into the sense of touch.

5. The sense of perception declines, then disappears inside.

Dissolution of the Sense Objects

This happens just at the point when one is ceasing to breathe.

1. External perception has disappeared and an internal perception

takes its place, which seems like moonlight.

2. An expansion state occurs – like sunlight radiating.

3. The state of Attainment occurs – this is a feeling of luminosity, which exhausts itself, then falls into a feeling of complete darkness or blankness. As the light radiates, then declines, it leaves a person with a feeling of space. This space becomes duller as the light fades and falls into darkness. Then the person becomes unconscious.

This succinct description of a process of dissolving was so vivid and consuming, when he finished, I felt myself grind to a halt, as if I could no longer breathe. I felt overwhelmed by a powerful memory of endings; different cycles in my life, where all around me I had witnessed an awesome sense of falling, as different aspects of a previous way of being were dispersing. I remembered faces, friends and places, images of something once familiar. In his revelation of the unavoidable process of death, Dr Trogawa had stirred me to my core. I realized how, in a sense, we were prepared for this great journey through the many different endings and beginnings we confronted in our lives. Again I wondered what this event in central London would come to symbolize for me and for this audience.

In the *Bardo*

Dr Trogawa proceeded to inform us of how, when the person became unconscious, a space would then occur. A space where lamas and great Masters would perform a special prayer or meditation called a transference. This was the point of entering the *bardo*, an interval or suspension like a bridge between two worlds. This post-death state occurred when outwardly the body had died, although Tibetans still referred to a state of unconsciousness within the deceased person. After one day of unconsciousness, the person was said to awake into a completely new experience. For the majority of human beings this would be a delusory state, but lamas could attain a more advanced condition, where they moved into a field of enlightenment. This was called the 'Buddha-field' experience. However, even with a degree of meditative or spiritual experience, a normal person could learn from this state if a spiritual ritual was performed at the post-death stage. This was the reason why death rituals were performed by Tibetans.

I marvelled at the idea that a person could achieve a certain measure of control within a state which to me appeared completely out of grasp, for by its nature death consumes us. Yet I had heard about the phenomena of certain spiritually advanced monks and high lamas, subtly informing others by means of various signs that daily life for them was about to end. They then would go into meditation and die in full consciousness. In the case of some who were particularly advanced in spiritual practice, miraculous phenomena had been witnessed, such as the body shrinking down to the size of a finger, or even achieving what was known as the 'rainbow body'. This meant that at death the body would actually dissolve into space like a rainbow, leaving behind only the hair and fingernails.

The Rinpoche then took us through the tantra on the stages of death to the ending of the *bardo* or the boundary we crossed between one life and the next, for he intended now to focus in more detail on the processes of birth. I felt relieved to see a light appearing at the end of the dark tunnel that had formed within my mind. He said we should never underestimate the precious opportunity offered to us through being born a human, for this presented us with a real chance to dispel ignorance. Birth held the basis for pleasure and pain, for suffering and happiness, and thus the extensive range of human experience. Once one had taken birth one entered the entire life process, the transformation from birth to death. It was the inevitable ups and downs of existence that actually provided the proper environment needed to help dispel complacency, increase awareness, and achieve insight into fundamental reality. Without such insight, the cyclic process tended to perpetuate itself, and dying would just lead to more ignorance which would lead us into life and yet more ignorance. Thus there would be a continuing cycle of ignorance, death, birth, ignorance, death, birth – ad infinitum.

His words emphasized for me how much time we tended to waste, complaining about our lives at every corner, wishing that we could be somewhere else. 'I'd rather die....' was an expression that we often fell to using when the chips were going down and we proclaimed our life a nightmare. So we would blame it on the sun, and on the god who had forgotten us. We would pray that we might peacefully bow out of this performance and be given something dreamier and easier within another world. Yet Dr Trogawa was presenting human life as so unique, we should not waste a single second. There was a speed we could achieve along a lifetime's evolution. Human life gave us the speed, the great potential, if we only could accept it and try to celebrate the pain as well as pleasure.

He explained that it was the winds of karma that brought us into existence. At the time of sexual union of the parents, our conscious-ness, which had been wandering in the *bardo* and was ripe for rebirth, would enter the combined reproductive essences. So at the moment of conception we flew in to take our place in human life, and there began our new formation, new creation. Once again the cosmic energies, or five elements, would begin to do their work and build our bodies for the new life. These were the building blocks, and the science of medicine sat upon these cosmic energies. From the very moment of conception, foetal growth within the womb and through our life we were affected by these energies. The fundamental knowledge of the three humours or vital forces, *rLung*, *Tripa* and *Badkan* was reinforced for me by Dr Trogawa as he presented these as translations of the basic cosmic energies into the human body. The balance of these humours was crucial for achieving inner health, just as within the greater world, the symmetry of energies or elements needed to be maintained for planetary life to flourish and survive.

His exposition powerfully linked us all with the environment and the need to protect it. It gave a greater emphasis to the danger we were witnessing through the destruction of precious fauna, forests, indeed nature in its entirety. If we could somehow gain respect not only for the world at large, but for our bodies as containers of the very same elements as everything around us, we might make a step towards greater harmony and health and not see ourselves as separate from the force of nature which we typically tried to defeat and master.

A Description of Creation

According to Tibetan medicine, the doctor said, the birth of all beings occurred in four different ways: miraculous birth, birth by humidity, by eggs or by the womb. He said the ordinary person entered the mother's womb completely ignorant of past and future lives, and would remain so throughout life. High bodhisattvas, by comparison, those beings who dedicated their lives to helping every sentient being within the world, could retain the knowledge of their past and future lives. These sacred beings who were high upon the path of evolution were at liberty to choose their own conditions of rebirth, for they had spiritually practised over many, many lives to reach this stage, and were powerfully motivated to disseminate the highest Truth to all humanity.

These beings, therefore, were not brought to life by karmic winds as with an average person, but were borne into the world upon the higher wind of wisdom. Their births were usually extraordinary. In 1905, the birth of the Venerable Kalu Rinpoche was heralded by extraordinary happenings. Rainbows formed within the sky and snow fell upon the ground. He was born feet first and immediately on being born recited the mantra: *Om mani padme hum.*

Dr Trogawa progressed to a description of the stages of development of the foetus in the womb. This most unusual, medically insightful, and clear account was quite absorbing, and I marvelled at the level of sophistication running through these texts. A most profound, exact description of the baby's growth within the mother's womb was presented as a fact known by the ancient doctors of

Tibetan history 2,000 years ago. They had described the embryonic development week by week, with such precision I was amazed at how accurate and clear they had been in their portrayal of the foetus. The sophisticated level of this view of embryology was utterly astonishing, for they had integrated medicine, science, tantric texts, doctrines of karma and rebirth completely and perfectly. It was no wonder that they called these texts the *terma*, translated as 'hidden treasures', for the purity, sublimity and wholeness of the knowledge was breathtaking.

He began with the uniting of the semen and the ovum at conception and then took us through the subsequent thirty-eight weeks. Just as from a pond one built a small canal, so that the water ran onto the waiting field and would then drop by drop begin to nourish it through irrigating systems, so the process of development must also take its time, and the capacity of what he called 'the winds' within the body would change across this length of time. As he spoke about the progress of the foetus, the rhythm of his words were beating in me like a poem of becoming and I felt as though a new birth was occurring in me through his lecture.

In the first week then, the foetus is like a piece of curd which floats on milk, and in the second week this curd begins to change as its consistency solidifies, becoming just like yoghurt in the third week. At this point, and only at this point, an influence can be exerted on the future gender of the child through special mantras and through diet, amulets and various methods linked to knowledge of astrology. If, for instance, a family have always had a tendency for daughters, then this specialized approach can thus assure them of a son. In the fourth week, characteristics of the foetus can already tell what sex the child will be, and it is now an independent form.

So, day by day and week by week this tiny life within the mother's palace of becoming will begin to take its shape; its distinct form will now expand quite rapidly. The navel first appears within the fifth week. From the navel in the sixth week then appears the life-force passage. All sense organs are the next week's task until the head makes its appearance in the eighth week. Now the body is appearing in the ninth week.

On and on, divine unfurling and expansion, like the 'big bang' of the universe, creation is occurring. Shoulders, neck and general form, internal organs, feet and hands, the fingers, toes, the nerves and passages, the flesh and fat, the muscles, tendons, bones and marrow, skin is now appearing. Across the cosmic light-weeks of the body universe, the body planets, stars and sun are manifesting in this personal zodiac, uniquely and precisely to the infinite degree. The womb of heaven arches over this new life who sits within the night surroundings of the mother, waiting for the moment when the dawn, the very first dawn of a life will come.

This miracle of gestation had been traced in its entirety by doctors of Tibet without the vision of an ultrasound, or any interference in the body. Inner knowledge, gift of deities, enlightened intuition, texts from heaven, all together had translated foetal language into processes which doctors, mothers and fathers could relate to and engage with, thus to assist the cosmic hand in its creation.

It was interesting to hear the doctor tell us that the sixth month is the time at which the foetus would experience the feelings of both pleasure and pain, and the capacity of memory and even mental clarity steadily develops. During the seventh month the body does not grow, but is more lucidly defined, then in the eighth month an inevitable conflict begins. This is the conflict between the mother and the child, for if the mother is much stronger than the child, her body takes the strength of her own child and causes weakening. Conversely, if the child is stronger than the mother, then she will feel weaker and the child will feel much stronger.

This account of inner wrestling, which he said could often fluctuate, was new and quite astounding, so much so that several members of the audience were visibly affected, slightly shuffling in their seats. As for me, I started wondering who'd been stronger in my inner battle for supremacy. He added that the child will now begin to feel some sadness and feels crowded, just as if something displeases him. If the mother drinks something too hot or very cold, or if she jumps or jars the body very suddenly, this all will feel unpleasant to the child, who will be shocked.

As an audience, we were transported by the words of this great doctor to our very first experiences of life within the mother. Responding to our need to be released into the world just like the baby from the womb of claustrophobia, the doctor then revealed that as delivery approaches, so the child develops the idea to leave the womb and finally in preparation for the birth the child turns itself completely upside down within the thirty-eighth week. Thus, by the end of nine months, usually the baby has been born, but in Tibet they say that pregnancy can go on even longer and continue to the tenth month.

Traditional Tibetan Birth

If the stomach of the mother is significantly higher on the right than on the left, and if her body is feeling light to her, and if she is seeing men within her dreams and if the milk is appearing in her right breast first, these are the signs she'll have a son. But if she has a marked increase in sexual desire, then quite suddenly starts wearing lots of jewellery – it's a sign she'll have a girl.

Birth and certain actions to consider at the time of birth became the doctor's focus now. He said that any woman or midwife called to assist the birth should always be a mother herself. In Tibet a child was never born within a hospital for every birth was held at home. A woman reaching her full term should walk a lot, and circumambulate a stupa or a temple just before the baby is born.

Tibetan medicines could assist the actual birth and had two functions: firstly cooling all the tensions that a pregnant woman might have; and in the second place preventing any possible infection. The approach was very simple and effective, with advice on the behaviour and the diet of the woman. Eating chicken during pregnancy was something to avoid at all costs, so the doctor said, for chicken makes the pelvic bones become too rigid, thus the birth can be more difficult. In Tibet, it is far too cold for pregnant women to go swimming, but in water that is warm enough, such exercise is good as swimming stretches all the nerves, the veins and passages.

During labour, medication would be given to ease the birth. The woman ready to give birth should keep quite warm, especially within Tibet where it is cold, and should particularly steer away from getting any cold right at the bottom of the spine. In Tibet there is a garment called a *gichi* that is used for such protection. It is like a belt but wider and is worn around the waist to keep the lower body warm.

Prior to the birth, the woman rubs the stomach and the genitals with oil from time to time. She will perform this by herself whilst sitting up, not lying down, by rubbing oil upon the hands, then holding up her hands before an open fire and then massaging. A position where the woman crouches on her knees is usually recommended as the posture suited to the actual birth according to Tibetan medicine.

After birth, the umbilical cord is tied in two particular positions using woollen threads, four finger widths out from the navel. Then it is cut between the threads to leave a piece of umbilical cord to rest upon the newborn child. Finally, the baby is washed completely with a mixture of some milk with warm water.

The power of the focus of this doctor on the audience was such that at this point we all were visibly relieved to hear the child had now been born. I knew this doctor's lecture was symbolically a 'birth' on some level for us all. Together, so it seemed to me, we shared responsibility to safely see this birth of knowledge from the land of snows begin to grow and root itself within the West. As if ensuring this transition, Dr Trogawa then told us how a sacred, metaphysical impression could be marked upon the child. To promote intelligence and health, a letter was written delicately on the baby's tongue. Of course it is difficult to write upon the tongue of any child, so in practice it is done by firstly cutting the letter's form into wood the right way round. The person giving the impression to the child will

103

wash one finger very well, and put some ink onto the wood, then press the finger on the wood, so that the image goes onto the finger backwards. They then touch the baby's tongue with this one finger, which impresses on the tongue the sacred letter the right way round. Special substances are used to make this letter of impression. Finally, a minute quantity of yoghurt, milk and butter mixed together with a consecrated medicine and a tiny bit of jewel pill is placed upon the baby's tongue to be the earliest nourishment of this, the newborn child.

Throughout the first few months, specific chosen medicines will be given to encourage clear intelligence as well as life-long health. A great variety of these at different periods in the first year are prescribed to increase courage and intelligence and make the baby strong and very healthy. The child's astrological chart will be cast, and his or her year sign will be listed with the star of their first month, first day, first moment in the world.

It was interesting to note that contact with the mother's body was important, to satisfy desires and at the same time foster courage in the child, to give good health and help the infant move towards a much more natural, harmonious relationship between the baby's body and the mind. Breast-feeding was the best way to provide the energy to build the baby's body. At the same time, it was pointed out that closeness to the breast promoted development of strong character.

Enigmatically, the Rinpoche then closed his chosen lecture with the words:

> So this is a traditional description of pregnancy and a
> description of what happens at birth in accordance with
> Tibetan medicine and Tibetan custom, and, as said at the
> beginning, everything has a cause and whatever happens,
> what is a result has a result within the character of the cause.

We all fell silent for a moment, quite astonished at the pearls this doctor cast before us. At last, applause erupted out across the room, but this great doctor in humility just blessed us with his palm outstretched before him. In one final act of mystery, he then declared he wanted to be photographed with all of us around him. Miraculously, though he had not brought along a camera, someone present had a polaroid and promptly took a snap which was given to the doctor.

I was sure this was symbolic and fell once again to thinking how fortuitous, auspicious and significant this Rinpoche's delivery had been. I also wondered if the photograph allowed this humble doctor to send healing at a distance to help us all and heal our wounds. This ancient jewel of the East had flown into our world; through him, the breath of the Medicine Buddha had been blown upon our bodies as his words, which were as blessed prayers, showered down upon our heads.

Somewhere deep inside I promised I would take this seed of wisdom very seriously and nourish it, allow it to grow into a flower of abundance, with a wish upon the winds that this same flower would itself beget more seeds to bring the Medicine Buddha's garden to the West.

Chapter 8

The Medicine Buddha Empowerment Ceremony

S EVERAL YEARS LATER, as if to confirm my inner promise made at the end of Dr Trogawa's lecture, I attended a Medicine Buddha Empowerment Ceremony given by the Rinpoche on another of his visits to the United Kingdom. It was held in a small, unprepossessing building in north London, which for years had been devoted to Tibetan wisdom. After threading through the bustling streets, filled with people, dogs and ever moving traffic, I stepped into the entrance hall where receptionists were standing to greet and register the participants. Once tickets were confirmed, we made our way along a corridor and left our shoes at the open door of the hall where this empowerment would be conducted. When I placed my shoes amongst the growing pile, I inwardly prayed that I might succeed in truly leaving something of my petty ego on the floor and enter this blessed ceremony without resistance.

Immediately on entering, I realized I had stepped across a threshold, for in this saffron coloured hall there was an atmosphere which hung in the air like early morning mountain mist. All the prayers and daily focus on the deities of Tibet had left their traces in the ether of this hall and today a Rinpoche had brought the blessing of his presence as a consecration. Simple cushions were arrayed in several rows before a dais where the Venerable Dr Trogawa Rinpoche sat deep in meditation. He was sitting cross-legged on a cushioned seat and a *thangka* of the Medicine Buddha hung behind him. Framed by most exquisite silk brocade and hung above an altar filled with photographs of lamas, sacred images and deities, the Medicine Buddha seemed to reign supreme. The Rinpoche was perfectly serene. He seemed to merge into the *thangka*. He must have been in meditation for some time in preparation for this sacred ceremony of empowerment.

His saffron robe was draped across his shoulders and left arm in a most particular way, as if each fold within his garment was an expression of his stillness. Underneath this was a red chemise; his bronzed right arm emerged to gently lie across his lap. His eyes were almost closed, yet I could feel that he was sensing every movement of our minds and with his presence was embracing us with peace to gently welcome us into this hallowed hall.

Purification

To his right was a raised section of the dais on which he had arranged, in perfect symmetry, the various instruments and texts required to perform the ceremony. He remained completely focused inwardly until at last the hall was filled and everyone had settled in their seats. Then, through his devoted apprentice and translator, he welcomed us and explained that he would be leading us through this empowerment ceremony with chanting, prayers and various visualizations. But before commencing anything, a process of purification was required, for the body must be like a purified vessel in order to receive the initiation.

A liquid mixture of sacred pills and saffron soaked in mineral water would be circulated round the audience. Whilst drinking this we should try to visualize the purifying deity, Vajrasattva, as if this divine being was residing at the apex of the head. We should envisage a certain purifying mantra rotating in the heart chakra of this deity and imagine that a stream of nectar was flowing from this point through the crown of the head, cleaning the whole body.

As the Rinpoche began to chant the mantra, the purifying liquid was circulated by his assistant around the audience. Poured into our proffered hands from an exquisite Tibetan teapot with a peacock feather sprouting from its lid, we gratefully received this holy water. The Rinpoche's chanting seemed to caress us from the depths of his being as if the sounds that he transmitted resounded in our hearts, minds and souls. As the last of us was served, he then took hold of an ancient Tibetan hand bell and gently rang it. These penetrating sounds that seemed to shatter any last traces of impurity revolved around the room as he looked up and gazed upon us before continuing.

He explained that prior to doing any spiritual practices like this it was also necessary to ward off any evil influences or negative vibrations. He said it was like giving the evil spirits some kind of gift and asking them to go away from here. This time, whilst chanting, he rotated a small hand drum strung with beads that rattled on its sides to clatter loudly, helping to disperse any harmful influences. Like a cadence at the culmination of this short but powerful practice, his words fell into a whisper as if a very secret mantra finalized the process.

We then would need to make an inner, mental offering, by visualizing precious gifts from all the different realms and various planes of existence. These gifts should be the very best. So if we'd chosen gemstones they should only be the purest in quality, or if we were envisaging a sacred creature, then this creature should be of the finest kind. For example if it were to be an elephant, then not only should it be the great white elephant, but it should be a whole herd of great white elephants. In this way we would gain merit and the more we visualized, the more meritorious would be the offering. Within my mind I formed and offered up a flock of glorious birds of paradise. Their sweet, melodious voices were rejoicing as they vanished into heaven as my offering, whilst the Rinpoche was chanting to assist them in their passage.

Request for Teachings

It was explained that as an integral part of this initial stage within the ceremony, a background to the history and lineage of this teaching of the Medicine Buddha was to be revealed through chanted verses. This was the tale of how Bodhisattva Manjushri had requested this particular teaching from the Buddha Shakyamuni. After going into meditation, the Buddha Shakyamuni manifested as the Medicine Buddha along with seven Medicine Buddha brothers in order to give this special teaching. Many other bodhisattvas, gods and holy spirits were there and all gave their word that whomever was to recite the name of the Medicine Buddha, or do the practice of the Medicine Buddha, would be protected in the future.

Through oral transmission these teachings were passed by Manjushri to the Indian pandit, Bodhisattva Shantarakshita. This pandit, it was said, had lived to over 990 years of age due to his capacity for prayer. In the eighth century he came to Tibet, where he passed the teachings on to the king at that time, and from there the lineage remained within Tibet. The Rinpoche said that even just to hear the name of the Medicine Buddha would be of benefit to a person. So to participate in this initiation ceremony was of immense benefit to all.

Once again his chanted tones began to fill the room as he exposed this history. The quality of his words was tender like a feather sent to stroke the very fabric of our hearts. He then led the whole audience through a short prayer asking everyone to fold their hands and repeat after him the words in Tibetan to request the initiation of the Medicine Buddha.

Dedication

Humility in everything and absolute dedication to others was vital. To ensure this, the Rinpoche led us through a special vow, which he said should infuse our minds with the most appropriate attitude. The aspiration here was to seek perfection in oneself for the sake of all beings in the world. The attitude required was like admitting one is ill and taking the support of the doctor and his medicine. The words quoted by Dr Choedrak came again into my mind:

> *Noble one, think of yourself as someone who is sick,*
>
> *Of the dharma as the remedy,*
>
> *Of your spiritual friend as a skilful doctor,*
>
> *And of diligent practice as the way to recover.*

The Rinpoche pronounced us ready to receive the initiation and asked us to retain the feeling already generated in our minds as we proceeded. He said one should have the proper vessel to receive the initiation and this vessel should have joy. Coming to the main part of the initiation he pointed out a key difference between the Buddhas and the human beings on this earth. The Buddhas were like someone who was fully awake and we humans on the earth were like a person who was sleeping very deeply. When the Buddhas saw these sleeping sentient beings, who remained in an illusion for they hadn't yet begun to realize the true meaning of emptiness, this generated great compassion from the Buddhas to the humans. Emptiness, or *shunyata* in Sanskrit, I understood was a state of non-separation or of having no independent nature, and created a sense of interconnection with the people surrounding us.

Visualization

With his finger raised respectfully towards the sacred *thangka*, the Rinpoche then fixed our vision on the Medicine Buddha, who he said embodied emptiness and compassion. The colour of his skin was blue because it resembled the sky which was vast without any boundaries. He was also called the King of Radiant Light, for it was said that he was brighter than the other Buddhas. This focus on the Medicine Buddha was particularly appropriate because he was the one who had created great kindness for human beings. In his right hand he held out the medicinal fruit, the King of Medicines, the first seed of which had descended from the heavens. In his left hand he was holding a container filled with nectar.

The visualization process of the Medicine Buddha must, he said, be conducted as if we saw him as an image in a mirror. The image in the mirror was really empty, but that emptiness we saw as being his form. When visualizing, colours were important as were various sacred syllables impressed upon the chakras, or points of energy in the body. The letter *Om* should be envisaged on his forehead inscribed in white, the letter *Ah* in red residing at the throat chakra and the letter *Hung* in blue upon the heart. These three letters represented the body, speech and mind of the Buddha. Each one was known to contain a healing power through visualization and sound. *Om* brought peace and clarity; *Ah* brought energy and expansion; whilst *Hung* brought enlightenment, oneness, and infinity. I understood that together they brought strength, openness and oneness. The Rinpoche said that the colours associated with these letters should be perceived as full of lustre. This visualization practice, whereby one focused in this way upon the Medicine Buddha, should be approached as if one transformed oneself immediately into the Medicine Buddha like a fish that springs abruptly from the lake.

Although it seemed beyond me to achieve this most extraordinary inner transformation, whilst the Rinpoche was chanting I could feel he was supporting us and guiding us towards this sacred goal. His description of the next stage of the process was breathtaking in its beauty. We had to visualize blue rays of brilliant light emerging from the heart chakra of the Medicine Buddha, pervading all the Buddha realms, invoking and inviting all the Medicine Buddhas of different shapes and sizes, which would come down and submerge into the Medicine Buddha visualized within the space in front of us. To do this we should consider that our body was like an ocean, and the gods were just like snowflakes. When they fell into the ocean, they of course became inseparable.

The sense of merging now was very powerful. I had lost all sense of time and place. His chanting, bell and drum became the beat within my heart as we moved on to request the blessing of Medicine Buddha's body, speech and mind to come into us. From the brow of this blue Buddha, visualized within my mind, I saw the forehead chakra and the letter *Om* in white. White rays of light just like the moon came forth and entered my whole body through the crown of my head. This served to cleanse me of my physical negative deeds. I heard the Rinpoche advising us to see in our mind's eye that we had received the body of the Medicine Buddha. Once again, his powerful chanting led us on as did his potent description.

At each stage of our receiving this great blessing of the Medicine Buddha's body, speech and mind, we should imagine that we heard sounds of auspiciousness which rang out from the heavens. Flowers and different musical instruments were raining down upon us from the deities who blessed us. Now the Rinpoche was chanting sacred prayers and spraying grains of rice into the air. From the centre of the chakra in the throat of this radiant Buddha in my mind, red rays of light just like a rising sun came forth from the letter *Ah* and entered through my mouth to cleanse me of the negativities polluting my speech. We had received the blessing of the speech of the Medicine Buddha as the chanting, bell and drum continued like an underlying stream, a ground bass rhythm to support us.

From the heart chakra, the letter *Hung* in rays of bright blue light came pouring forth into my body through my heart to cleanse me of my mental negativities. We had received the blessing of the mind of the Medicine Buddha as the chanting, bell and drum continued like an underlying river rising up to bear us on. This sacred imagery was flowing through my mind into an ocean of great wonder as the Rinpoche recited various prayers. Now the rainbow in its splendour was appearing. We were required to visualize the different coloured rays of light, just like a rainbow entering through the navel chakra, entirely filling the whole body and clearing the negativities of the body, speech and mind.

Blessings, Contemplation and Homage

With all the blessings of the Medicine Buddha fully visualized as deep within us, the Rinpoche led us in a request for the blessing of his mantra. His voiced Tibetan was repeated by us all as we approached the special moment where his mantra would be given. At this point we were encouraged not only to visualize the Medicine Buddha in the space in front of us, but this time to try to visualize ourselves as being the Medicine Buddha. In this way we could envisage bright blue rays of brilliant light within our mouths, and in our heart the rays were issuing forth whilst we could see the mantra rotating in a clockwise direction around the letter *Hung*.

At last the sacred mantra of the Medicine Buddha was carefully presented to us in its longer form. The sounds resounded deep inside me, this most extraordinary mantra – an elaboration of the name of the Medicine Buddha, praising him in Sanskrit as being so very great:

> *Om Namo Bhagavate Bhekhadze*
>
> *Guru Baidurya*

Prabha Rajaya

Tatha Gataya

Arhate Samyaksam Buddhaya

*Tadyatha Om Bhekhadze Bhekhadze Maha Bhekhadze
Bhekhadze Raja Samudgate Svaha*

This was then repeated seven times in its short form by the Rinpoche
for us to follow faithfully:

*Tadyatha Om Bhekhadze Bhekhadze Maha Bhekhadze
Bhekhadze Raja Samudgate Svaha*

*Tadyatha Om Bhekhadze Bhekhadze Maha Bhekhadze
Bhekhadze Raja Samudgate Svaha*

*Tadyatha Om Bhekhadze Bhekhadze Maha Bhekhadze
Bhekhadze Raja Samudgate Svaha*

*Tadyatha Om Bhekhadze Bhekhadze Maha Bhekhadze
Bhekhadze Raja Samudgate Svaha*

*Tadyatha Om Bhekhadze Bhekhadze Maha Bhekhadze
Bhekhadze Raja Samudgate Svaha*

*Tadyatha Om Bhekhadze Bhekhadze Maha Bhekhadze
Bhekhadze Raja Samudgate Svaha*

*Tadyatha Om Bhekhadze Bhekhadze Maha Bhekhadze
Bhekhadze Raja Samudgate Svaha*

This mantra was so powerful that its essence filled the atmosphere
completely. When we'd finished chanting solemnly, it seemed the air
within the hall was magnetized as if the mantra still revolved around
its walls. To bring this initiation to a close we sat together in
meditation, for the Rinpoche informed us that now we had received
the blessing of the Medicine Buddha's body, speech and mind we
should sit comfortably and keep our minds quite still, relaxing whilst

we contemplated for awhile in this pure state. For several minutes we remained in deepest silence until more chanting from the Rinpoche completed this absorbing meditation.

He then explained that every day it would be beneficial to recite the mantra one hundred times, or twenty-one times or at the very least seven times. Before recitation of the mantra we should always say a short prayer in homage to the Medicine Buddha. The immense benefit of this mantra extended through and beyond ourselves to patients and to other people and was not just for this life but also for future lives. The merit of this practice had been cited in the sutras of the Buddha Shakyamuni. He led us in a vow which promised recitation of the mantra every day and emphasized a spirit of dedication and devotion. At all times we should remain in keeping with the very highest principles.

To complete this ancient ceremony of empowerment, we visualized an offering to the mandala of the Medicine Buddha in thanksgiving for the blessing he'd bestowed upon us. The Rinpoche then voiced some prayers for peace and requested from the Medicine Buddha that there would not be many more new diseases appearing on the earth.

Before we left, we were invited to come forward to receive the blessing of the Medicine Buddha through the Rinpoche. Queuing up with the traditional Tibetan white silk scarf, called a *katak*, which was to be blessed and placed around our necks, my inner mind felt cleansed, renewed and open to the Rinpoche. I bowed before his blessing, felt the wave of his compassion soothe my being as I inwardly gave thanks to him for the jewels of Tibetan wisdom he had brought into the West and into my heart.

Part Two

The Basic
Concepts of
Tibetan Buddhist
Medicine

Introduction to Part Two

*T*HE GREAT PHYSICIAN, the Buddha, spent his whole life in the service of others, giving constant teachings with the aim of alleviating all suffering in the world. As Tibetan doctors, we humbly follow in the footsteps of this enlightened physician who healed others of their illnesses. Our ideal is to practise compassion at all times, equally towards every human being without exception, to perfect our medical skill for the sake of others and to always remember that we are continuing a sacred lineage of physicians who are acting as ambassadors for the Medicine Buddha.

It is for this reason that a Tibetan doctor's ability to heal is directly related to the level of his wisdom and compassion, for it is these inner capacities that manifest in an ability to bring about a cure, whether this is required on the physical, emotional or spiritual level. Historically, the greatest physicians have always been held in high regard within Tibet and accordingly been given such titles as *Menpa*, 'The Benefactor' and 'Emperor of the Kings', for kings give respect to a great physician just as they would to an emperor. Indeed, doctors acquire respect and renown not through any form of advertising or a long list of qualifications, but through their level of sensitivity shown towards the patient, the quality of their compassion, selflessness and innate wisdom combined with a pure focus on the source of all healing, the Medicine Buddha.

This is the ideal to which my wife, Yeshi Khando, and I attempt to aspire. By aligning ourselves with the exalted and holy model of the Medicine Buddha, we endeavour to skilfully serve the physical, emotional and spiritual needs of our patients. This in itself offers a powerful impression to the younger generation. My own daughter, Tenzin Yangkyi, who already holds a BSc degree, has been so inspired by the effects of Tibetan medicine that she is now studying Tibetan medicine at the Central Institute of Higher Tibetan Studies in Saranath, Varanasi, India. In fact, many young Tibetans are developing a great interest in the Tibetan culture in general, and in particular Tibetan medicine.

In the years since my wife and I graduated as doctors, we have observed a growing interest in Tibetan medicine. During my travels throughout India, Europe and America, I have personally witnessed a tremendous expansion of awareness in relation to our unique medical system, and believe that it brings hope for the preservation and rebuilding of our Tibetan culture – a culture which, as many will know, was all but destroyed by the Chinese.

Since going into exile, His Holiness the Dalai Lama has worked tirelessly to preserve our Tibetan culture. As an essential element of the establishment of Tibet in Exile he entrusted the task of re-establishing the Tibetan Medical and Astrological Institute to an extremely accomplished physician, Dr Yeshi Dhonden, with whom I was later most fortunate to be granted an internship. Under his great guidance, together with the various esteemed doctors and directors who were to follow in his footsteps, and with the magnificent support of His Holiness, the institute has steadily grown to its current level of excellence.

In fact, it has expanded to such a degree that several Tibetan physicians have journeyed to the West to present this 2,500-year-old system to the world. The many conferences and seminars they have conducted have led to a tremendous exchange of medical ideas between East and West. This wonderful cross-fertilization has been apparent in the emergence of much written and visual information now available on Tibetan medicine. Naturally, due to the complexity and profundity of our medical system, such information can only offer the West a glimpse of the depth of Tibetan medical science, which is one of a number of fields of science deeply rooted in Tibetan culture and tradition.

Nevertheless, this presents a wonderful opportunity to impart the rich seeds of Tibetan medicine, developed by the highest minds as a system of great depth, profoundly linked to Buddhist thought. It has a completely explicable and definable logic. Results may seem miraculous, but thorough study will reveal the truth of this science. However, to immerse oneself in this medical system without careful forethought, or to begin a course of study and then practise it as soon as one has reached the very minimum of years, can very easily lead to a superficial understanding of the system. For example, Western texts translate the fundamental energies, or humours in the body according to Tibetan medicine as wind, bile and phlegm. But these terms, although attempting to attain an understanding, are relatively gross and superficial. Indeed, to fully realize the exact science and design behind these energies can take a lifetime spent in contemplative study linked to practice and research. Yet exploration such as this will yield great fruits for the physician who is genuinely seeking a much deeper understanding.

Once in Calcutta a newspaper reporter asked me to read his pulse. After careful examination I told him what his problem was. Next morning, I saw my photograph in the paper and above it the headline read 'Miracle Man'. Yet, although pulse-reading in general may seem like a miracle, behind it there is a very real science and perfect logic. It may be seen as similar to the fact that we can speak to someone on the telephone who may be as far away as the other side of the world. This may seem quite miraculous, but there is a scientific explanation behind this apparent miracle. Tibetan medicine is not a system based on empty belief or hocus pocus, as the original dismissive and destructive reaction of the Chinese implied, but a system with a profound logic at its roots.

More recently, the Chinese have begun to admit that there is some value in the Tibetan medical system and have allowed the remaining Tibetan doctors to establish medical clinics and institutes in occupied Tibet. This is a great step forward scientifically for Tibetan medicine, which has managed to withstand the ungrounded attack of ignorance and blind prejudice levied against it. It is also a step in the right direction for the Chinese who are beginning to comprehend an enlightened system of thought.

Between 1998 and the year 2000, I visited London annually in order to offer consultations and give lectures on Tibetan medicine. These visits marked the beginning of a long and fruitful relationship between myself and the two co-authors, Janet Jones and Terence Moore, for it was during these visits that the work on this book began in earnest.

The presentation which follows introduces the basic concepts of the Tibetan medical system. These concepts have been diligently and faithfully translated and are accompanied by insights and clarifications drawn from Western experience, knowledge and psychology in order to facilitate a greater understanding and integration of the system as a whole. As far as the medical texts are concerned, it is inevitable that a certain degree of dilution occurs in translation, but I have aimed to minimize this as far as possible.

Certain fundamental concepts are repeated throughout Part Two. This is deliberate, in order to allow these concepts to be more completely understood and assimilated by the reader. At the end of each chapter, I have also inserted a short practice or note designed to help the reader integrate something of the essence of the Tibetan medical system into daily life. Finally, as part of this introduction, the following is a short summary of the topics covered: Tibetan medicine is being spread all over the world. This is enormously helpful for humanity, for it focuses on the essential root of all suffering – the *mind*, which must be tamed, for it is veiled by a form of ignorance that is blind and unenlightened, and leads to the arousal of what are termed the 'three mental poisons' of desire, anger and closed-mindedness. These in turn negatively affect three fundamental energies in the body called 'the three humours' and thereby their twenty characteristics. These humours are termed *rLung*, a mobile energy, *Tripa* responsible for heat in the body and *Badkan* which is cooling.

The two main causes of disease are lifestyle and diet, for through the ingestion of foods we take the five elements into our bodies. Indeed, from birth the ingestion of foods by the mother and the effects of parental lifestyle help to produce three body types, relating to the three humours. In order to maintain health we must maintain a balanced approach to everything, looking beyond the symptoms of disease to the root of the illness; respecting the fact that the body is a vessel for transformation of not only our various foods through the digestion process, but also our life experiences and emotional responses.

However, place, time and age also affect us, so we need to be aware of our environment and position in life. Over and above everything, Tibetan medicine is a science of equilibrium. Balance is at the heart of the system, which facilitates the normal production of the body elements, termed the seven constituents, which are produced successively through a particular process of digestion, involving the separation out of nutriments from wastes.

Disease is disorder in this system and the various humoural diseases will enter the body through specific pathways related to the locations of the three humours. Restoring ease, or health, is to be achieved by considering the humoural characteristics, tastes, qualities and inherent powers, and utilizing food and medication to restore balance in these essential qualities, which must be carefully handled to minimize side effects.

Tibetan medicine is a reflection of nature, and if we abuse nature we abuse ourselves and vice versa. An integration of the balanced, natural approach of Tibetan medicine and its inherent spiritual guidance can be of help in the creation of a more positive future for humanity.

Tibetan medicine has been revealed to the world through ancient, sacred teachings called the rGyu-shi. The characteristics of all studying physicians are considered to be paramount. There is a particular approach to study which must be applied diligently. There are certain important differences between Tibetan medicine and Western medicine. Tibetan medicine has specific diagnostic techniques and forms of treatment.

To conclude, there have been many seeming miracles of healing through Tibetan medicine, and continuing attempts to truly integrate it into the Western psyche, yet fundamentally it is the simple fact that Tibetan medicine *works* that increasingly draws patients from all over the world to seek its healing powers.

It is hoped that this description of the clinical reality behind Tibetan medicine will help to inform the average Western patient of the fundamental differences between the Tibetan system of medicine and the Western medical approach.

Doctor Pema Dorjee

Chapter 9

The Mind – the Root of All Suffering

*T*HE TEACHINGS OF LORD BUDDHA are essentially based on the fact that suffering can be alleviated and its root cause transformed, if we can control the mind. His doctrine was to tame the mind and attempt to change negative, limiting thoughts and feelings. He did not attempt to set himself apart in any way, declaring that deep within us all we have the key to open up the gates of freedom from our suffering and pain. Buddhists therefore view it as a supremely important life task to rediscover and awaken this inner state of Buddhahood, for as the Buddha himself said: 'Our body is precious. It is a vehicle of awakening.'

What is the mind?

- How is the relationship between body and mind formed?
- We feel we have a human mind. Is there somewhere where the mind is based, or not?
- Is the mind within us, or outside of us?

- Is it near or is it far?
- We refer to 'my body', so indicating that we feel that our mind is based in our body. Indeed, no one can deny this on a temporary level.
- Where is the main abode of the mind in the body?

It might be thought to be in the heart, in the head, in the throat; in fact it seems to be rather unstable. For example, one could say that one experiences the world through the senses and that this is communicated by the nervous system to the brain. Thus, the mind seems to be in the head.

We consider that in our own system of Tibetan medicine, the chief abode of the mind is in the heart. In the centre of the heart is a group of special passages or nerves which are not truly physical. They are called nerves of light and are very fine, about the thickness of a single hair from a horse's tail. The central, hollow part of each nerve is of course even finer.

The 72,000 channels

The mind, or consciousness, is pure and stainless, clear and understanding. According to Tibetan medicine it has the nature of the five elements thus connected to the body which is also built from the five elements. The senses within the body are derived from the consciousness during the formation of our body.

In fact, there are a total of 72,000 channels in the body, divided up into three sets of channels related to the three fundamental energies in the body, which will be described later, but are called *rLung*, *Tripa* and *Badkan*. The three divisions of channels are as follows:

1. 24,000 channels of *Tripa*, the solar nature energy, flow in the right side of the body. This set of channels is called *Roma*.

2. 24,000 channels of *Badkan*, the lunar nature energy, flow in

the left side of the body. This grouping of channels is called *Kyangma*.

3. 24,000 channels of *rLung* flow in the central channels of the body, called *Uma*.

The mind or consciousness is supported by one of the five types of *rLung* energy, called *Srog-zhin rLung* and located in the *Uma*, the central channels. The channels located in the heart are the final refinement of the body in its relationship to the elements and represent the most subtle aspect of the elements.

The Tibetan medical texts describe the heart, the abode of the mind, to be like a flower with petals radiating the six senses to their respective organs as follows:

1. anterior	east sense of ear	black in colour
2. lateral	south sense of eye	red in colour
3. posterior	west sense of nose	yellow in colour
4. lateral	north sense of tongue	white in colour
5. superior	upper sense of body	green in colour
6. inferior	lower sense of mind	blue in colour

If the channels remain clear and without obstructions, then this will lead to positive health. However, any obstructions, or a disordered energy entering the channels, will cause mental as well as physical disorder. For we consider these channels to be the main support of the mind and from this centre radiates the whole of one's being. This is like a light from which rays radiate. For example, in the case of the sun, it is this sun which is the source of light and from it radiates a great immensity of light. So it is with these passages and the radiating of the whole of one's being. Thus the mind is related to the body.

Since body and mind are seen as a composite whole in the Tibetan medical system, all manner of diagnosis and treatment take this into account. On the most physical, organic level, the body is understood in terms of three primary energies, or humours:

- *rLung* (translated as wind)
- *Tripa* (translated as bile)
- *Badkan* (translated as phlegm)

The relationship between the body and mind is fundamental. The taming of the mind should essentially go hand in hand with the balancing of the three humours in the body, which if soundly balanced promote a healthy body, but conversely in imbalance lead to disease. The balance of the humours is affected by a range of influences, including seasonal changes, personal diet, behavioural habits, psychological traits and emotional upheavals together with the less visible forces of karma and astrology.

The importance of taming the mind assumes a very particular significance where the physician is concerned, for the relationship between the doctor and the patient crucially affects the prognosis of any disease. A good physician is very much aware of this ability to influence the state of the patient positively, through the medium of his own state of being and state of mind. This is where the spiritual evolution of the physician, his powers of meditation and pure focus on the higher healing powers are very important, almost like an inner, invisible yet extremely potent essence which can be transmitted to the patient during the consultation. Mantras, meditation, prayer and visualization are considered a vital part of the healing process, running like a thread through all aspects of a physician's practice.

So, when studying any medical system it is very important to examine one's own state of mind. In devotion to healing the sick, a physician's primary aim should be to develop compassion for the patients, particularly those who live in poverty. It is a serious mistake for him to take advantage of the power he may have over a patient. Human beings may accumulate great wealth in their life, but on their last day in this world, they cannot take this wealth with them.

However, they will certainly be able to take all the goodness they have given to others. It is therefore so important to try to understand the real meaning of being a *menpa*, a person who truly benefits others.

The rGyu-shi, or Four Tantras, has remained a secret teaching handed down by oral methods. This word 'secret' means that it must not be revealed to any student with an unsuitable or tainted attitude of mind, but given to serious students with honourable intentions. The meaning of the word 'tantra' in this case actually means 'to protect the body'. For this system of protection to survive intact, the teachings are essentially preserved within a perfect stream of continuity, an ancient oral lineage system. Giving teachings in this way is, by itself, an action which brings a protection to the body.

The Power of the Mind

The mind sits at the heart of everything, the prime mover of our body towards a state of health or disease. It is through the portals of our own perception that we view the world and it is the movements of our inner minds, our subconscious, which ultimately can easily erupt in the form of a disease. Consequently, the Tibetan approach to healing is about raising our awareness and lifting our minds above the maelstrom of our own limited perception which is so often simply a recipe for illness.

The mind is the state of consciousness at any one particular moment in time. It is not simply the engine of thought but is the summation of all our inner impulses, thoughts, fears, desires, aspirations, emotions, reactions and sensitivities to everything around us. The mind has an all-consuming, powerful influence upon our vision. Indeed it is directly linked to all our senses as the gift of perception, our aid to touching and understanding the experiences of life. Esoterically, it has often been likened to a mirror upon which everything is reflected, yet it is vital to understand that this is not simply a passive object of reflection. The need for controlling the mind is emphasized as a means of achieving inner stillness and calm. But this is no easy task. For as Arjuna said in the Bhagavad Gita:

The mind is more difficult to control than the wind and
how difficult it is to control the wind.

Perfectly in step with the senses, the mind is always steadily building up a picture of everything around us. As the various sensations and perceptions pour in, a process of absorbing, sifting, organizing, editing and projecting is continually occurring. The mind is indeed our own personal film director and as such has the power to influence and ultimately determine exactly what kind of film we are watching. For the mind links the various images together, not merely in some predetermined stream of reality, but in a personally chosen order, directly in relation to our inner predilections. And just as certain parts of a film end up on the cutting-room floor, if there is something in the outer world that we cannot face, or do not want to, we simply cut that experience out.

So inevitably, when we approach a person's state of health, the state of mind of that person is a powerful mover along the path towards sickness or to health. Unfortunately, modern medicine far too often becomes a form of disempowerment, whereby the remedy is sought from an external authority as a 'quick fix', without considering how one's state of awareness, inner attitudes and intentions have contributed to the situation in which we find ourselves to be ill. Without addressing this all important factor in the process, medicine can only offer temporary relief, until the powerful thought patterns, which might be fixed in a particular, negative direction inexorably drive the body back into a state of disease.

So one cannot emphasize enough how critical our state of consciousness is within the healing process, for our hopes, dreams, fears and expectations will have a powerful effect on the outcome. We would therefore benefit enormously from increased attention being given to this essential element and how we may turn it to our advantage, rather than suffer endlessly from the vagaries of mental unrest. It is for this reason that Buddhists meditate upon the nature of suffering and discontent. We can indeed learn much from this and try to rise above our often trivial feelings and inflexible beliefs to reach a broader view of life, an all-embracing contemplation and awareness. For every action follows thought and through our thoughts we determine our future.

> *Man is the creator of thought,*
>
> *What he thinks about in this life, that hereafter he becomes.*
>
> **Upanishads**

According to Tibetan medicine, suffering and illness are related to the mind and to its level of stability, or instability. Chaotic, stressful thinking disturbs the life force in the channels and the nerves, and so of course results in damage to our physiology. All so-called reality is subject to personal perception, so we never really see the world just as it is, but always through the tinted, tainted spectacles of the mind. If we can truly understand and accept this, then the power of positive or negative thinking assumes much greater importance, for we have it in our hands to improve or impair our lives, to build or destroy our environment. Positive thinking is the cultivation of a better frame of mind, a frame for health and a wider horizon rather than a limited perspective.

The cultivation of a positive attitude is of course a lifetime's work, for the mind is mercurial and volatile, turning upon a whim and constantly veering between the path to health and the route to disease. However, we can assist our situation by choosing to meditate upon positive impressions such as the essence of compassion found within the Medicine Buddha, effectively following in his footsteps. It is said within the sacred texts that Gautama Buddha went into the forest to meditate and attain enlightenment. There are a range of titles given to the Buddha. One is *Julai*, meaning 'he who has gone likewise', or rather he who has followed in the steps of those before him. In this way, we might consider just whose footsteps we are following and who we seek to glorify or idealize, for our mind reflects this and aims to actualize it within our life.

What seems vital is to realize the actual significance of our motivation. Is what we idealize and act upon aimed at increasing suffering or reducing it? This kind of self-examination means looking at the effects one produces. We are creating or destroying all the time, but very seldom credit that we are indeed the problem and solution. If we really want to benefit the world we must begin on our own doorstep, with our own bodies and our own minds. If we can cultivate our minds we may begin to rid ourselves of our disturbed emotions and distorted views. With a positive approach, and some attempt to gain enlightenment, we may at last attain a wider view, realizing our own inherent better nature.

It was a wonderful reflection for Tibet and indeed for the whole world that His Holiness the Dalai Lama was presented with the Nobel Peace Prize. For it recognized that with his inner attitude and tireless outer energy, he had made an enormous contribution to the vital cause of peace within our time. His inner focus was the key, and quite beyond the norm of many in the world. Who can seriously pretend to have compassion for the enemy, the murderer, the torturer, the tyrant and oppressor? Yet His Holiness knows deeply that the only route to peace lies in practising compassion for others. For the root of all our problems in the past, the present and the future lies in man himself, in his confusion and his ignorance, the erroneous conceptions in his mind.

Our Inner World

The eminent enlightened psychologist from the West, Dr Carl Jung stated that in the end, all reality is psychic reality. He pointed out that the inner psychic atmosphere within each one of us ultimately always determines the patterns of our behaviour and experience. Our thoughts and attitudes, inner potential and personal resources powerfully pervade the very air we breathe, to the extent that we cannot help but live out our own psychological nature as if it were reality. Jung went so far as to suggest that we do not in reality experience the outer world at all, for we are always only really experiencing the atmosphere within ourselves, the potent atmosphere of our own inner world, which suffuses everything within and around us.

Taking this further, he pronounced that the real catastrophes threatening modern man were not physical or biological but were what he called 'psychic epidemics', manifesting on a large scale as wars and revolutions. These catastrophes could take various forms, from a personal breakdown to mob violence, from a general sense of unease and disquiet to a widespread loss of meaning in life. He indicated the root of the problem to be an inner split between the head and the heart which was steadily widening within us and therefore within society as a whole, creating a dangerous vacuum from which would inevitably spring very serious events. Modern calamities were therefore, he asserted, stemming from the inner emptiness rife within modern society.

Accordingly, Jung was convinced that the key to healing the sickness of our time must urgently be addressed by more attention being paid to understanding human nature through a psychological approach:

> ...the only real danger that exists is man himself. He is the real danger and we are pitifully unaware of it. We know nothing of man, or far too little. His psyche should be studied, because he is the origin of all coming evil.

Face to Face – BBC Interview with Dr Jung in 1959

This powerful statement made by Jung, resonates with the Tibetan Buddhist approach exemplified in the teachings of His Holiness who emphasizes how important it is, when faced with outer adversity, to turn within, practise inner principles and diffuse disturbing emotions. He views these disturbing emotions as real destroyers and the root of timeless suffering:

> *External enemies, however brutal they are, only affect us*
> *during one lifetime. They have no power to harm us*
> *beyond this life. On the other hand, disturbing emotions*
> *are our inner enemies and can definitely cause disaster in*
> *future lives. These are, in fact, our worst enemies.*

Stages of Meditation – The Dalai Lama. pp. 20–21

Thus, our own worst enemy, according to His Holiness, lies within ourselves, within our minds. So when the enemy appears to manifest before us on the outside, we can generate a positive vibration for ourselves and for mankind through the control of our responses, inner feelings, strong emotions and reactions. By curtailing, containing and transforming these responses we create a better future for ourselves and for the world. This is the inner Everest that has to be climbed. No-one will ever say that it is easy, but either we spend our time thinking about the climb and entertaining it as an attractive thought, or we actually begin a real attempt to reach the top.

Spiritual ignorance is fundamentally the main obstruction to a future free from suffering, for it effectively blinds the person to reality. It promotes the illusion of 'I', 'me', 'mine' which separates and severs a person from the surrounding world. The blind man who trudges round the Tibetan wheel of life is a symbol of this ignorance. He is trapped in a seemingly endless round of mindless existence. All possibility of self-awareness and any attempt at achieving even a modicum of wisdom is way beyond his grasp. Ignorance sits upon him like the blinkers on a horse. His narrow vision traps him conclusively. Thus, even the most advanced and efficacious medicines, treatments, therapies and more, cannot restore and cure the root of the problem if we continue in our ignorance. For as long as ignorance remains within each one of us, emotions which arise from our attachment to the body will produce our future misery, depression and disease.

There are many Tibetan medicines and therapies that can assist everyone, but the best personal advice to give to someone who wishes to maintain good health is as follows:

- Think before you speak.

- Think before you eat.

- Think before you decide.

- Think before you act.

The Taming of the Mind

Essentially all-pervasive, and lying at the very heart of Tibetan medicine is the philosophy of Buddhism. Tibetan physicians adopt a holistic approach to their patients, whereby they are not only looking at the presenting signs and symptoms of a disease, but are encompassing within the medical consultation the patient's entire psychological perspective. With the teachings of the Buddha forming the nucleus of Tibetan medicine, it naturally follows that great emphasis is placed upon the crucial task of taming the mind and therefore negative emotions.

According to Tibetan Buddhist medicine – whether the illness is physical or mental, the exploratory investigation into the nature of the root of suffering is the most important part of the healing process. Then one applies the correct treatment to relieve the suffering. The whole treatment requires an answer to the simple question:

'From where does the suffering originate?'

According to Buddhist philosophy, the answer will always be 'The Mind'.

Our relationship with others, including the environment, our sensory, intellectual and conceptual experience, all determine our mind and body interaction. Buddhist medical philosophy is one of those ancient systems which deal with these relationships and concepts in great detail. The basic cause of illnesses according to Buddhist philosophy, psychology and medicine, is the ego, full of trivial pursuits and clinging attachments. It is this clinging nature that ultimately produces a confused mind and thereby all suffering and disease.

The mind is the petty throne of the usurping king: ignorant, inflated and full of self-cherishing tendencies. This is the all important 'I', or ego, which lives within all of us and which attaches the greatest importance to itself. The illusion upon which the reign of this 'king' is based is that it is fundamentally different from all other egos. This false sense of value sits at the very centre of our consciousness, pontificating to all around. Naturally this arrogance and pride makes the ego easily insulted, offended and hurt by even the tiniest occurrence when it is perceived to be experiencing personal disturbance. The pain, tension and stress arising from this thought of 'I' is so extreme, yet we refuse to let go of this suffering, perpetuating a need to isolate and separate ourselves. This form of pride is the biggest obstacle we all face on the path towards true emancipation.

All human beings are the same, wanting to be happy and to lead a comfortable life. Yet on a day-to-day basis we encounter situations which activate mental and physical stress and which negatively affect our inner basic energy system, steadily propelling the body on a path to related illnesses. Desire is a universal driving force within all of us. We see something of value, of great beauty, or attractive in some other way and immediately we wish to possess it as our own. Naturally such desire cannot always be satisfied, whereupon pain is immediately activated. Our mind in this state is completely deluded, tethered to suffering in its ignorance and generating negative thoughts.

So unless we attempt to tame and control the mind, we remain forever at its mercy. Worldly affairs can unremittingly and increas-

The Medicine Buddha. Thangka Painting by Ugyen Choephell

Above: The Leaders of some of the Spiritual Traditions on the Central Platform at the Rainbow Festival.

Below: The Rainbow Healing. Watercolour painting by Janet Jones.

Palace of the Medicine Buddha. Tibetan Thangka Painting. Artist unknown.

The Medicine Buddha, Seven Medicine Buddha Brothers, Deities and Protectors.
Tibetan Thangka Painting. Artist unknown

The Venerable Dr Trogawa Rinpoche preparing for the Medicine Buddha Empowerment Ceremony.

Dr Pema Dorjee and Dr Tenzin Choedrak.

The Venerable Dr Trogawa Rinpoche conducting the Medicine Buddha Empowerment Ceremony.

Left: Constant Devotion –
Monastery at Boudhanath,
Kathmandu, Nepal.

Right: The First of the Three
Roots of the Tree of Medicine,
from The Tibetan Medicine
Text Book. Part 1.

Below: The Tibetan Medicine
Text Books.

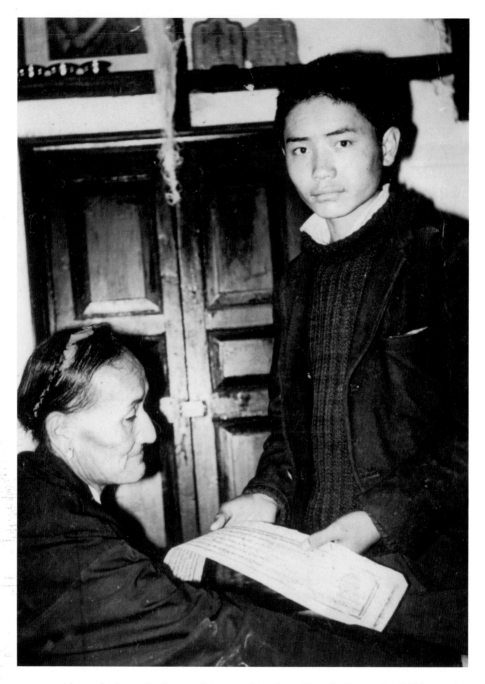

Above: Dr Pema Dorjee receiving teaching from Guru Professor Barshi Phuntsok Wangyal, 1969.

Right: Dr Yeshi Dhonden, at a workshop on Tibetan Medicine held in France. Dr Pema Dorjee is seated to his right.

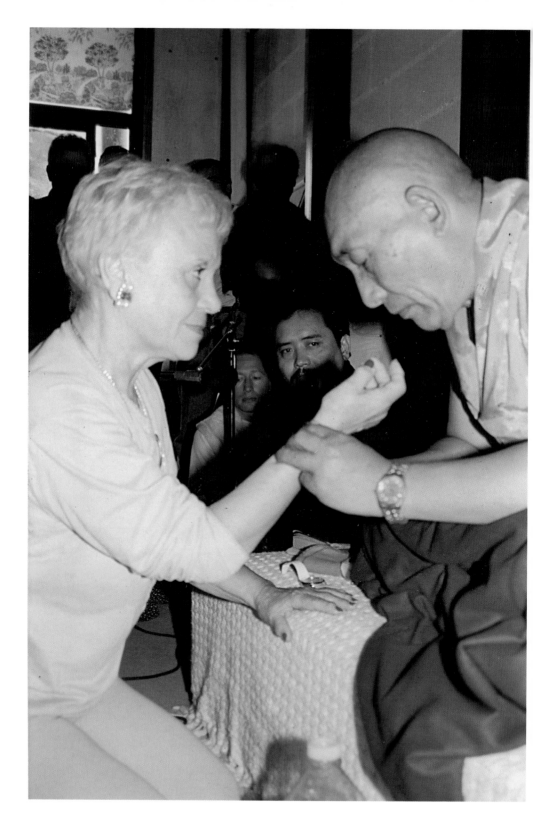

Above: Dr Pema Dorjee taking the pulse of co-author Janet Jones.

Left: Dr Yeshi Dhonden taking the pulse of one of the participants at a workshop on Tibetan Medicine in France, with Dr Pema Dorjee observing.

His Holiness the Dalai Lama with Dr Pema Dorjee.

ingly close in upon us, and overwhelm us if we do not retain some sense of mind control and inner balance. It is common to find the modern-day mind replete with perpetual ruminations and worries. These constant fears and thinking 'If I had done so and so I would not be in trouble now' can definitely cause serious problems in our bodies and ultimately lead to disease. If we could change things by worrying then clearly there would be a point to it, but we cannot change things in the past, so endless recollections when there isn't a solution has no purpose.

Over-thinking, obsession with the past and constant worry about the future stirs up one of the three fundamental energies in the body, called *rLung*. An increase in this energy causes us to become unstable and susceptible to external occurrences, somewhat similar to acting like a flag which flutters in the wind. The mind will weaken and we find that we are increasingly vulnerable to sadness and depression. This can worsen like the coming of a cyclone which wreaks havoc with our lives. Here once again it is the mind that is the key to healing our worries.

It is a burden, all this brooding on the past, for people lie awake at night and worry over everything and more besides, when really we should let things go, release ourselves from the things we cannot alter in the past, and not spend agonizing days disturbed, distressed, perturbed, tormented by the things that we perceive might go wrong in the future. Self-oppression such as this will tire the mind, and accordingly our emotional nature weakens. Ceaseless mental racing wears us out, so mental steadiness is necessary if we want to live a life not blown about by every passing gust of wind. We must have courage and be brave within the mind, and face the trials of existence without fear. The mind can be a sword within our hands rather than a source of fear. But illness will indeed strike us if we let our thoughts run rife. This is the enemy within, which we have to face and fight and in our fighting, help our fellow man. Challenging our fears within ourselves, rather than challenging them within someone else who we imagine is against us, will inevitably change the world around us and disperse the darkened clouds we have created.

Inner Process

The concept of facing one's own inner enemy, one's own mind and making a real attempt to tame it, is a crucial focus shared between Tibetan medicine and Western psychology. For an important message in Dr Carl Jung's psychological approach was that man must, without fear, face the evil in himself and increase his awareness of this side of himself. However daunting the task, this would prove to be of immeasurable value for oneself and the wider environment. However, facing the inner enemy, which Dr Jung termed the 'shadow', is not at all easy. For it is a powerful inner battle for supremacy, which must at all costs be won if we are serious in our aim of taming the mind. Tibetan medicine points to the root of the problem as being ignorance, which gives rise to what are termed the 'three poisons' of desire, hatred and closed-mindedness. These poisons are directly linked to three fundamental energies in the body. It therefore follows that any attempt to uproot ignorance will have a correspondingly powerful and revolutionary effect on the total body, leading a person towards increased health, inner and outer balance.

Dr Jung called this ignorance 'unconsciousness'. He too made it clear that a concerted attempt to address this, by confronting the shadow, is essentially a very powerful process which will have a dramatic effect upon the total person. Taking this a stage further, he pointed out that such a supreme personal effort actually contributes to a reduction in what he referred to as the 'collective evil'. This was in fact one of Jung's most significant and far-reaching ideas, that one's own personal inner effort and courage in facing the darker sides of the personality would have a corresponding effect on outer events, helping to diminish, reduce and eventually halt the dangerous 'psychic epidemics'. He constantly warned the modern individual of the danger of what he termed 'projection', a psychological phenomenon occurring when we perceive in others the various elements in our lives that we cannot come to terms with in ourselves. Dr Jung was once asked about the atom bomb, whether it would be employed sometime within the future, and if grave destruction of the world was likely. He replied that everything depended on how many people in the world could bear the tension between the positive, lighter side and the 'shadow' or darker side of their nature.

Similarly, His Holiness the Dalai Lama, when addressing the need to reduce wars and serious rifts between nations, will always direct the audience towards an inner process as the key to helping the world. Indeed, His Holiness makes an inordinate amount of trips to various countries of the world, taking the Tibetan Buddhist message wherever he goes. In addressing the outer calamities and events which appear to beset us, he constantly refers us back to the power of good within ourselves, pointing out the very real effect of developing compassion and love for our fellow human beings. He talks of a process called *Tonglen* in Tibetan, a form of prayer whereby one visualizes the act of taking into oneself other people's pain and suffering, whilst giving back in return an essence of goodness. (See The Practice of Giving and Taking, p.224) He teaches that we should really lessen our selfish desires and increase our selflessness. He encourages us to extend this focus even to our enemies, who are equally deserving of our compassion.

Dr Jung's approach to the outer enemy was to state what he declared to be an irrefutable law, that whatever darkness we are unable to face within ourselves will manifest on the outside. He advocated true consciousness rather than a dangerous repression of everything we would rather not face within ourselves, for this inevitably leads to the projection of our own inner problem onto some other person, group or nation. In this way, our own anger, upset and tension is simply dumped onto the outer world, to increase the growing emotional maelstrom, whilst we sit back and proclaim our inner purity and goodness. During times of crisis, political or otherwise, he claimed that the balance is held and the problem contained in direct relation to the people strong enough to face their inner selves and thus not be swayed by the outer masses.

But he affirmed that individuals cannot complete this task alone and this is where a spiritual system can be supremely important, offering a mass religion with a power equal to the power that is pushing upon them from the outside. Christianity can offer this to Westerners. Tibetans look, of course, to Buddhism. Through this intense and powerful religion, every individual Tibetan Buddhist thus attempts to remain anchored in a higher power, Lord Buddha, for this can offer from within one's own resources a resistance to the outer destructive forces of the masses. From birth, the young Tibetan is so completely steeped within the teachings of Lord Buddha that his aim and sole desire is to accomplish the ideals proclaimed and lived out by Lord Buddha. By traversing this direction, and attempting to attain an inner, transforming experience of Lord Buddha, God, Mohammed or one's chosen deity, an individual develops much greater security in the face of the mass movements, wars and revolutions which appear to be all-consuming and inevitable. The maintenance of one's own inner spiritual position, and alignment with a higher power, is potentially a damming force against the tidal waters of the organized masses.

Making a Start

One may understand the strength of steadily developed, spiritual power if one considers how best to dam a force of rushing water. To merely meet the waters head on, damming horizontally in the face of the torrent is virtually impossible, for the water will prove to be too powerful for this, carrying away material as one builds. But if one starts above where one wants to dam the water, and works from that point on the bank downwards, slanting across the water, eventually the water begins to turn back on itself, until it actually stops itself and the dam can be easily completed. In this way, step by step, the spiritually-organized person can positively affect the outer mass. This should be a real incentive to all those who are aspiring to ideals found in religion, for whatever they are able to attain will be of benefit to many others.

Thus, within our daily lives, the taming of our own mind is a very real force, for what can happen to one person in a group will indisputably react upon the others, for good or for ill. In other words, if an individual can find within himself a real dimension which in depth is just as equal to the pull of the dimension of the mass, then this can indeed be the calm within the centre of the storm, where the potential for resolution lies.

Clearly medicines can help us, various treatments can support, but in the end we have to take it upon ourselves to tame the mind. Even Buddha said that he could not change the mind for someone else, but could only point the way for every person to pursue this vital path. Through meditation, conscious stilling of the mind, through visualization, prayer or the chanting of mantras we can make a start. Inner calmative processes such as mantras, the repetition of the names of God, or of a deity, produce a certain atmosphere both inwardly and outwardly. Yet the mantra and the spirit of devotion do not need to be limited to sacred places. You may often find Tibetans chanting the sacred names of chosen deities whilst walking on the road, or whilst waiting in various public places. A most particular vibration is produced within the mind by recitation such as this. Devotional thoughts become a habit over time, so that devotion is built into us, developing our character. Through the strength of inner focus on the positive, our thinking can become a powerful mover on the path of evolution.

The mistake we seem to make is that we do not give much thought to thought itself. The power of thought is as real and as definite as money, food and water. It can be given to friends, neighbours, in fact anyone. Each day we could be helping anyone we know in pain, by sending out a loving thought to give that person aid. Even if healing thoughts are sent out generally, and not focused on someone in particular, it will still find someone among the many who are suffering. Further to this, the act of sending out supportive thoughts of reverence and strength to those who are spiritually evolved, such as the high lamas in the world, not only rewards us with a blessing, but something is also added to their store of power, which they use for the good of mankind.

So when a Tibetan physician approaches the understanding of all diseases, a precise and informed observation of the interaction of the mind and body is the most important element to consider. All our experiences in life, whether great or small, pleasurable or painful, are not simply external occurrences which happen to us as mere victims of circumstance. Looking beneath the signs and symptoms one will always discover some form of inner discordance, stress or conflict which essentially needs to be resolved, along with a prescribed approach to diet and lifestyle. A state of health will only ever come about when harmony is restored within both mind and body.

In fact, it is impossible to truly control or eliminate any illness without an integrated approach to harmonizing the mind and body. Mind over matter is indeed a powerful element never to be underestimated. On a physiological level our activities are all controlled by the mind. Our mental attitude directly influences our actions. So a negative mind will produce a negative action with a negative consequence.

In summary, the cause of all our pain, suffering and disease is the ignorance of the human condition, just as a flying bird and its shadow, which falls upon the ground beneath, can never be separated. The root of all suffering is ignorance, which subsequently develops what Tibetan medicine refers to as the three mental poisons:

- Desire, or attachment

- Anger, or aversion

- Closed-mindedness, or obscuration

Each of these poisons can cause one of the three humours to become disturbed. In the individual who experiences the states of mind created by these three mental poisons, the arising, deficiency or imbalance of three energies occurs, respectively:

rLung

Tripa

Badkan

Practice – How to Give Ourselves Time

Within the West, the time when one is expected to work is very clearly defined, such as beginning at 9.00am and going on to 5.00pm. In the East this is not the case; one simply works until one is tired, then stops. However, although the Western theory is useful, practice can sometimes be very different, where one begins to use up more and more spare time, until there is none left. This tends to increase stress and worry, for the work becomes like the ripples on the surface of the river, which never cease. The problem arises because we never truly finish work and leave it to one side. It is therefore important to develop, as a habit, the process of true relaxation in our lives.

When you first wake up in the morning, it is important not to leap up and rush. It is much better to sit up and relax just for a few moments, without any thoughts on the day ahead, then get up slowly and gradually start the day. You should sit up and expel all the air from the lungs by sighing for as long as possible. Then repeat this two or three times more. Even if this is for only one or two minutes, this process of sitting will have an effect upon your day. In this way you subtly build up a habit. So the feeling quality of sitting perfectly calmly starts to infuse itself into the whole day, even during periods of great action. This is a small, but effective piece of general advice for maintaining a healthy mind and a healthy body.

Chapter 10

The Three Humours, the Seven Constituents and the Three Wastes

*T*HE TIBETAN MEDICAL SYSTEM is tripartite, in that it is based on three fundamental energies within the body. The specific combination of these energies and their particular characteristics produce the individual nature and unique stamp of every human being. In a state of harmony and balance, they act as pillars upon which the whole body is constructed. The three energies, called *nyespas* in Tibetan and commonly referred to as humours in English, are *rLung* (translated as wind), *Tripa* (translated as bile) and *Badkan* (translated as phlegm).

The use of the word humour stems from Greco-Roman and later mediaeval European medicine which all referred to different fluid types within the body. However, this translation is inadequate, for *nyespas* are really very subtle, pervasive energies, currents or forces which are vital to the body and which operate not only on the physical level, but also on the psychological and spiritual levels. The exact translation of *nyespas* is 'defects', or those which do harm. Whilst the normal function of the defects is to be supportive of and helpful to the body, mind and speech, problems occur because these three defects arise from a defective source, ignorance, which in itself leads to desire, anger and delusion.

Therefore the *rLung* energy overdevelops in the body in direct relation to the increase of insatiable desire. The *Tripa* energy overdevelops in the body when anger cannot be pacified. The *Badkan* energy overdevelops when a closed-minded attitude towards life becomes predominant. This tripartite relationship of the body – through the defects – to their source, ignorance, which is the root cause of all suffering and disease, is fundamental. So although on the one hand, the *nyespas* act as sustainers of the body, they remain potentially afflictive elements and ultimately their final action is to cause death and the separation of consciousness from the body.

In a healthy body the balance between the three *nyespas* is maintained and appropriate qualities of each are present. This balance, however, is a precarious one, and the increase, decrease or erratic movement from the usual location of any or all of the *nyespas* moves the body towards a diseased condition. As Tibetans we use the simile of firewood to describe how the humours always retain within them the potential to become defective, for the final purpose of firewood is always to burn it and make a fire. In the same way, wind, bile and phlegm always carry within them an inherent defect, for they all come from one defective source – ignorance.

These three *nyespas* are always present in the body, being the first three channels to develop in the foetus. The first channel goes up from the navel to the brain. It is developed by closed-mindedness and is called *Badkan*. A second forms in the centre of the body, linked to the blood, developed by hate and is called *Tripa*. The third goes down to the sexual organs, is developed by desire and called *rLung*.

In this way, *rLung* (wind) resides in the lower part of the body in the pelvic region where the reproductive seeds are located, and is developed by desire, lust and attachment. *Tripa* (bile) is located in the middle part of the body in the area of the liver and gall bladder and is developed by anger and hatred. *Badkan* (phlegm) resides in the area of the brain and is developed by closed-mindedness or delusion. The use of the somewhat limited terms wind, bile and phlegm needs further enhancement, since wind is indeed an aspect of *rLung*, but *rLung* is not simply wind or solely even a reference to air within the body in the form of gases. In fact, each of the humours is defined according to characteristics, which subsequently facilitate the process of diagnosis whereby a predominating humour may be identified in a particular condition.

rLung has, in fact, six characteristics, which are principally tactile in nature and named as: rough, light, cold, subtle, hard and mobile; one would not normally attribute these characteristics to the nature of wind. Similarly, bile, understood in the West as a secretion of the liver, which is stored in the gall bladder, is an aspect of *Tripa*, but *Tripa*, which has seven characteristics particular to itself – slight oiliness, sharp, hot, light, having a bad odour, purging and moist – cannot be simply translated as bile. Likewise phlegm can be explained as an aspect of *Badkan*, but *Badkan* is more than the translation implies. *Badkan* has seven unique characteristics all of its own: oily, cool, heavy, blunt, soft, stable, and having a sticky consistency. So although the terms wind, bile and phlegm reflect an aspect of the humour, they should be perceived as more of a convenient name for a grouping of specific characteristics which the Tibetan physician is trained to identify, in order to diagnose the condition of a patient.

Generally, *rLung* is responsible for the inhalation and exhalation of breath and for all types of physical movement in the body; *Tripa* is responsible for thirst, hunger, the digestive system and appetite. It develops physical heat, maintains the complexion and gives a person bravery and intelligence. *Badkan* maintains the stability of body and mind, induces sleep, lubricates the joints, produces softness in the body and gives us the quality of tolerance.

The three humours are constantly interacting together within the body and are interdependent. So, although for the purpose of differentiation and to achieve a thorough understanding, each of the humours will be presented in detail within separate chapters of this book, in practice they can never be considered in isolation from each other, for they are inextricably interconnected. To separate them from each other would be like shifting, expanding or diminishing one corner of a pyramid and assuming this will not affect the other corners. Unless a balanced approach to all points of the pyramid and its exact geometry is maintained, the whole structure will be unbalanced and become precarious.

Our bodies are just like this. When examining one of the three foundations in our system, we must always keep in mind the continuous effect any adjustments to this part of the structure will have upon the other two foundations and thereby the whole of the body. All human beings have the three humours within them, and are thereby directly subject to the three mental poisons. So, finding someone without the three mental poisons is virtually an impossible task. Only Buddha and the emanations of Buddha are free from the mental poisons. However, there are those who have attained a degree of enlightenment and rare exceptions who are said to have reached a state of 'Buddhahood'.

We will now proceed to look at each of the specific characteristics of the three humours.

The Twenty Characteristics of the Three Humours

Tibetan medicine has classified the twenty characteristics of the three humours in order to facilitate diagnosis. This allows the practised physician to pinpoint the state of imbalance within a patient in terms of the three humours. *rLung* has six qualifying characteristics, which are rough, light, cold, subtle, hard and mobile, which may be understood in the body as follows:

Rough

The rough nature of *rLung* means that the diseases will be quite unbearable. There will be roughness apparent on the skin, the tongue, and the quality of the blood will be rough.

Light

This means that the diseases will respond lightly, or easily to treatment, whereby even an oily massage or the inhalation of smoke from burned butter can cause the problem to subside. The patient may also experience a light sensation in the body and mind.

Cold

The patient will typically feel cold and have a desire for warm food and a warm environment.

Subtle

rLung is very subtle in nature, for it is not material and can easily enter any location of the body, however fine, such as the body hair, the teeth to cause toothache and blood circulation to cause numbness.

Hard

This means 'hard' in the sense of having no rotting nature. Therefore *rLung*-based growths do not form pus very easily, *rLung* fevers do not naturally mature and the bowels are often constipated and difficult to purge.

Mobile

rLung is continuously fluctuating in nature, therefore a *rLung* patient may suffer from delirium, hallucination and hysteria. Such a patient is typically talkative and always on the move. *rLung*-based swellings, growths, pain and even the pulse all fluctuate and change because of this mobility.

Tripa's seven qualifying characteristics are slight oiliness, sharp, hot, light, bad odour, purging and moist, as follows:

Slight Oiliness

The nature of *Tripa* is slightly oily, so the patient will generally have an oily complexion on the face and skin.

Sharp

The characteristic of sharpness means quick to act. Therefore *Tripa* diseases affect a patient very suddenly or quickly. Fevers mature quickly and swellings will easily suppurate.

Hot

Tripa is hot in nature, therefore it heats up the body to cause thirst, and generally increase the body temperature. The patient will desire cool food and drink and seek cool places.

Light

Tripa is light in responding to treatments, so even a strong fever will respond readily to cool remedies.

Bad Odour

A *Tripa* patient will generally have foul-smelling perspiration, breath, urine and faeces.

Purging

Due to its purging characteristic, *Tripa* causes patients to have loose bowels even with only a slightly unwholesome diet and irregular behaviour.

Moist, or Liquid

This characteristic means that there will be a liquid quality to the phlegm and blood in the body, and diarrhoea is likely.

Badkan has seven qualifying characteristics, which are oily, cool, heavy, blunt, soft, stable, and having a sticky consistency, as follows:

Oily

The oily characteristic of *Badkan* will manifest as an oily quality to any diarrhoea, vomiting, faeces or the blood.

Cool

This means there will generally be a lack of warmth in the case of a *Badkan* illness and the patient will seek warm places and desire warm food.

Heavy

Since *Badkan* is heavy in nature the patient will feel a heaviness in the mind and body, generally feeling lethargic, and will also respond slowly to any treatment.

Soft

Due to the soft characteristic, the tongue will have a soft quality, the skin will be soft to the touch and the blood will have a soft or smooth quality to it. Generally the symptoms are soft, in the sense that there is very little pain in a *Badkan* disease.

Stable

Due to the stable nature of *Badkan*, any swelling, growth or pain will not fluctuate very much.

Sticky

In this case, vomiting, diarrhoea, blood, phlegm and saliva will be very sticky in quality.

The three humours are, in themselves, a combination of the five elements. *Tripa* has the nature of fire; *Badkan* has the nature of water and earth; *rLung* has the nature of air, whilst space is the container of everything. So if the *Tripa* energy is imbalanced, it will 'burn' the physical constituents since it has the nature of fire and has a hot quality. Even though it is located in the middle part of the body it will produce burning symptoms in the upper part, just like the flame from a fire will lick upwards. There is not a single hot disease which does not originate from *Tripa*. Imbalanced *Badkan* degenerates the digestive heat since it has heavy and cool characteristics, being of the nature of earth and water. So even though it is located in the head, it will descend to affect the lower part of the body. There is not a single cool disease that does not have its origin in *Badkan*. *rLung* is extremely mobile and pervades both hot and cold diseases. Having the nature of air it can act like a wind which blows upon the fire of *Tripa*, thus helping it to burn. But it will also assist a chill by accompanying *Badkan*. Because of this, *rLung* is understood as the cause of all diseases.

Each human being is, therefore, an original tapestry – a unique combination of twenty essentially different characteristics, manifesting together as a unified, whole person. The task of the physician is to decipher the code of each patient in terms of the three humours. This requires a precise reading of the manifesting characteristics of the patient, and subsequent weighing of the balance or imbalance of the humoural elements within the body. It is important to understand *rLung*, *Tripa* and *Badkan* not just by their names but by their respective characteristics. If one is able to identify the characteristics of a disease, whether it be detectable in the behavioural traits, dietary tendencies or within the actual condition of the patient, the urine sample or pulse, one can apply the appropriate treatment, whatever the disease may be. Consequently it is not necessary to know every illness, only to have the ability to identify with precision the characteristics of that illness, which can then lead the physician to prescribe an appropriate treatment.

It is very difficult to give advice on diet, lifestyle, medication and therapy if one has no real knowledge of the true characteristics of the three humours, *rLung*, *Tripa* and *Badkan*, for it is rather like trying to understand a language without an alphabet. Accordingly, before treating a patient we have to develop a thorough and comprehensive understanding of their characteristics in order to identify which humour is primarily operating. The more one becomes familiar with the characteristics, the easier it is to recognize them immediately and to take appropriate action.

For instance, one may be practising medicine in a windy and cold environment which is naturally conducive to the arousal of *rLung* diseases. It may also be the rainy season which is most likely to elevate the *rLung* energy. To make matters even more difficult, one may already be addressing a disease caused by an imbalance of *rLung* in a person whose natural body-type already has a predomination of the *rLung* energy. The physician must clearly bear in mind all of these influencing factors, and take them into account when determining the severity of a disease, whatever the humour affected.

Once the physician has identified the predominating characteristics within a person and therefore diagnosed the disease in terms of the three humours, a treatment may be prescribed in order to balance the humours within the body and restore the body's health. The path to rebalancing the patient's condition will typically include advice on diet and lifestyle, together with appropriate medication. Particular symptoms will require particular medicines, normally having the opposite qualities to the manifesting characteristics, i.e. a condition with light characteristics would require medication known to have a heavy quality. There may be corresponding advice on the management of the person's emotions, due to the high sensitivity of the balance of the humours within the body to powerful emotions which inevitably have an adverse effect on these humours. All other injurious influences, including the climate, will be considered in order to restore or preserve the inner balance of the humours, so that health is maintained.

The Seven Constituents and the Three Wastes

In terms of the body, balance is primarily expressed as the harmony of the three humours. However, in addition to the three humours, there are other aspects of the body that must be balanced along with them in order to maintain health. The medical text says that:

> It is the balance or imbalance of the three classifications of
> the three Humours, seven Constituents and the three
> Wastes that causes the body to thrive or be overcome.

The three humours are potentially three harmers of the body. The seven constituents and three wastes are the processes within the body that can be harmed by the humours. These ten processes together refer to the stages of digestion within the body, as the nutritious elements of the food and drink ingested are separated from the waste elements. From the time one first takes in food and drink, the formation of the seven constituents begins to take place, whereby at succeeding levels of digestion each constituent is formed from the one that precedes it across a period of six days. The seven constituents are the nutritional essences, blood, flesh, fat, bone, marrow and reproductive essence. The three wastes are faeces, urine and perspiration.

When the food we eat reaches the stomach, it enters the first part of the digestive process. A process of refinement begins here as elements of nutrition are separated from the waste. In this way the food ingested is separated into refined and unrefined parts, the refined portion being the nutrients and the unrefined portion being the waste.

During this process of gradual refinement the body produces three primary waste products: *Shangwa*, or faeces, which are solid, *Chin*, or urine, and *Nyuel*, or perspiration which are both liquid. The production and elimination of these is absolutely vital to health, for these three major wastes purify the system and keep the body healthy. In respect of both *shangwa* and *chin*, they perform two basic functions: firstly to act as a means of retaining food substances in the body long enough for all nutrition to be extracted and used for the benefit of the body; and secondly to expel the final waste from the body.

The seven constituents are seven basic and vital tissues, responsible for the entire structure of the body. They maintain the functions of the different organs, systems and vital parts of the body, and play an important role in the development and nourishment of the body. These seven constituents, also called the seven supporters of life are as follows:

Dangma, or nutritional essence

This is the nutritious essence extracted from the food, which goes to the liver and transforms into blood, while the waste matter from this part of the process helps in developing the decomposing aspect of *Badkan* in the stomach.

Tak, or essence of blood

The blood is a vital transporter of the life force throughout the body and also supplies moisture to the body. The essence of blood transforms into flesh and the gall bile is developed by the waste.

Sha, or essence of flesh

Flesh fills out the body form. Its essence transforms into fat and the wastes are the excrements discharged from the orifices of the body such as the nose, mouth, etc.

Tsil, or the essence of fat

Fat is an essential lubricant within the body. The essence of fat transforms into bone and the waste matters are the body grease and sweat.

Rue, or the essence of bone

Bone is responsible for the frame and firm structure of the body skeleton. The essence of bone transforms into marrow and the waste forms teeth, nails and pore hairs.

Kang, or the essence of marrow

This important source of vitality transforms into the reproductive essences of both male and female. The waste develops skin, faeces, body grease and discharge from the eyes.

Khuwa, or the essence of the reproductive seeds

The reproductive seeds are the semen in men and ova in women. The body growth is supported by the reproductive seeds during the first twelve years of life. Thereafter, up to the age of fifty, the body is strengthened by them and in pregnant women they develop milk in the breasts. After this age, the body gradually becomes weaker because the energies are reduced within the body, and there is a decline in the production of reproductive seeds.

However, although the texts refer to the seven constituents as named above, there is an essential eighth stage in the process, whereby the essence of the reproductive seeds is even further refined to become the super-essence of the body which resides in the heart as *mDang-chhog.* From here this highly refined essence is distributed throughout the body. This all-pervading, extremely important essence is responsible for the maintenance and longevity of life, and actually shines out of a person as a healthy glow, particularly noticeable in the complexion. It can be kept in good condition by following a healthy diet full of nutrition, and by maintaining a generally happy disposition, free from anxiety and stress as much as possible.

The importance of the digestive process cannot be overemphasized and we will return to this topic later. The seven constituents are seven basic and vital tissues, responsible for the entire structure of the body. They maintain the functions of the different organs, systems and vital parts of the body, and play an important role in the development and nourishment of the body. Any disorder within the process will naturally have a correspondingly negative effect upon the body.

The digestive process always remains reliant on the balance of the three humours, which in the next chapter we will proceed to investigate in detail. Each of the three humours subdivides into five different major categories with their own specialized function and distinct location, in the various tissues, organs or other parts of the body. Tibetan medicine describes these fifteen types of humour in terms of five *rLung* energies, five *Tripa* energies and five *Badkan* energies. Together they provide an integrated system of energies which sustain the body and all of its functions.

The Practice of Meditation

One exercise generally helpful to both body and mind and thereby to the three humours, the seven constituents and three wastes, is meditation. There are a number of different ways in which we can meditate, and each person should find the way that feels best for them personally. In essence, the aim of meditation, whatever method is used, is to achieve tranquillity of mind, which is so very important, not only to ourselves but also to our surroundings. The Tibetan Buddhist approach to meditation is to gradually develop levels of concentration. As a way of beginning, we simply allow the mind to rest upon a small object such as a stone or a piece of wood.

Allowing the mind to 'rest upon' something is the key phrase here, for as Buddha advised:

In your meditation practice you should not impose anything too forcefully on your mind, nor should you let it wander.

When the mind is peaceful and calm, this very state of tranquillity exudes a kind of radiance or luminosity, a feeling of happiness. This is of course very good for ourselves, but more than this, it can help others around us, for we actually communicate this tranquillity and feeling of inner joy to others, promoting it in the atmosphere.

11

rLung – the Mobile Energy of Life

*I*N LIFE, NOTHING ever stands still. Everything is subject to the laws of change, movement, transformation and evolution. The great wheel of life inexorably turns and the cycles of nature and the seasons turn with it, in constant ebb and flow, expansion and contraction, rise and fall. Our attempt at fixed views upon the world and on ourselves can only ever be snapshots in time, for when we look upon form, we look upon energy and from one split second to the next the world has irrevocably changed. From the rise of the sun at dawn, to sunset and the emergence of the moon, into the night through our sleeping state into our waking once again, we participate in the dynamic energy of life which is constantly in motion. From the first gasp of the newborn infant to the last gasp of the dying aged person, the force of life, the force of *rLung* is always with us. The constant movement of all that is, may at times appear to be in a state of chaos, yet beneath everything there is a precise universal pattern.

The energy of *rLung*

I normally translate *rLung* as 'mobile energy', and its exact meaning is 'movement'. All movement is *rLung*. It is the force of the exhalation and inhalation of the breath. The movement of the body, mind and speech comes from *rLung*. Any movement that takes place in our body, whether it be the movements of the hands and legs or in fact, of any organ in the body, originates from *rLung*. Both voluntary and involuntary movements come from the *rLung* energy. Its force is responsible for the elimination and retention of faeces, urine and mucus and for the pervasive movement in their pathways of the seven constituents, respectively: the nutritional essence of food, blood, flesh, fat, bone, marrow and reproductive essence.

It is very important that the process of the formation of the seven constituents is not restricted or blocked in any way. For example if the transformation of blood into flesh were to be inhibited, then muscle wasting would occur. Thus, muscle wasting can be attributed to a malfunction of *rLung*. *rLung* has the characteristic of drying up things when it is not functioning well. In this way, polio is a kind of drying up of the muscle, when the malfunctioning of *rLung* results in lack of blood flow to certain parts, causing difficulty in movement. *rLung* also facilitates the functioning of the sensory organs towards their respective objects. Thus, in its normal, balanced state, *rLung* maintains the body.

Located around the genital organs, hips and waist it is linked to desire, lust and attachment. The pathways through which *rLung* chiefly moves are the bones, ears, pores of the skin, heart and the colon. Strong desire or attachment will cause disturbances in the *rLung* energy which will manifest as overtalking, stretching and sighing. A strong desire eventually transforms itself into the physical *rLung* energy as a law of nature. For instance, if I see a beautiful house, a desire to have that house will immediately arise in my mind, for I assume that this cherished possession will enable me to live happily. Likewise, if my bank account is low, I will either simply try to forget about it, or work hard to increase the money in the account.

Stress and *rLung*

Despite trying everything possible, if these desires are not fulfilled, they can lead to mental stress. Gradually, this stress will increase, giving rise to sleepless nights because excessive thinking or mental concentration will tend to induce insomnia. In turn, insomnia causes tiredness and a change in facial expression. If one attempts to reason with someone caught in this high state of anxiety, their mental block, having affected the sensory organs, obstructs clear perception, resulting in them only hearing part of the conversation. As the *rLung* disturbance gradually progresses the individual loses his or her appetite, and in this way the situation worsens.

When the *rLung* energy is in this way unbalanced, it plays tricks with the mind, making it difficult to function properly. The person becomes restless and fidgety, and will constantly change his or her mind. It therefore becomes impossible for the person, thus affected, to make any real decisions. We can compare the effect of the disordered *rLung* energy to that of a hurricane, which twists and uproots trees, and collapses buildings. The benefit that accrues from a normal state of mind can be compared to the effect of a gentle smooth flowing breeze on a beautifully balanced flower. Whereas a beautiful flower destroyed by violent winds is the perfect image of the damage caused by a *rLung* disordered state of mind.

rLung imbalance

Tibetan medicine considers disorders of the nervous system to be directly attributable to an imbalance of the *rLung* energy, whereas other systems regard these nervous disorders as being purely psychological. In fact, other medical systems don't seem to be able to give a satisfactory explanation to manifestations of a disruption of *rLung*, such as tension and stiffness around the neck, general nervousness, depression and other mental problems, which may include having nightmares, visions, hallucinations and suffering from mania. For *rLung* is mobile, erratic, and causes numbness. By erratic, we mean that it can send wrong information to the sense organs. Tibetan medicine understands the heart as the vital organ and seat of consciousness where one of the five *rLung* energies resides. From the heart there is a channel which connects to the brain, and in this way to the sense organs. The erratic nature of *rLung* can thus result in double vision, seeing ghosts or hearing abnormal sounds. Memory, which is supported by the heart, may be impaired, and the disordered *rLung* can also produce fearful dreams. As *rLung* is connected to the nerves, a disorder in this energy can affect the blood circulation, and produce the sensation of numbness.

rLung has been translated as wind, for like the wind it cannot be seen, yet its effects are very real. It moves largely in unseen pathways, most of which are not visible on dissection, although some of these channels are part of the nervous system. As already said, *rLung* is responsible for all movement in the body and this naturally extends to the movement or spread of disease. The multiplying of an element in the body, the formation of a growth and the scattering of diseases – all these are due to the force of *rLung*, for the *rLung* energy assists both the hot and cold energies within our body. But when it becomes unbalanced, it can disturb everything within the body. Consequently, *rLung* can be the cause of every single disease.

The beginning of illness

The importance of *rLung* cannot be exaggerated, for all diseases begin and end with *rLung*. *rLung* can inflame and incite both hot (*Tripa*) and cold (*Badkan*) diseases. Just as oxygen is needed for a fire, otherwise it extinguishes, the hot disease can only begin with *rLung*. Similarly, cold diseases begin with *rLung*, for without *rLung* nothing can develop. Any disease, such as a fever with a temperature is always initiated by *rLung*. The signs of *rLung* can be noticed in the very shivering at the beginning of a fever, which is the indication of rising temperature and is initiated by *rLung*. This shows how the humours never work in isolation. They are like three brothers, and if something goes wrong with one brother, whereby he is hurt, then the other two brothers are affected and disturbed.

Such careful observation of the interaction of the three humours at the beginning of a disease is also necessary towards the end of an illness. For instance the reduction of a fever to a point of stasis may be likened to finding the exact juncture of where the hill descends to meet the plain. Just as the fever comes down, the greatest caution is needed, for *rLung* can suddenly rise up again, and create problems. In this respect, correct administration of medicines is very important, for an overprescription of a cooling medicine, designed to reduce the heat of the fever, can bring up *rLung*, because the *rLung* energy is attracted to the cooling nature of the treatment. This seemingly minor *rLung* will invite a further increase in *rLung* to a more major degree, and seriously disturb the mental balance of the patient. For even a small portion of the temperature can be blown up by *rLung*, just as when you blow on a small fire you bring the fire back into life. This manifestation of *rLung*, which is called 'empty channel inflammation' must be guarded against in the final stages of the treatment of any illness, otherwise *rLung* may suddenly rise up and cause a different problem.

The slightest trace of mental stress, tension and pressure will provoke *rLung*. Once *rLung* becomes disrupted, it affects the functions of both *Badkan* and *Tripa*, finally affecting the normal functions of the body to create an unstable and poor digestion, irregular bowel movements, etc. Hence it is very important to keep the mind happy and content, as this is the way in which we can help to maintain *rLung* and keep the physical system in a state of good health.

rLung and diagnosis

Diet is always a major factor to consider when diagnosing any illness, for *rLung* diseases may be due to the excessive ingestion of food, drink or medication with the tastes or qualities known to affect the *rLung* energy. In terms of tastes, those affecting *rLung* are the bitter or astringent tastes and in terms of qualities, those substances having the qualities of light, coarse, subtle, hard, absorbent, mobile and cold can be injurious to *rLung*. Aside from this, other specific causes include exhaustion, fatigue and excessive sexual intercourse. Not taking enough food, overfasting or eating food that is not nutritious will cause *rLung* problems, as will general sleeplessness and strenuous activity of the body and speech on an empty stomach. Loss of essential body fluids such as excessive blood loss due to injury, severe vomiting or diarrhoea will all negatively impact *rLung*.

As already stated, the *rLung* energy is increased by desire, or attachment, and this can affect the nervous system, producing disturbances. Conversely, mental stress, tension and depression can cause *rLung* disease, as will excessive shouting, screaming or talking for very long periods. Tibetan medicine counsels against the withholding or forcing of natural bodily urges and in the case of *rLung* this applies to urine, faeces, semen, hiccoughs, sneezing and belching, as excessive restraint or pressure will negatively affect this humour.

Some *rLung* symptoms

Because of its responsibility for all movement within the body, when this energy is out of balance, involuntary movements such as shuddering, shaking and twitching may occur. Such movements stem from obstacles in the *rLung* energy pathways and will occur either when the body is moving further out of balance in a worsening disease, or when moving towards a more balanced condition, for instance when emerging out of a crystallized traumatic condition.

The problem with mobility and its link to the mind can be clearly seen in such conditions as Parkinson's Disease, which is an abnormal functioning of *rLung* in the body. If you question people who suffer from Parkinson's Disease, they will confirm that their tremors are increased when they are depressed or worried. This again demonstrates the *rLung* and mind connection. Therefore we need a deeper understanding of *rLung* in order to treat this condition.

rLung and the heart

Attachment can negatively affect the nervous system, and will also affect the heart. A person with lots of worries and responsibilities is very likely to suffer from a heart attack. According to Tibetan medicine, a heart attack is the result of a depression of the *rLung* energy, which is responsible for the circulation of the blood and lymph in the body. This builds up pressure within the blood, and results in a serious obstruction in the blood flow.

Within the body there are five specific types of *rLung* with their own specific location and function.

The Five Different Types of *rLung*

Life-Sustaining *rLung*, or *Srog-zhin rLung*

According to the Tibetan medical tradition, consciousness is supported by *Srog-zhin*, or life-holding wind, which is known as *prana* in India. All other *rLung*s develop from this *rLung* which holds and supports the life force. It is localized at the crown chakra, and moves down through the throat into the chest and back into the head. It carries out the actions of eating, drinking and salivating, in that it enables us to swallow food and liquid. It also carries out the actions of exhalation and inhalation of breath, spitting, belching and sneezing. It gives the feeling of clarity to the mind and sensory organs, clarifying the intellectual power and the sense of seeing and hearing etc. and holds consciousness. It sustains the body functions and protects the consciousness. *Srog* means 'life', and *zhin* means 'hold'. Thus, when *Srog-zhin* is in disorder, or disrupted, for example by poor food, poor health or a defective lifestyle, this in turn can negatively affect the consciousness. *rLung* may play with consciousness and make people behave strangely, producing restlessness, the inability to think by oneself and other mental problems such as stress, anxiety and depression. Such disturbances can be controlled by both medicine and meditation.

Consciousness without *rLung* is like a man who cannot move his legs, whilst *rLung* without consciousness is like a horse with no eyes. In this way we can see that consciousness and *rLung* are interdependent, and if there is no Life-Sustaining *rLung* then it is impossible for consciousness to exist, or act on the body. *rLung* is the supporter and holder of life, like a tree which supports the nest of a bird. The bird (consciousness) depends on the tree (*rLung*) for stability and life. An imbalance in *rLung* can therefore lead to severe mental problems just as a bird may be forced from its nest during a cyclone. Ultimately, the image of the tree falling and the bird flying away is the departure of the soul from the body at death.

The causes of disruption to the *Srog-zhin rLung* are: the taking in of poor quality, malnutritious food; fasting or starving for long periods; and forcibly withholding or pressurizing faeces, urine and hiccoughs. This disruption can manifest in dizziness, hallucinations, hysteria, insanity, difficulties in inhalation of breath and problems in swallowing food or beverages.

Ascending *rLung*, or *Gyengyu rLung*

The Ascending *rLung* is localized in the throat chakra and chest. Its energy moves upward from the chest past the mouth and as far as the nose. It moves around the nose, throat and tongue and produces the voice, enabling us to speak and to sing. It clears the sensory organs and the mind, assisting the capacity for memory and gives the body physical strength, the characteristic glow of a good complexion, and the willpower to do our daily work.

Disruption in *Gyengyu rLung* may be caused by forcibly withholding belching or vomiting, crying or laughing loudly and lifting and carrying loads which are too heavy. This disruption may show itself in vocal problems such as stammering, difficulty in speaking or even the complete loss of the ability to speak. It can also produce a loss of physical strength, facial paralysis or the loss of one's memory.

Pervasive *rLung*, or *Khyabjey rLung*

Localized in the heart chakra, the Pervasive *rLung* pervades the whole body. It facilitates the movement of our extremities such as walking, lifting, stretching, bending, opening and closing of the eyelids and lips, and its energy spreads to all areas of the body. It is responsible for blood circulation and the lymphatic system. All physical, mental and vocal functions depend upon this *rLung*.

Disruption in *Khyabjey rLung* can be caused by overwalking or extensive trekking, sitting too long on wet ground and excessive physical work, exercise or sport. It can also be disturbed by an attack of sudden, powerful fear within the mind, or depression caused by mental tension and worries. Poor food also has a negative effect on *Khyabjey rLung*. The disruption of this *rLung* in the body can manifest as: a feeling of discomfort in the heart; unconsciousness or fainting; meaningless talking; the desire to keep moving; ever increasing fear and stress in the mind; and strong reactions to sounds which are perceived to be unpleasant.

Fire-Accompanying *rLung*, or *Menyam rLung*

Localized in the navel chakra and stomach, this *rLung* accompanies the digestive heat which is one of the *Tripa* energies. It is called Fire-Accompanying *rLung* and moves within the entire abdominal canal and in the pathways related to the body elements. This *rLung* is responsible for the movement of the bowels. It aids in digestion, separating the essence from the waste, and assists in the maturation of the seven constituents as already mentioned, together with the three waste products (faeces, urine and perspiration).

Disruption in *Menyam rLung* is caused by the intake of heavy foods such as stale foods, and sleeping during the daytime. The disruption can manifest as poor digestive heat, loss of appetite, vomiting and difficulty in digestion.

Descending *rLung,* or *Thursel rLung*

The Descending *rLung* resides in our genital chakra and the rectum. Its energy moves around the colon, urinary bladder, thighs and genitals. It facilitates the expelling of semen, urine, and faeces. It is responsible for menstruation and can also cause retention in all of these actions. It also helps in child delivery.

A disruption in *Thursel rLung* is caused by forcibly withholding or pressurizing faeces, urine, wind or semen and can manifest as an aching and burning sensation in the hips and bones, muscle wasting, paralysis and loose joints, constipation, dysuria and gas accumulation in the stomach. It may also result in the person wishing to keep moving, the development of ever increasing fear and stress in the mind, and disproportionate reactions to hearing something unpleasant.

CASE STUDY:

On one occasion, when I was conducting consultations in Europe, a young lady visited my clinic. This particular lady was restless and generally very distracted. She was not very attentive, and moved about all the time, constantly needing to stretch her limbs. She sighed a great deal, had a pale complexion and seemed unhappy. On questioning her, I discovered that the main cause of her problem was a separation from her boyfriend, whom she loved very much.

I checked her pulse and found it to be superficial, bulky and that it disappeared on slight pressure. Her tongue was rough and dry and her urine sample was thin, watery and had large bubbles. These being typical *rLung* signs, I then checked certain *rLung* points on the spine, crown of the head, shoulders and shoulder blades and certain points on the sternum between the breasts. All these were unbearably sensitive and painful when touched.

At the end of a thorough diagnostic procedure, I came to

the conclusion that she was suffering from a *rLung* disorder. Since she was young, pretty and well educated, I tried to help her to realize the good qualities within her, assuring her that she could have many good friends. However, because she was so full of worries and upset, this was having a bad effect on her, covering over her good qualities and thus leading nowhere. We had a long discussion and finally she accepted my suggestion to try to calm her mind and live a normal life again.

I also asked her to smile three times a day, to help her inner state and mood, which she promised to do without fail. I also advised her not to take in foods that would increase *rLung*, such as bitter foods or generally strong-tasting foods and pork. I asked her to take in warm and nutritious food, prescribed Tibetan medicines and also advised her not to overuse her mind by dwelling on things too much. I treated her *rLung* points with a warm, oily fomentation (cloth soaked in heated butter).

When I returned one year later, a young, well-dressed, gently-spoken and pretty lady came into my clinic. At first, I could not recognize her but then realized that she was the same lady whom I had treated the year before. The warmth of feeling and gratitude from her was immense, as if she had been given a new life. Tibetan medicine had really helped her to enjoy a normal, happy life.

The Practice of Sky Gazing

In the fast pace of the modern world, increasingly more and more people are developing high levels of tension and stress, which have a negative effect upon the *rLung* energy in the body. It is therefore most important to find ways of counteracting this with moments of peace and calm. One way of doing this is by gazing at the sky.

In the morning when the sun rises, we can sit or stand facing the west, gazing into the clear sky. From here we should exhale all the air out of our lungs, sighing as we do so, for two or three times, gazing calmly into the sky. This can also be performed in the middle of the day by gazing into the northern sky and at sunset by gazing into the east.

The reason that this has such a beneficial effect is because of the impression of light in the sky. The impression created is of the vastness of the sky which seems very far away. It is the vision of the reflection of light in the sky that produces this effect. If we can give ourselves five minutes in the morning and five minutes in the evening to perform this simple practice it will be immensely valuable. But even if we can only spare one minute, however much tension and stress surrounds us and makes us feel we have to rush, this will have a positive effect.

Chapter 12

Tripa – the Sun at the Centre of our System

The origins of *Tripa*

The sun sits at the heart of our universe, emanating the power of heat and light essential for our existence. The earth has its orbit around the sun and also spins around its own axis. These two motions are fundamental to the earth, regulating all life upon the planet. The daily cycle and seasonal round are determined by the movement of the rotating earth which travels around the sun. All living organisms essentially are sensitive and adapt to the resulting basic rhythms of periodical change which affect the quality of light, heat and humidity available at any one time.

The radiation of the sun's energy is paramount and all life feeds upon it through a process of transformation of its radiant energy at a cellular level. The resulting energizing and multiplication of cells allows the plant to grow, the foetus to develop, the creatures to roam and humanity to exist. The seasonal cycle is our annual companion, from the burst of spring shoots to the midsummer blooms, from the autumnal colours to the roots in their winter cold storage. The temperature changes profoundly affect all behaviour and appearance, for without solar power there is no life, no warmth and no vitality. An apple ripens, becomes red and looks beautiful due to the solar heat. In the same way, internal heat ripens everything within our body, because the humour *Tripa* is similar in nature to the heat of the sun.

The energy of *Tripa*

The real meaning of *Tripa* is 'inflammation'. Generally located around the middle part of the body in the area of the liver and gall bladder, the *Tripa* energy is hot in nature. Its primary pathways are via the blood, perspiration, eyes, liver, gall bladder and intestines and the *Tripa* energy could be said to be linked to the secretory and endocrine systems. It gives the heat to our body and is the warmth we feel when we touch our forehead.

Tripa aids digestion and is the cause of hunger, thirst and the general appetite. It is responsible for a good complexion, giving a certain gloss to the skin. For just as the element of fire, through the action of the sun, is responsible for ripening and changing the colour of fruit, the heat of *Tripa* underlies the layers of the skin, producing and maintaining its colour. Heat naturally rises, so during an imbalance of *Tripa* a person will experience heat in the upper part of the body. Unnatural heat will 'burn' the body, thus negatively affecting the seven constituents and three wastes, whereas in a balanced state it serves to help them mature and ripen.

Where does this heat in our bodies come from? As already mentioned, the three mental poisons influence the nature of a person very much and *Tripa* is linked to the mental poison of anger, or hatred. Positively utilized, the heat of *Tripa* within the body gives a person the mental strength, courage and fortitude to face life's various endeavours. *Tripa* also provides the foundation for intelligence and is linked to the ability to think ahead and have a sense of ambition in life. Imbalanced *Tripa* energy is always linked to anger, however this anger may have arisen, for in the case of all human beings who are not liberated, like Buddha, from the three mental poisons, anger is always a form of self-grasping, which occurs when anything goes against our personal desires.

When the all-important 'I' is challenged or thwarted, petty pride raises its ugly head demanding personal success and launching into aggression and competition, effectively closing off from others in a form of inflated isolation. Here, the 'I' becomes all-consuming to the extent that it can now only see and hear itself. There is no possibility for rational discussion as the 'I' refuses all external offerings which are only perceived to be personal attacks. Such a negative attitude of mind stirs up the fires of hatred until violence inevitably erupts, bringing with it an explosion of harsh words, and even the hurling of insults and objects. Such actions of hatred intensely overheat the body, and increase the *Tripa* disorder to an excessive degree.

Angry responses and intensely possessive feelings of 'mine not thine' stem from ignorance and delusion which close the door on anything that does not fit in with a neatly boxed, blinkered vision of the world. In such a world there are only two possibilities: 'I am right' or 'They are wrong'. So encounters with others immediately produce a feeling of uneasiness. This uneasiness heats up within the closed-off world of the ego in perpetual conflict. Like a kettle on the boil, the *Tripa* energy heats up into anger which has a terrible potential to be destructive both personally and globally if it is not appeased.

The *Tripa* of ego

The day becomes replete with catastrophe upon catastrophe as this exclusive inner world of hatred manifests without fail on the outside, in a multitude of perceived threats to its existence. The growing inferno is based on a grand illusion, that this is my body, my will, my desire, my life, my needs. In short, the tiny ego has us in its grasp so that instead of being open and friendly to others, we have closed off into a negative state of mind, which revolves in upon itself as we decide that the world is peopled with aggressors and enemies and we must fight for survival at all costs.

The resulting body heat is powerfully increased, having an inevitable burning effect upon the whole system. One can easily see when a person is under the influence of strong anger, for perspiration occurs and heat develops in the middle part of the body. Like the rising flames that lick upwards, the upper part of the body is also affected, with obvious heat signs such as redness in the face and sweat upon the forehead. When this humour is unbalanced, it produces many types of fever.

In the case of *Tripa*, what is happening is that the heat and anger develop alongside each other in a worsening negative spiral of aggression in the mind and body, destroying peace. Maintaining peace is about not being angry, aggressive and agitated, or agitating. Aggressive mental and physical action will destroy the peace and happiness within oneself and others. Conversely, a nonviolent, peaceful and unaggressive mind and body will develop peace within oneself and others.

Aside from the overall, powerful effect of anger, other conditions can lead to the arousal of a *Tripa* disease. These include the excessive ingestion of food, drink or medication that is rich, hot, spicy and peppery or having the qualities of sharp, hot, oily, light or malodorous; for example old wine, butter or oil. In general, the intake of too much alcohol, butter and meat will negatively affect *Tripa*. Sleeping during the daytime, especially during the summer, is not good for *Tripa*, nor is sudden, excessive physical exertion after a period of resting, and long-distance running. The lifting of very heavy objects and physical labour in extremely hot conditions will exacerbate *Tripa*, as will a sudden accident, fall or attack from someone else.

The Five Different Types of *Tripa*

Digestive *Tripa*, or *Jujey Tripa*

Digestive *Tripa* is located between the stomach and intestines. This *Tripa* is responsible for digesting food and drink; it separates the essence and waste in the seven constituents and develops body heat. It promotes strength and supports the function of the remaining four *Tripas*, energizing them, for it radiates heat to all other parts of the body and this heat maintains life.

The digestive process is where the three energies of *rLung*, *Tripa* and *Badkan* come to meet. Therefore, Tibetan medicine understands the digestive system to be a very important body process. The medical text says:

> *The stomach is like a field; one must maintain its heat as a farmer who desires an abundant harvest, keeps the fields fertile. A person who understands what constitutes the nature of digestive fire, who is able to maintain this heat, and who knows how to recover it, can indeed be called a physician.*

Consequently we need good food for good digestion and good digestion for good food. Good digestion is the root of good health and is the basis of a happy life.

A child from a rich family who can afford the best quality food may fall ill, whilst a child from a family with fewer resources, where simple less expensive, food is eaten, can be strong and healthy. The answer to this apparent paradox lies in the comparative abilities to assimilate and absorb the food. If the food is digested well by the digestive heat, then the essence of the food will be absorbed into the body. Digestive heat can be maintained by eating light and nutritious food. Also different parts of the body require different types of food; for instance *rLung* cannot be developed with overly rich food.

A good digestive system leads to good health; a malfunction

causes abdominal disorders. In fact, most abdominal disorders originate from indigestion, or poor digestion resulting in undigested particles of food remaining in the body. Undigested food becomes toxic, and develops impurities within the body. For example, food remaining undigested in the stomach ferments and produces gas, and thus pressure which pushes up towards the diaphragm. This in turn can produce a choking sensation, palpitations, dizziness, blurred vision and dryness in the throat. In many cases, these disorders are mistaken for coronary and pulmonary problems. But all of them are actually due to a weak digestive system. The toxins eventually enter into the system and can cause eruptions and cancer growths.

The physician needs to be an expert in treating poor digestion. Like the farmer who wants a good harvest from the fields, he first needs good quality seeds and soil, and then needs to ensure that no unnatural calamities will befall the crop before the harvest is completed. In the same way, if you keep digestive heat intact with an appropriate attitude to the food and drink you ingest, and do not allow the mental poison of anger to overrule your condition, then you will not have problems.

Clearly it is important to take care of the digestive system. The medical tantra cautions one to 'remember the two principal causes of disease and always manage to avoid them'. The two principal causes are defective food and defective behaviour. Most of us never pause to consider whether our stomach is accustomed to taking a particular food which we are about to consume, possibly in large quantities. We also neglect to check on the actual time of ingestion, as to whether this is appropriate for our digestive system. For instance a late night feast just prior to sleeping is certainly not advisable for anyone. We also do not consider whether it is healthy to put a complete stop on one's typical diet and immediately change to dramatically different food, nor do we look more closely at the particular combination of foodstuffs, and whether these are really nutritious for our body. We do not think carefully before we eat in excess as to whether our digestive system can cope with the sheer volume of food and properly assimilate it within the body.

There is a common saying in Tibet which sums up this important issue, stating that 'while you are a guest at a party, do not forget that the stomach is yours, even though you know that the food is served by others'. During such gatherings people become ill either through overeating or through unaccustomed intakes of food.

The digestive power is a heat which is understood to be the main material required to obtain true inner wealth, the preservation of the body's health and thereby facilitate personal transformation and enlightenment. If food is not digested well, the basic body elements will not develop. Also, a weak digestion will not be able to assimilate and absorb medicines, rendering them ineffective. Therefore, in most cases of a disruption to any humour, to facilitate the healing process the patient is typically given three different types of medicine, addressing different aspects of the disease, and one of these will always be related to the digestion.

The disruption in *Jujey Tripa* can manifest as a yellowish tongue, thirst, difficulty in digestion and loss of appetite.

Colour-Regulating *Tripa*, or *mDangyur Tripa*

This resides in the liver and is responsible for producing the colours of all the body constituents, particularly the white and red colours, such as the redness in blood and the whiteness of the bones. It also lends colouring to the hair. This *Tripa* also provides the warmth of the internal organs.

A disruption in *mDangyur Tripa* can manifest as an excessive amount of fluid in the stomach, a heaviness in the body and loss of physical strength.

Determination *Tripa*, or *sDrubjey Tripa*

Determination *Tripa* is seated within the heart. It gives strength and energy to our mind, to determine the physical or mental activities we need for accomplishment in life and promotes pride. If this *Tripa* is weak, one will lack motivation, be cowardly and have an inferiority complex. However, when this *Tripa* is strong and in balance, it is like a light shining in the darkness, so we can derive courage and strength from it.

A disruption in *sDrubjey Tripa* can manifest as a sense of discomfort in the heart, breathlessness, thirst and loss of appetite. It can also result in physical tremors or shivering and a pinching pain in the heart and lungs.

Vision *Tripa*, or *mThongjey Tripa*

This resides in the eyes and facilitates eyesight, enabling us to see objects clearly, establishing their spatial dimensions and helping us to identify colours and shapes. The quality of light is an aspect of *Tripa* as it is considered to be an aspect of the fire energy.

A disruption in *mThongjey Tripa* can manifest as a headache, severe pain after drinking alcohol, yellowish eyes and poor eyesight.

Poor eyesight is linked to the Digestive *Tripa*, which is not functioning correctly due to an increase in the elements of water and earth, the elements which make up the cold energy of *Badkan*, and therefore is not distributing heat to the other *Tripa* energies as it should. This leads to problems with the liver and through this, the kidneys. The problem with the liver negatively affects Vision *Tripa*. This underpins how important the proper functioning of the Digestive *Tripa* is, and how our digestive system is fundamental to health.

Complexion-Clearing *Tripa*, or *mDoksel Tripa*

This *Tripa* is located in the layers and pores of the skin and gives us a good, clear complexion. It is also responsible for the colour of the skin.

A disruption in *mDoksel Tripa* can manifest as a rise in body temperature, a darkening of the complexion, painful sensation in the skin and roughness in the skin's texture. In this way a number of skin disorders are due to a malfunctioning of this *Tripa*.

CASE STUDY:

Once whilst in my Dharamsala clinic, a Western gentleman entered. He had noticeably yellowish eyes and skin. The area of the body around his liver was very tender, and he was suffering symptoms of anorexia, headache and general weakness. His pulse was thin and tight; his urine sample was dark yellow and had a bad odour. According to Tibetan medicine, he was suffering from a *Tripa* disease.

I immediately advised the patient to cease taking in any oily, fatty, buttery, spicy and fermented food. I said he should not take alcohol, refrain from physical exertion and keep generally cool. He was prescribed Tibetan medicines and in a relatively short time found that the jaundiced colour in his eyes and skin disappeared, and his urine returned to normal. There was no longer any tenderness in the liver and stomach region. His appetite improved and he was able to return to enjoy his travels.

Advice when Preparing to Eat or Drink:

The intake of any food and drink should always be regulated by bearing in mind the state of the digestive heat within the body. There is a simple approach to ensuring that you do not compromise or harm your digestive fire, which is as follows:

Do not eat unless you feel hungry.

Do not drink unless you are thirsty.

Do not eat when you feel thirsty.

Do not drink when you feel hungry.

If you feel hungry, then this is a sign that your digestive fire is operating successfully and prepared for the ingestion and digestion of food. However, if you then proceed to drink at this time, it is no different to pouring water on a fire, thereby extinguishing it completely. Taking in liquid at this time actively reduces the digestive fire, making it more difficult for the food to be properly digested and thereby increasing the risk of particles of food not being digested properly, causing other problems within the body.

In essence, the whole of this approach acts to help preserve a good digestive fire.

13

Badkan – the Lunar Liquid of the Body

What is *Badkan*?

In *Badkan*, the cold, lunar power meets the dominant liquid of the planet, the medium through which the whole of the cosmos affects us – water. The tides within us and around us are turned by the power of the moon and its gravitational pull. Gravity is an awesome force which no-one can escape. Indeed the sun, moon and planets are constantly exerting their effects upon us all, dictating the diurnal and nocturnal rhythms, the constant ebb and flow of life. Our monthly cycles are tuned to the pulsation of the universe which pulls upon our body waters, moving us formidably and inexorably, at the particle level, around the great wheel of life.

The human body is approximately 65% water. This fluid life, through which the cosmic forces act upon us, permeates our anatomy entirely, running through the arteries, veins and vessels as blood and lymph and providing all moisture and body fluids. From our very first beginnings, suspended within the amniotic fluid of the mother, to our complete subjection to the magnificence of the oceans which rise and fall at the command of the universe, we remain at the mercy of the moon and its magnetic cooling potency.

The real meaning of *Badkan* is 'liquidity' and 'cold'. *Badkan* is a combination of the elements of earth and water. It is the body's inner liquidity and is cold in nature. The term 'liquidity' is not simply the physical manifestation of water at the molecular level, for as with all of the humours they are forces and energies, much more than the terms which are inevitably limiting in their description. Thus, liquidity is an active force within us, sharing the same characteristics as liquid and bringing about a moistening, cooling quality. Like the moon that salutes the sun, the cooling nature of *Badkan* counteracts the heat of *Tripa* and prevents the body from being scorched and burned. It moistens the organs, and the body weight and body fluids depend upon it. It develops firmness in the body, induces sleep and helps to lubricate the connecting joints. It brings a softness and oiliness into the body. In its positive aspect it is linked to the aspects of relaxation, patience and tolerance.

Badkan in the body

With its main location in the upper part of the body, in particular the head, *Badkan* originates from a mind which is dull and closed, so much so that it has no self-awareness and thus has not the ability to see and accept its own faults. This dazed and confused mind cannot separate the good from the bad, virtue from vice, merit from its opposite. For it is as if the ability to draw a line between what is right and what is wrong has totally disappeared within the fog of the mind in its closed condition.

Consequently, when the ego is in such a bewildered state, the ability to assimilate information, form decisions, arrive at conclusions, grasp ideas, concepts and intuitions in order to progress, is impaired. There is no learning from the past, integration in the present, or creative and informed planning for the future. Inevitably, this leads to totally inappropriate actions and the law of cause and effect takes its toll, producing unfortunate results. Such outcomes all stem from a heavy, dull, closed quality in the mind which ultimately leads to *Badkan* in its diseased form.

In its balanced state, the *Badkan* energy serves as a crucial foundation of the body, providing wet and moistening factors as part of the body's cooling system. As has been noted in the last chapter, one of the primary functions of *Tripa* is to provide the heat necessary for transformation of the food and drink we ingest, through the all-important digestive fire. This must be maintained for the body to function correctly.

Whilst *Badkan* can serve to keep heat in balance, when its cold energy is adversely elevated, the digestive heat will immediately begin to suffer and degenerate. This is a fundamental problem, for the whole cycle of transformation is affected, effectively frozen by the increase of cold. With the digestive system malfunctioning in this way, we can feast upon all kinds of wonderful, nutritious foods, yet receive no nourishment. An impaired digestive heat will then lead to the accumulation of undigested particles of food which are dangerous and become toxic.

Long-term poor digestion will have a serious effect upon the body. For instance, if over a period of time an excess of oily and fatty foods is continued whilst the heat of the digestion is not functioning correctly, the resulting undigested food particles will become impurities in the bloodstream. Normal circulation of the blood will be negatively affected, for effectively the blood has become clogged up and has a sticky, oily consistency. The sluggish motion of the blood has its resulting effect on the body, leading to all kinds of problems, including skin eruptions, problems in breathing and heart pain. If left untreated, tumours may form.

The heart pain mentioned here refers to the cardiovascular system. However, as with everything in Tibetan medicine it is important to look for the root of the symptom. For instance, heart pain may arise from an obstruction of the Fire-Accompanying *rLung* energy. Here due to indigestion or a reverse movement of the Descending *rLung*, which moves upwards instead of its normal downward movement, disturbances are created in the flow of the blood, in the other *rLung* energies, *Badkan* energies and the body's constituents. This kind of disorder causes pressure and pain in the diaphragm, the heart and the arms. It is therefore important to identify the root of the heart pain in order to obtain relief.

The energy of *Badkan*

The pathways of *Badkan* in the body are through the essence of the food digested, the flesh and muscles, fat, marrow, reproductive seeds, faeces, urine, nose, tongue, lungs, spleen, stomach, kidneys and urinary bladder. Therefore, *Badkan* could be said to be linked to the organic and inorganic masses of the body.

Anything that increases the cold energy in our body, such as sitting and sleeping in damp and cold places, or consuming salad sandwiches, potatoes, soft drinks or fruit juice increases *Badkan*. Any uncooked food, anything raw, has the nature of earth and water, therefore is cold in nature, and will increase *Badkan*. The bread used for sandwiches is baked, so is not a problem, but a filling such as salad is cold. Potatoes in general are cold in nature, but if roasted or boiled will be not so cold. Roasted potatoes are lighter than boiled potatoes. But whatever the temperature of the potatoes, compared with other vegetables they are cold in nature.

A disorder in this humour could then manifest as pain in the lower back, abdominal rumbling, general dullness, frequent urination and tinnitus in the ears. Any of these symptoms are an indication that the body is asking for something hot as a remedy. The kidneys, being the site of the cold energy, are responsible for filtering the water in the body. The ears are affected, because they are linked to the kidneys, just like flowers are connected to their roots.

With respect to diet, there are a number of foods which can lead to the arousal of a *Badkan* illness. The excessive consumption of foods, drink or medication having a bitter taste, such as dandelion or bitter cucumber, and sweet foods such as candy or milk will ultimately cause problems, as will over-ingestion of unripened fruits, fresh grains, nuts and peas, radishes and wild garlic. The heavy intake of poor quality meat, fats and marrow, oil, butter, rotten, stale, uncooked, half-cooked or burnt food is also injurious, as is too much cold milk, cold water and tea. As far as the qualities of substances are concerned, one should not excessively take in those having heavy, cool, oily, blunt, soft and firm qualities.

Badkan and illness

Lying down or sleeping immediately after a meal can precipitate a *Badkan* disease, as will remaining too long in wet, moist, damp places, particularly if lying down. Immersion in cold water during winter is also not advised in this respect, for this will increase the *Badkan* energy, which will also be affected by chills due to wearing too light clothing during the cold seasons or in air-conditioned places.

Badkan is also directly linked to the increasingly prevalent disease of asthma. In fact the Tibetan medical texts describe five different types of asthma, all fundamentally *Badkan* diseases and the main one is due to an excess of the *Badkan* energy in the body, which produces a sensation of general heaviness in the body, excessive sputum and saliva, feeling of cold, lethargy, heavy sleep, sneezing and difficulty in breathing. Basically, what happens is that the increase of the cold *Badkan* energy in the body decreases the heat of *Tripa*. Once the *Tripa* is decreased, it means we cannot digest and assimilate the food properly within the stomach. This poor assimilation affects other parts of the body. The lungs are directly affected where a particular phlegm and sputum arising from the cold will develop.

Gradually there will be an increased obstruction in the lungs by this particular type of phlegm. People affected in this way will suffer more from asthma either early in the morning or in the late evening as these are the cold times of the day. These people are also liable to experience an attack of asthma during the full moon. The reason for this is that the external cold power of the moon, which is at its height when full, adds to the internal accumulated cold energy. The accompanying increase in phlegm will give rise to more serious obstructions to the windpipe and as a result there will be wheezing and difficulty in breathing.

The Five Different Types of *Badkan*

Supporting *Badkan*, or *rTenjey Badkan*

This resides in the chest, in particular around the upper ribs and breastbone and supports the other four *Badkan* energies. It supports the elements of earth and water in the body and acts as a substitute for water helping us not to feel thirsty all the time.

A disruption in *rTenjey Badkan* can manifest as a loss of appetite, a bloated or filled sensation in the chest and upper back, and burning and acidity in the chest.

Decomposing *Badkan*, or *Nyagjey Badkan*

This is located in the stomach and transforms undigested food into a semi-liquid in preparation for the next stage in the digestive process, conducted by the Digestive *Tripa*.

A disruption in *Nyagjey Badkan* can manifest as difficulty in digesting food, poor assimilation of nutrition by the body, frequent belching and a hard stomach.

Experiencing *Badkan*, or *Nyongjey Badkan*

This *Badkan* is located in the tongue. It gives us a distinctive sensation for each of the six tastes and enables us to experience the various textures in the food we eat.

A disruption in *Nyongjey Badkan* can manifest as a lack of experiencing taste in any food, a feeling of a cold sensation on the tongue, pain in the lips, a hoarse voice and loss of appetite and thirst.

Satisfying *Badkan,* or *Tsemjey Badkan*

Satisfying *Badkan* resides in the head, from the neck upwards. It helps the sensory organs to function, enabling each one to reach the object and be satisfied. For example, if we stare at an object long enough eventually we become satisfied and turn our gaze away. This *Badkan* is also linked to tears, for when this energy is very strong it is said to 'melt' *Tsemjey Badkan* in the head, so that tears begin to flow.

A disruption in *Tsemjey Badkan* can manifest as a loss of balance experienced within the head, blurred vision, blocked ears, frequent sneezing with much mucus, a susceptibility to flu and a heavy sensation in the forehead.

Connecting *Badkan,* or *Jorjey Badkan*

This is located in all the joints, connecting and lubricating the joints so that the body can stretch and bend freely.

A disruption in *Jorjey Badkan* can manifest as difficulty in stretching and bending the legs, cracking sounds in the joints, bulky joints and pain and swelling of the joints.

CASE STUDY:

A Tibetan patient came to me one day with poor digestion, swollen face, body and legs. He was anaemic, with a general heaviness in the body. He had a full sensation in the stomach and felt very cold. His pulse was weak, slow and sunken and his urine sample was whitish, with no smell or steam. It was also foamy with saliva-like bubbles on the surface. My diagnosis was that this was a patient suffering from a *Badkan* disease.

I advised the patient to stop eating raw, cold, heavy, oily, fatty foods and drinks. I asked him to avoid cold places and do regular exercise, especially fifteen to twenty prostrations a day and to take boiled water in the morning and evening. He was prescribed Tibetan medicine and finally recovered. After that, I often saw him circumambulating the temple in Dharamsala.

Physical Exercise to Alleviate *Badkan* Diseases

Any form of exercise is good in treating a disorder of *Badkan*.
Our customary Tibetan form of exercise is a devotional one
known as performing prostrations. These involve beginning from
a standing position as a form of prayer to one's chosen deity.
One then crouches down until one is squatting, then
immediately kneels forward onto the ground and, keeping the
body as close to the ground as possible, with the palms
smoothly running along the ground in front, one stretches out to
full length – prostrated in surrender to the same deity. From
there one pulls the body back to the kneeling position and
stands up again to complete the exercise.

Ten to fifteen of these prostrations every morning and evening
are excellent for *Badkan* diseases. They help muscle problems,
spondylitis and tapeworm. For a practising Buddhist,
accompanying visualization of the deity is particularly helpful.
There is also a mode of relaxation for when one is exhausted.
For example, when one is doing prostrations, this is very
physical. So in between several prostrations a person stops and
sits. It is important not to become distracted during
prostrations.

Tibetan communities often perform devotional exercises such as
prostrations and circumambulations whilst chanting mantras
typically, but not exclusively, conducted at dawn and dusk. This
is considered to make a real contribution, not merely to the
individuals, but more particularly to the world at large. Of
course, some people practice different forms of exercise purely
for reasons of health. But whatever the form of exercise, it is
very good to define times of sitting and relaxing. This is equally
good after having walked or jogged a long distance. This is a
general consideration no matter what state of mind exists.

Chapter 14

The Two Principal Causes of Disease: Lifestyle and Diet

Accanding to Tibetan medicine, the two main causes of disease are a person's lifestyle and diet. These are held to be of paramount importance, so naturally when considering the remedy for a disease these factors are listed as the first two considerations. Third on the list is medication and fourth is therapy.

Lifestyle and diet represent the first two stages in the treatment of disease, for an unwholesome lifestyle or unhealthy diet will lead to problems. In the Tibetan texts we refer to the 'avoidance of overuse, misuse and disuse' as important ethics by which we can maintain our health.

When considering our lifestyle we should look at our mind, body and speech. If we exert ourselves too much, this will increase the heat in our body, and give us a hot disorder. If we relax too much, this will increase the cold, and produce a cold disorder. If the mind thinks too much, this increases the *rLung*, and will affect the nerves, heart and mental health. If we talk too much, this also increases the *rLung*, affecting the movement of our mobile energy. In all cases of the body, mind and speech we should not exhaust ourselves, thereby losing our strength, and developing more problems.

Further to this, the Tibetan Buddhist approach counsels against negative thought, word and action as having a profound effect upon us, not just in this life but in future lives. There are direct links to illness through specific negative tendencies such as arrogance, attachment, hatred, slander, gossip and even pointless conversation. As a general rule, one should accept that every thought, word and deed is a cause which will irrefutably lead to an effect. Therefore, consideration should always be given to the effects one produces, for by noting these, we may begin to assess ourselves in a more accurate light. Specific negative tendencies are listed according to our Buddhist system as the ten non-virtuous activities. On the physical level these are: the act of killing, sexual misconduct and stealing. As far as speech is concerned they are: slander, abuse, lying and idle gossip. On the level of the mind they are: avarice, malice and holding false views. All these will indeed be harmful to others but particularly harmful to oneself.

When considering diet, we must look at our normal food and beverages. Tastes are very important, whether something is sweet, sour or astringent for example. The sweet taste is based on a mixture of earth and water. Too much of this sweet taste will lead to diabetes. We should therefore not eat too much food that has been grown under the ground, for such food has a predominance of earth and water, and is cold in power and sweet in taste. Such food in excess, aside from causing diabetes, will also affect the digestive heat. Too much alcohol damages the liver because alcohol is hot in nature. The liver is a hot organ, and becomes oversensitive to excessive heat.

Excessive ingestion of foods and beverages which have cold and heavy qualities, such as potatoes and salads, will gradually result in a degeneration of the digestive fire, or heat, leading to indigestion.

Undigested particles within the abdominal area can cause serious diseases such as heart and kidney problems.

Therefore, when wondering if food is healthy or not, it is useful to think of the taste, and whether the food is hot or cold. In the morning and evening, it is better to take food that is hot in nature, or simply heat your food up. This is because in the mornings and evenings the solar effect is less, and the lunar effect is stronger. Conversely, during the daytime we can eat salads, or cold things, because the solar effect is greater, and also because we move about during the day.

In this way we should always try to live a balanced and healthy life, for any misuse, disuse or overuse will give us problems. Sometimes we neglect certain tastes, for instance the bitter taste, which according to Tibetan medicine is important for the protection of the liver. Diseases such as hepatitis and jaundice require a treatment that involves a bitter-tasting medicine, which has a cooling effect. However, if we have too much of the bitter taste, this will increase *rLung*, leading to lack of sleep.

Patients in the West complain about the bitter taste of medicines, but in Tibetan medicine the taste of the medicine regulates many disorders. For instance, any disease connected to the liver needs the bitter taste, and if you try to disguise the taste, the power of the medicine will simply not be the same. Our medicine states that the substances that are taken as nourishment and medicine as well as the substances of which the body is made up, are essentially of the same nature. Therefore, a genuine scientific approach to Tibetan medicine demands that one has the knowledge and can analyse the qualities and characteristics of the six tastes.

The use and nature of any medication is determined by taste and potency. Taste is determined by the power and qualities of the plant chemical constituents. Each taste is linked to a combination of the five elements, as follows:

- Sweet – If something tastes sweet, the predominant elements are earth and water.

- Sour – In the sour taste the predominant elements are fire and earth.

- Salty – In the salty taste the main elements are water and fire.

- Bitter – In the bitter taste the main elements are water and air.

- Hot – The hot taste comes from a combination of fire and air.

- Astringent – The astringent taste comes from earth and air.

The Five Elements

The five elements are the fundamental energies of the universe, and are symbolically represented in the structure of the Tibetan stupa, or sacred monument, which is a devotional symbol of the whole of creation throughout the cosmos. The square base of the stupa is in fact a cube, representing solid earth, upon which the whole stupa, or *chorten* rests. This symbolizes the element of Earth. Upon this cube rests a large sphere, or circle, which in the shape of a drop of water represents the element of Water. Upon this sphere is a spiral-like or triangular, flame-shaped structure, representing the element of Fire. At the very top is a crescent shape, like the inverted vault of the sky, symbolizing the element of Air. Within this crescent shape rests a small sphere to symbolize the ether, or element of Space, which is considered to be the primary force from which all other elements flow.

Thus the five elements: earth, water, fire, air and space, are responsible for all known things within the universe. They operate at all levels of existence as an integral part of the microcosm and macrocosm. This includes all plants, minerals, fauna, animals, and of course, humans. However, as with the humours, the actual translated terms applied to the five elements are very limited when applied to nothing less than the basic laws of the solar system. For instance, water is said to contain all five elements. They are really cosmic, powerful forces which are in constant cyclical movement, interacting with each other. They exist throughout the whole being and essence of man and woman, from the particle level up to the larger body form, yet there is nothing fixed or inert about them. They are in a constant state of flux, exchange and interchange, residing at the basis of everything in existence, which naturally includes all the food and beverages we ingest. Above and beyond this they unite humanity with the universe, the microcosm with the macrocosm.

In the natural world of plants, it is the earth that provides the base in which the seed will germinate and thus begin its journey. To develop, it needs water to provide the moisture and fluidity. The fire element in the form of the sun is a warming agent that matures and ripens the plant, so that the flowers will eventually appear. The actual movement and process of growth of the plant needs the air element, whilst the space element literally provides the space within which the creation of the plant can take place.

As far as the human body is concerned, the five elements are essential for the formation and development of the foetus. They are present in the mingled reproductive essences of the parents and their qualities pervade the new consciousness. If one of the elements is not present, then life will not be possible, for without the earth element it is not possible to produce the physical form of the body. The water element is necessary for the formation of different shapes in the body and for general moistening. The element of fire is essential for the ripening process, and air for hardening and mobility, whilst space contains everything and gives room for the process of development. The elements are also required for the development of the sensory organs. For example, earth develops the sense of smell, water the sense of taste, air the sense of touch, fire the sense of sight and space the sense of sound.

The five elements manifest as the three energies or humours, *rLung*, *Tripa* and *Badkan* which carry out the various functions of the body and which form the basis of all diagnosis and cure. *rLung*, or wind, is the air element and responsible for the movement of the breath and body fluids throughout the body. *Tripa*, or bile, is the heating element of fire within the body, whilst *Badkan*, or phlegm, contains both the earth and water elements as a cooling agent which provides the substantial forms of the body. Space is needed as the container for all three humours, offering space for the body to exist and specifically manifesting in such body cavities as the ears and nostrils.

Ultimately, the five elements are responsible for the formation, maintenance and destruction of the body and are known as *Jungwa nga* in Tibetan. Since the human body is formed from the five elements, the Tibetan healing remedies are also based on the nature of these elements. Therefore, proper maintenance of the body is possible only if the intakes of food and medicine are taken with the correct proportion of the five elements in mind. According to Tibetan medicine, a balanced diet contains the correct combination of earth, water, fire, air and space.

The five elements of earth, water, fire, air and space have specific functions and interact individually as well as collectively. The elements determine the inherent qualities, power and action of an ingredient. Tibetan doctors understand them in terms of their particular characteristic qualities, which are listed below. For example, for anything to be called water it must be blunt (in the sense of being 'slow to act') or moisturising. For anything to be called fire it has to be sharp (in the sense of being 'quick to act') and hot in nature.

The Qualities (*Yonten*) and Actions of the Five Elements

Earth, or *Sa*

The qualities of the *Sa* element are: heavy, stable (firm), blunt, soft, oily and dry. This element gives things an odour, and its actions are to firm and harden the body, make the body stout and to bring or assemble things together. Medicines in which the earth element predominates are used mainly to eradicate *rLung* diseases.

Water, or *Chhu*

The qualities of the *Chhu* element are: liquid, cool, heavy, blunt, oily and soft. This element develops taste in things, and its actions are to moisten the abdominal area, generally soften the body and help bring things together. Medicines in which the water element predominates are used mainly to eradicate *Tripa* diseases.

Fire, or *Meh*

The qualities of the *Meh* element are: hot, sharp, dry, coarse, light, oily and mobile. This element is responsible for the form within the body, and its actions are to increase body heat, digest the food, ripen the body elements and help to keep the complexion clear. Medicines in which the fire element predominates are used mainly to eradicate *Badkan* diseases.

Air, or *rLung*

(note: the air element and wind humour share the same Tibetan name)
The qualities of the *rLung* element are: light, mobile, cold, coarse, absorbent and dry. This element gives things texture or feeling and its actions are to harden the body, develop its mobility and assist the seven constituents to pervade the body. Medicines in which the air element predominates are used mainly to eradicate *Badkan* and *Tripa* diseases.

Space, or *Namkha*

Space provides the container for all the medicines of the other four elements and provides space within the body. It pervades all the four elements and accommodates them within itself. Medicines in which the space element predominates are used to eradicate *rLung*, *Badkan* and *Tripa* combined diseases.

In this way, the five elements of earth, water, fire, air and space are the very building blocks upon which our body and indeed the whole world is built, because everything is created from them. In view of this, all plants and minerals have some medicinal value. If one knows the taste, inherent power, post-digestive taste and qualities of anything the body ingests, remedies and dietary advice can be scientifically formulated, based on the nature of the five elements.

By way of example, we might consider a carrot. The element earth gives the carrot its firmness and form and the element water is the unifying factor, holding the carrot together. It is ripened by the heat of the element of fire, assisted in its growth by the air element and given room in which to grow by the element of space. In considering the carrot as a food, the predominant elements are earth and water, which produce a sweet taste, and thus the ingestion of a carrot increases strength in the body. However, if we continue to just eat carrots, the body will then begin to steadily suffer the depletion of the other three elements which it also needs for the purpose of existence. According to our medical system, the balanced intake of food, drink and any medication is essential, ensuring the correct proportion of the five elements manifesting as the six tastes. If the six tastes are not ingested in a balanced way, or if any of them are taken in excess, we become ill.

Although it is not easy for a Tibetan doctor to know all the different types of food in each of the countries he visits, he can offer clear advice on diet by simply dividing every food into six tastes. Too many sweet things will lead to diabetes; too many hot things will damage the liver. Yet conversely, not to have hot things at all will overdevelop the cold energy in the body, thus disturbing its harmony. Excessive intake of the hot taste develops fire and wind elements in the body which will cause diseases such as liver problems, blood disorders and ulcers. The most common cause of a liver disorder is the excessive intake of alcoholic drinks. An excessive intake of the bitter taste develops the wind and water elements which results in diseases such as nervous disorders, mental depression, insomnia, heart problems etc. The element of water is the basis for the sensory experience of taste; therefore, the tongue must be wet in order to taste a substance.

Because of their direct link with the five elements, herbs and plants in nature have great potential to correct the imbalances within our system. Tibetan medicine offers many explanations of the effects of nature's wonders and especially the medicines that are prepared from herbs. This makes it easier for even a poor patient to afford treatment from such natural and readily available remedies. Clearly our whole body has been formed by, and is very much dependent upon nature, to the extent that all human beings can be classified according to seven naturally occurring body types.

The Seven Natural Classifications of Humanity

Humanity is a product of the womb of the earth and inextricably connected to the planet's evolutionary development, its geological structure, the chemistry of its atmosphere and plethora of diverse environmental conditions. The chain of evolution, which stretches back millions of years, has determined the current form of humankind. The human race is entirely dependent upon the atmospheric and magnetic forces of the earth that contain, support and protect all life. At any point on the earth's crust, one may focus in upon a particular geographic environment, particular nation, particular race, particular household and particular person, there to reveal a set of identifiable characteristics which classify that person according to the various influencing conditions.

Each person is inevitably influenced by the immediate surrounding geographic and cultural environment and is a fusion of the biological forces inherited from the parents at the instant of conception. The myriad of ingredients that surround and inform the development of the newborn child are constantly at work upon his or her condition, propelling the child in a particular physical, emotional, spiritual and psychological direction.

From the moment that the foetus is developing in the mother's womb, the food she eats and the lifestyle she chooses, is already having a powerful effect upon the unborn child. This effect naturally continues beyond the physical womb into the post-uterine period, where the embrace of the mother's unconscious realm remains all consuming. All kinds of nonverbal signs and signals particularly from the mother, but also from the father, family and friends, are nudging the child in certain directions. These early stages in the life of a human being crucially inform and develop the unique stamp of the personality, body type and temperament.

According to in-depth astrological charts, the precise moment of birth determines a unique human being, ultimately with a unique destiny, driven by the particular forces of the universe at that time. Yet, just as the zodiac groups together individual signs with common emotional and psychological tendencies, so humanity can be classified according to certain characteristics, body types and temperaments, presenting an important and defining frame by which to measure a person's natural leaning. Such a frame offers the skilled practitioner a benchmark by which to view a presenting person, before moving more deeply towards the specific individual condition.

Considering the impact of different physical and environmental factors which result in the multitude of potential variations in human behaviour and temperament, Tibetan medicine has classified each human being according to three naturally occurring 'body types' or temperaments, related to the three humours. These types present the physician with a vital starting point by which to measure the manifestations of the three fundamental energies within the patient, facilitating a basis from which diagnosis can begin. This is of particular importance, for the practitioner must have an understanding of the natural tendencies and elements within any presenting person before assessing what imbalance in the person's condition may have occurred. When considering the characteristics of the body types, the movement, behaviour and speech can also be likened to particular animals who share similar characteristics. This may be understood if you recall occasions when you meet someone who, for some unknown reason, reminds you of an animal or bird. The humoural type also essentially presents important considerations when offering dietary or behavioural advice, together with medication and therapies, for adjustments must be made in line with the natural tendency of the person.

The *rLung* Type of Person

rLung type persons will typically have a thin and slightly stooped, or bent body, a bluish complexion and are not tall. Their joints often make a cracking noise on movement. They cannot tolerate the cold, wind, air conditioning and fans. They do not become rich and have a short life span, sleep lightly and are easily distracted. They are very talkative, and like music, singing and laughter. They have a tendency towards arguments and enjoy a good fight, according to the ancient texts typically being associated with archery. Their favourite tastes are sweet, hot, bitter and sour. With regard to their similarity with particular creatures, they are likened to a vulture because of their energetic, mobile behaviour. Also, like a fox, they are restlessly moving here and there and tend to have a harsh sounding voice like the crow.

The *Tripa* Type of Person

The *Tripa* energy facilitates digestion, which will be a quicker process in this body type. Therefore, they are always feeling hungry and thirsty. They have a slightly yellowish complexion, are fair haired and are bright, eloquent, competitive and proud. They perspire easily which causes a bad odour. They have a medium height and medium life span, and their favourite tastes are sweet, bitter and astringent. They like cold things and in some ways resemble such animals as a tiger, due to their aggressive energy, or a monkey, which as a creature is very quick and light. They are also said to be like devils, tending towards being proud and power loving.

The *Badkan* Type of Person

These type of people are tall. As *Badkan* is cool in nature, they have less body heat. They are typically overweight, so that the articulations of the bones are not particularly visible. They have a whitish complexion and usually have a straight back. They like to have a long sleep and generally have a long life span, easily accumulating wealth. They are quite jolly; in fact, it is difficult to arouse them to anger, for they can tolerate tension easily and their reactions are slow. They can tolerate hunger and thirst, so can fast for long periods. They enjoy helping others, so much so, that such persons are often found amongst social workers. They prefer hot, sour, astringent tastes and things with a course, rough quality. They have the characteristics of such animals as a camel, lion, bull, eagle or an elephant, for like these animals they have majestic tendencies, relatively long life spans and a greater level of tolerance.

Naturally, people rarely fall simplistically under the exact description of these body types. So from these three single character types, we need to understand that a person's nature can also be classified as a combination of two characteristics or can be a mixture of all three. So to the three humoural types already described we can add four more, being a *rLung/Tripa* type, *Badkan/Tripa* type, *Badkan/rLung* type and a *rLung/Tripa/Badkan* type. These are the seven natural classifications of the human being, which help the physician to establish a measure by which accurate diagnosis and treatment can be conducted.

On Positive Health – How to Apply Oneself to the Notion of the Six Tastes and the Five Elements

Negative health, as far as diet is concerned, is unfortunately all too rife within modern society, with its emphasis on artificial elements in food, fast foods, eating purely in order to pamper the taste buds, eating for appearance, eating as an opulent activity and not at all for health. Such an approach may indeed bring a temporary feeling of wellbeing, although this is really the result of a form of intoxication and overindulgence. Unbeknown to our carefree approach to diet, such indulgence inseminates itself into the system as a habitual tendency, which gradually begins to build up toxins within the body. Ultimately, the only thing to bring this dangerous dietary spiral to a halt is the onset of illness, when the system has indeed become poisoned and in need of treatment.

Putting it as simply as possible, positive health is the balance of the fifteen different types of humours, the seven constituents (the nutritious essences, blood, flesh, fat, bone, marrow and reproductive essence) and the three wastes (faeces, urine and perspiration). We can help to maintain this balance by taking in a balanced diet of foods with a variety of tastes, for these are the indicators of the five elements. Our body is formed by the five elements. Diseases are due to the disruption of the five elements. Restoring the balance of the five elements in the body is positive health. Therefore we emphasize the danger of misuse, disuse or overuse of the five elements in our diet. Much of this approach towards a balanced diet is actually common sense.

Chapter 15

Tibetan Medicine as a Reflection of Nature

AT HEART, ALL HUMAN beings naturally seek freedom from suffering, pain and disease, wishing to be happy, content, in comfort and at peace. Yet our earthly condition dictates that we move through varying states of ease and disease, order and disorder. Rather than seek to avert disorder and disease at all costs, we might do well to understand that the seeds of order can be found within disorder. Indeed, the most important step towards health is to first admit that one is sick. This of course relates directly to the three mental poisons of desire, hatred and closed-mindedness which lie at the root of all suffering as emanations from an ignorant state. The first step to enlightenment is to admit that one is ignorant; otherwise inflated pride in oneself will block all possibility for improvement.

So if we can accept the fundamental flaws within us or the presence of disease within our system, then we can begin to re-establish order and balance from within and return our body to a healthy state. In Tibetan medicine the concept of health is fundamental to the understanding of disease. 'Dis' means 'away from', 'the reverse of' or 'deprived of' and 'ease' means 'comfort' or 'freedom from pain'. Therefore, before discussing disease, we must understand the meaning of comfort or health.

The chief metaphor used within the ancient texts of Tibetan medicine, as part of the learning and memorization process, is that of the tree of medicine which has three roots, nine trunks, forty-seven branches, 224 leaves, two flowers and three fruits. Each part of the tree corresponds to particular aspects of the system of medicine. The very first of the three roots has two trunks, the first of which represents an exact description of the body in a state of health. This highlights how vital the complete understanding of the state of health within the human condition is, before one can begin to approach a realization of what is a state of illness.

The body is healthy when the three humours, the seven constituents and the three wastes are in a state of perfect equilibrium. Whilst in equilibrium, these vital functions, which relate directly to the ability to resist disease and develop immunity, can ensure that even the most virulent infections cannot penetrate and disrupt the healthy body. Therefore the disease process begins the very minute any of these systems becomes in any way disrupted or imbalanced, leading to physical and psychological pain and suffering.

Our inner world is constantly responding and reacting to the impressions flooding in upon us from the outer world. When we are healthy and in balance, there is no conflict between these two worlds; they are in harmony with each other. Disorder and disease occur when the internal environment and the external environment are out of balance. The process of disease, in the end, always stems from the mind, so in order to successfully change one's disrupted inner world, one must form an understanding of the beginning of the disease process within the mind. Tibetan medicine offers a template by which we may understand the beginnings of disease and thereby how we might begin to restore order and health from disorder and disease.

To repeat, ignorance lies at the base of all our problems and manifests as three negative states of mind: desire, hatred, and closed-mindedness. These faulty mental states cause an increase and imbalance in the three humours rLung, Tripa and Badkan. The manifestation of the mental poisons in the conscious state may be ascertained through a predominating negative tendency in thought, word or deed. This tendency may be an outer symptom of a deeper unconscious rage, hatred, envy, overwhelming desire, greed or stubbornly closed mind. These repressed forces breeding in the mind will inevitably infect the body as a form of illness. So, if a person is constantly overwhelmed by a powerful desire, this will cause a disturbance of the rLung energy. Deep-seated anger will cause the Tripa energy to arise excessively, whilst the stubborn refusal of the mind to open up to new possibilities, preferring to remain in ignorance will strengthen the Badkan energy to an unbalanced degree. The disturbance of the humours immediately blows a hole in the body's natural line of defence against illness, and we are immediately open to the attack of disease.

The Entrances of disease

Under a set of particular conditions the body will become prone to disease, which will manifest and develop through a number of stages. There are, according to Tibetan medicine, specific entrances for the disease, which will then spread to other parts of the body. There are also explicit areas where the disease will localize and begin to settle more deeply. The main pathways by which the disease will spread are the seven constituents, i.e. the nutritious essence, blood, flesh, fat, bone, marrow and reproductive essence. Consequently, the power to support or destroy the body lies within this essential digestive system of the seven constituents together with the three wastes. Once the disease has settled in a particular part of the body, it can spread to other parts through the main pathways.

Disease can appear in the body via a number of different routes. When *rLung*, *Tripa* and *Badkan* become unbalanced, there are six entrances by which the diseased energy can enter into the body. From the skin the disease can penetrate into the flesh and start to circulate around the channels and blood vessels. From there it sticks to the bones and settles into the five solid or vital organs of the heart, lungs, liver, spleen and kidneys from whence it also can reach the six hollow organs of the stomach, small and large intestines, gall bladder, seminal vesicle and urinary bladder.

The Location of the Three Humours

According to the medical tantra, *Badkan* is supported by the brain and located in the upper part of the body; *Tripa* is supported by the liver, bile and blood and is found in the middle part of the body. *rLung* is supported by the hips, waist and genital organs, and remains in the lower part of the body.

However, even though these are the main places of residence of the three humours, there is no place within the body where all three cannot be found. It is somewhat similar to the fact that the main residence for a particular nation does not mean that this is the only place where you will meet the people of this nation, just as Spanish people chiefly live in Spain, yet you will find Spanish people living all over the world.

Badkan is supported in the brain because of its characteristics which are similar to the brain. Hence closed-mindedness and dullness are located there. We can all see the snow on top of a high mountain. It is the same with *Badkan* in our heads. When the sun gets hot, this snow will melt and go downwards to bring water to the plain. Thus, even though *Badkan* is in our head, the effects of the disease will show in the lower parts of the body such as the stomach and kidneys. An excess of water in the body will accordingly lead to a feeling of heaviness in the legs, and produces swelling of the feet.

Tripa remains in the middle part of the body. As the flame of fire goes upward, the tantra says that the first area to be affected by a *Tripa* disorder will be the upper part of the body, such as a headache caused by a fever. Whenever we become angry our body temperature increases, and we feel some kind of heat in the middle part of the body. Generally, a glass of cold water is needed to help cool us down.

rLung is found in the lower part of the body, and is represented by sexual desire. Someone with a strong sex drive, if it becomes excessive, will be more susceptible to *rLung* disease because the powerful sexual desire naturally develops the *rLung* energy in the body. Both men and women become naturally aroused when they are sexually attracted to someone, and experience this feeling in the genital area.

The Pathways of the Three Humours

The *rLung* energy moves in the bones, ears, skin, heart, life-channel and large intestine respectively.

The *Tripa* energy moves in the blood, eyes, perspiration, liver, small intestine and gall bladder.

The *Badkan* energy moves in the nutritious essence, flesh, fat, bone marrow, reproductive seed, faeces, urine, nose, tongue, lungs, spleen, kidneys, stomach and urinary bladder.

From the different pathways of the three humours, one can understand the similarity between the nature of the humour and the paths it takes. *rLung* could be said to be linked to the nervous system in the body, *Tripa* to the secretory and endocrine systems, whilst *Badkan* is associated with the various masses in the body, whether organs or otherwise. The pathways have the same nature as the humour, and when a humour is unbalanced, its pathway is affected.

Tibetan medical literature covers all aspects of disease. It is stated within the texts that there are 1,616 diseases, which can be condensed into 404 approaches to treatment. Tibetan medicine also accepts the concept of parasites, or bacteria within our body, which are specified as 80,000 different types.

There are diseases which can ultimately be fatal, but even if diagnosed as such, there is no sense in which we should ever then abandon our patients. We can still help them, for according to the Tibetan Buddhist system, survival will always depend upon life span, karma and merits accumulated. In certain cases, despite all medical treatment, there may be no relief appearing for the patient. For such persons, we may focus on helping the person's mind with spiritual advice and teachings. This assistance may also be given by spiritual lamas who specialize in such situations.

The Interaction of the Three Humours

At first glance, when reviewing the three humours and in particular the humoural body types, one may think that the approach to the humours is rather simplistic. However, although the texts present clear, methodical divisions of the humoural energies and their various manifestations and locations in the body, in actual fact the topic of the three humours when applied to the human condition is much more subtle and quite complex.

Indeed, it is rare to find any illness that can simply be described as a single humour disease. The three humours are constantly interacting with each other in a finely balanced triangle of energies. In fact, visually one might appreciate the precarious nature of this relationship by imagining a triangular seesaw with the humoural energies perched at each of the three points. As one energy goes up or down, so the other two are affected. If a single energy completely leaves the scene, then the whole seesaw will be static and inoperable.

So, when approaching diagnosis, the physician will be establishing the condition of each of the three humours in relation to each other, for it is their particular combination that is manifesting as disease. Typically there may be one humoural disorder predominating as the primary condition. But beyond this there can be a secondary humoural imbalance, tertiary imbalance and more issues to be included within the overall diagnosis and subsequent treatment. Over and above this, there will be a consideration as to whether the illness is cold or hot in nature, or whether the disease appears to be hot, but in reality is cold, or vice versa. Such considerations are crucial to understand before medication is prescribed, or we can easily worsen the condition.

Other factors to be included may be psychological or environmental, taking into account the seasonal cycle together with any particular imbalances manifesting at the time. Indeed, mankind is constantly subject to the law of opposites which in these modern times can manifest as particularly dramatic changes. Some countries may be subject to excessive heat and drought for long periods of time. Others may be subject to torrential rains and serious flooding. Still other countries may experience both drought and flood in close proximity to each other, with no warning of the change to come. It seems that due to humanity's meddling with the environment, the seasonal cycle has been affected, with no longer a smooth transition from one season to another.

The Consideration of Tastes, Characteristics, Qualities and Inherent Powers

When practising Tibetan medicine, the physician seeks to map out the exact 'terrain' of the patient, creating a precise picture of the body's imbalance in detail, adopting the reference points given through the medical system of the three humours and their characteristics. The approach to treatment therefore involves a method by which the practitioner can rebalance the humours. Putting this in its simplest form, the imbalance will relate to the excess or deficiency of certain elements in the body. Accordingly, by prescribing the ingestion of certain elements, whilst decreasing the intake of others, by means of food, herbal medicines, prescribed behaviour, including an approach to the effect of the seasons and therapies, a balance can be reconstituted.

This, of course, requires an in-depth knowledge of the various qualities, tastes, and energies associated with the humours, with all forms of medication, food, lifestyle and environment, relating this to the five elements and applying this to our body which is formed of the five elements. Of course, there is nothing in the universe that is not produced out of the five elements, therefore the possibilities are quite literally limitless.

There is a most instructive story, related in the Tibetan medical texts, which elucidates this fact perfectly. One day, the legendary Kumar Jivaka (called Tsojey Shunu in Tibetan), who became personal physician to Lord Buddha, was instructed by his teacher, Drangsung Gyunshebu, to go out into the forest with his colleagues to collect whatever they could find which they deemed to be of use as a medicinal substance. At the end of the day, all returned with numerous, particular substances with different degrees of healing power which they enthusiastically laid before the teacher. However, Kumar Jivaka walked in completely empty-handed, to the surprise of all his colleagues. When challenged on this point, he replied that he had searched high and low throughout the land, but had not found a single substance that could not be used as a medicine. As he could not bring everything in the forest back with him, he had returned empty-handed.

This simple tale emphasizes the fact that everything within the universe is formed by the five elements and therefore can potentially be used as a form of medication.

The Twelve Side Effects of an Unwise Treatment

In the prescription of dietary and behavioural advice, medication and therapies, the physician must take a precise, balanced approach to the restoration of humoural balance, taking into account the interrelationship of all three humours, otherwise a secondary or tertiary problem may arise and complicate the situation. For instance, a treatment may be prescribed to deal with a disorder of the *rLung* energy in the body. This treatment may indeed correct the *rLung* imbalance, but without appropriate attention to the interdependence of all three, the *Tripa* and *Badkan* may arise as a result of the treatment. Again, taking the analogy of the triangular seesaw, one point has been restored without any thought to its effect upon the other two points. Worse than this, the unskilled approach may have no effect on restoring the *rLung* imbalance, yet succeeds in creating problems with the *Tripa* and *Badkan* energies.

This same approach can of course be similarly applied to each of the other two humours, and is detailed within the medical texts under the title 'The Twelve Side Effects of an Unwise Treatment'. This relates to the particular tastes of the substances prescribed. For each humour, or *nyespa* must be treated very carefully and wisely in order to ensure that the other *nyespas* are not disrupted by the excessive intake of a particular taste. An unwise treatment may lead to the arousal of other diseases through a particular taste without pacifying the original problem, as follows:

rLung

The prescription of a particular diet and medicine having a bitter and hot taste for a *rLung* disease in excess, may cause a *Badkan* disease to arise (through the bitter taste) and a *Tripa* disease to manifest (through the hot taste) whilst the *rLung* is not pacified.

Tripa

The excessive intake of food and medicine having a salty and hot taste prescribed for an excess of *Tripa*, instead of pacifying it, causes an imbalance of *Badkan* (through the salty taste) and *rLung* (through the hot taste).

Badkan

The prescription of both bitter and salty food and medicine for a *Badkan* disease in excess, can cause a *rLung* (through the bitter taste) and *Tripa* (through the salty taste) imbalance, without correcting *Badkan*.

An unwholesome prescription may, in these ways, cause disruption in all the three *nyespas*. Also, an excessive intake of particular foods and medication may indeed pacify the original disease, but cause the arousal of other diseases through an imbalance in the other two humours, as follows:

rLung

Taking an excess of certain foods and medicine with a sweet and salty taste may pacify the *rLung* imbalance, whilst unfortunately causing the arousal of *Badkan* (by means of the sweet taste) and *Tripa* (salty taste) respectively.

Tripa

Excessive usage of sweet and bitter tasting diet and medication may pacify *Tripa*, but the sweet taste may cause the arousal of *Badkan* and the bitter taste the arousal of *rLung*.

Badkan

The intake of an excessively hot and sour diet and medicine may lead to the pacification of *Badkan* along with the arousal of *rLung* (hot taste) and *Tripa* (sour taste).

The subtle use of tastes in the treatment of diseases is a very complex topic, beyond the scope of this book to elucidate fully, but the description above demonstrates how sensitive the humours are to specific tastes, and how important it is therefore to ensure that none of the twelve side effects arise through an unwise and unskilled form of treatment.

The Seventeen Qualities

According to Tibetan medicine everything in existence, including organic and inorganic matter, thoughts and actions, can be categorized according to seventeen different qualities. When assessing what particular advice or medication to give to the patient, the physician will firstly establish how the humours are imbalanced through their manifesting characteristics. Then the practitioner will prescribe remedies according to their qualities and how they interact with the characteristics of the disease.

This approach is fundamental to Tibetan pharmacology, therapeutics and food preparation. The exact understanding of the complexity of action and reaction of the seventeen qualities to the manifesting characteristics, enables the delicate balance of the three humours to be restored and maintained.

The seventeen qualities of all existing things are: (1) smooth, (2) heavy, (3) warm, (4) oily, (5) stable, (6) cold, (7) blunt, (8) cool, (9) flexible, (10) liquid, (11) dry, (12) absorbent, (13) hot, (14) light, (15) sharp, (16) coarse, (17) mobile.

Each of the seventeen qualities can be chosen by the diagnosing physician as remedies for characteristics manifesting according to the three humours, as one can see from the table overleaf.

Once again, this topic is most precise and of considerable complexity, but an understanding of it can be approached by means of simple examples. For instance, if someone is suffering from a *rLung* disease, manifesting with such light characteristics as light-headedness, then the physician will aim to prescribe medication which is known to carry within it a heavy quality in order to reduce the lightness. Conversely, a heavy or lethargic condition, as typically manifesting in a *Badkan* disease, may require the administration of medicines having a light quality. A person suffering from an arousal of the *rLung* energy may be exhibiting signs and symptoms which are highly mobile, such as aches and pains that are constantly moving around the body with no fixed location. To counteract the mobile characteristic, the practitioner will prescribe a medicine with a stabilizing quality and thus address the disease.

Imbalances of the hot *Tripa* energy will naturally tend to be eased by medicines that are cooling in quality. The *Tripa* energy also normally manifests with a sharp characteristic, basically meaning that imbalances can arise extremely quickly. It would therefore be beneficial for the physician to prescribe medication with a blunt quality, i.e. slow to act. Further to this, a pronounced *Tripa* imbalance may manifest in such symptoms as sudden diarrhoea with the characteristics of purging and liquid. This diarrhoea can accordingly be arrested and transformed through the application of medicinal substances with a drying quality.

Humour		Characteristic	Quality of the Remedy
rLung	1.	coarse	smooth
	2.	light	heavy
	3.	cold	warm
	4.	subtle	oily
	5.	hard	
	6.	mobile	stable
Tripa	7.	slightly oily	absorbent
	8.	sharp	blunt
	9.	hot	cool
	10.	light	heavy
	11.	bad odour	liquid
	12.	purging	dry
	13.	liquid	
Badkan	14.	oily	absorbent
	15.	cool	hot
	16.	heavy	light
	17.	blunt	sharp
	18.	smooth	coarse
	19.	stable	mobile
	20.	sticky	coarse

Badkan diseases are related to the cold energy, so are often pacified by advice to the patient that he or she should keep warm and drink hot liquids, thus applying the hot quality to the cool characteristic. Advice such as this would naturally include warnings against increasing the cold energy by taking in food and liquid straight from the fridge. An imbalance of *Badkan* may also manifest in phlegm arising in the chest, thereby having a sticky characteristic. The physician would therefore seek out remedies having a coarse quality to combat this.

With an understanding of the qualities of foods in relation to disease characteristics, similar principles can be applied in terms of what to avoid as far as diet is concerned. Therefore, fruits such as banana, grapefruit, apple and peach have a heavy quality, so would be inadvisable in the case of a *Badkan* disease, as they would increase the heavy characteristic of the illness. Pork has the qualities of cool and light, so would aggravate a *rLung* imbalance. Green and red peppers are both hot in taste and have within them a sharp quality, so would be injurious to a *Tripa* illness. The physician would therefore recommend avoidance of tastes exacerbating the characteristics of a disease through their respective qualities and would recommend foods carrying opposite qualities.

The Inherent Powers

In many ways, this approach may be understood as applying the universal law of opposites to a treatment. Linked with this concept, each of the seventeen qualities contains within it an inherent power, or potential energy, which needs to be taken into account. These inherent powers can be categorized according to the law of opposites. For just as the masculine and feminine principles exist and function together as opposite forces, so this may be applied to the whole universe. According to ancient alchemy, this universal manifestation of the two basic opposites, male and female energy, was known as Sol and Luna, King and Queen, which as opposites must be understood, balanced and ultimately integrated.

Thus, it is possible to understand the universe in terms of the interactions of opposing forces that manifest as eight inherent powers arising out of these seventeen qualities. These inherent powers can be further condensed into two energies: the cold, lunar energy and hot, solar energy:

The Cold Powers

The cold, inherent powers which relate to the Lunar effect are: heavy, oily, cool, blunt.

The Hot Powers

The hot, inherent powers which relate to the Solar effect are: light, coarse, hot, sharp.

These two major powers, hot and cold, are primary motive forces within the body, just as they are within nature, where they appear to transform one element into another. The heating power will result in the evaporation of water into the air, whilst the cooling power can change water into ice, similar to the element earth in its solidity. However, in reality the elements themselves do not change. For elements are really changing states, and not fixed. It is matter which moves through the states of the elements. If we view the body from this perspective, it operates no differently to nature with its dependency upon the sun and moon.

Therefore, having obtained some understanding of the complexity of the tastes, characteristics, qualities and inherent powers with their inevitable effect upon the human condition, we can approach an understanding of how, in the end, Tibetan medicine is always a profound reflection of nature.

Following the Natural Laws

In the modern world, alongside some signs of increased awareness of the importance of what we do to our bodies and what we put into our bodies, there unfortunately still runs a widespread disregard for these two factors which dramatically affect our condition. For human beings still, it seems, persist in thinking that they can abuse their minds and bodies through an irreverent and irresponsible approach to nutrition and lifestyle, whilst remaining in a perfectly balanced state of health. Of course, this is far from the truth.

Nature has always demonstrated the natural way for us to follow. We need only observe the animals and birds that operate in harmony with nature and follow its basic laws to understand the importance of behaviour and diet. Indeed, Tibetans have studied much of nature in the approach to the development of medication and how it can maintain health and restore balance to the body.

Yet humans remain the only creatures on the earth to blatantly ignore the natural laws. The combination of lack of exercise and fast food is only one obvious example of modern self-abuse, resulting in the problem of obesity, which has become a particular concern where children and young people are concerned. Wrong eating, overeating, under-eating – this lack of a balanced approach to diet does not simply remain as a problem on the physical level, but worms its way into our inner psyche to poison our whole being, thus seriously affecting the future of mankind as the issue transfers itself from the individual illness to the collective disease.

At the individual level, if we take in too many sweet things, then the water and earth elements will develop excessively in the body, because sweet-tasting things are predominantly constituted by the elements of earth and water. *Badkan* has the nature of earth and water, so *Badkan* will increase in our organism. Being cold in nature, an increase in *Badkan* means an increase in the cold energy which in turn affects the heat in our body which is *Tripa*. The digestive heat will then be affected, and this might result in undigested food being found in our excrement.

An abuse of the bitter taste will affect our sleep because this taste has cold and coarse properties. Thus, foods such as cucumber, coffee and strong tea, which have a light and coarse power, increase *rLung* which is mobile and light, causing sleep disturbances, restlessness and impatience. Alcohol tastes hot and an excess of it chiefly attacks the liver which is hot in nature. It gradually affects the blood and as a result *rLung* increases. The brain and kidneys become affected, and that is when people become generally shaky.

Oily and fatty foods are helpful in suppressing *rLung*. However, if *rLung* decreases too much in the body we suffer from lethargy. People who live on non-nutritious food will suffer from ringing in the ears, a light sensation of the body and dizziness. Loss of blood, strong vomiting or diarrhoea will also weaken the body and thus *rLung* increases.

There are people who are very happy during the daytime, but when night comes they begin to feel restless and anxious. During the daytime the heat of the sun has suppressed *rLung*, but at dawn and dusk they tend to feel more of the *rLung* type afflictions due to the lack of heat. We therefore need to pay attention to the responses of our bodies, recognize that these bodily responses are warning us of an inner imbalance, and look at our dietary and behavioural trends to see how we might be initiating or exacerbating the problem.

Tibetan medicine offers a route to enlightenment and liberation through a balanced and harmonious approach to the mind, body and spirit. This is based on the assertion that one of the most fundamental steps we can make towards a better world is to work upon ourselves, balancing our condition on all levels – physical, emotional, mental and spiritual, to promote a positive essence within ourselves which can, in a very real way, be given to others, either consciously or through a process of osmosis, where others are naturally affected by, and absorb something of our inner qualities. For just as the bees buzz around a honey pot, certain people naturally attract others to them as a result of their inner goodness and health.

A sound mind and sound body are very important to the human condition, for this holistic approach to health will plant the seeds for a disease-free future. Conversely an abusive approach to health will have a negative impact on our prospects, just as indifference to the condition of constipation in the system will result in a build-up of toxins in the intestinal system, which will be absorbed into the blood and steadily poison the whole body. Such poisoning of the body inevitably goes deep into the psyche and is directly linked to the whole inner condition of mankind. Our diet is a reflection of our inner emotional and psychological drive, in the same way that our thoughts and feelings are always reflected in what we choose to eat and drink. It is therefore crucial to maintain a balanced diet and lifestyle. To abuse, misuse or overuse anything which affects our food and lifestyle will lead to illness, and contribute to the gradual onset of disease within the whole of society.

The Practice of Giving and Taking

Further to the work we can do upon ourselves, there is a practice whereby we can give help to other sentient beings within the world. According to our tradition this is called *Tonglen*, or the practice of giving and taking.

It is a form of meditation whereby, in its simplest form, we imagine that we are taking into ourselves the suffering and pain of others, whilst giving back in return feelings of goodness and happiness. It can be practised as a means of helping a specific person we know to be in pain, or can be a more general practice for the good of humanity.

This practice goes to the very heart of Buddhism and indeed other religions such as Christianity, for it is about developing the capacity to take upon oneself the suffering of others. It is the very essence of what is meant by true compassion. Its effects are real and should never be underestimated.

Chapter 16

The Study of Tibetan Medicine through the Four Tantras

*H*AVING CONSIDERED A NUMBER of fundamental elements of the Tibetan medical system, we will now move to reflect upon the actual medical teachings, how they are laid out and what topics they cover, before proceeding to look more closely at the characteristics of a Tibetan physician, how this system is studied and its essential differences from Western traditions. Finally, we will proceed to look at diagnostic techniques and methods of treatment.

Within the region of Tibet, which remained isolated for thousands of years, this unique civilization developed its own culture, customs and particular system of medicine. Taking the law of the five elements as a context within which all things, including the human body, could be understood, a system of tantric medicine developed. This was a medical system whereby the elements in the body could be purified and transformed, with the ultimate goal of bringing the body to an enlightened state, free from all disease. The purification and transmutation of the body was facilitated by the guided ingestion of specified substances with medicinal qualities. Utilizing the various herbs, minerals and other substances purely for healing the body was considered a very basic step to make, allowing the person to reach a balanced condition more conducive to prayer, meditation and spiritual realization. The formulation, prescription and ingestion of all healing substances was therefore always accompanied by spiritual practices such as the recitation of mantras, religious incantations and invocations of healing deities.

The Four Tantras

All medical teachings are held to be sacred as transmissions from the Lord Buddha, revelations from certain deities, and the result of tireless research and development by renowned Tibetan physicians over a period of many, many years. The primary text of Tibetan medicine as practised today was produced in the twelfth century by the great physician, Yuthog Yonten Gonpo the Younger, who took all previous teachings and revelations and drew them together as four medical texts or tantras, called the rGyu-shi.

Advanced Tibetan medical students are expected to memorize all 156 chapters from the rGyu-shi. When they graduate, student doctors serve as assistants to senior doctors in order to observe how all topics learned are applied in practice. It is not a difficult medical system if one takes the time to experience it fully, so that the system develops naturally within. For this, the correct learning attitude is essential. As the word tantra means 'the knowledge that protects the body', it is of utmost importance that students develop a positive attitude and pure motivation, when applying themselves to their studies.

Whilst numerous books, journals and research papers have been written and continue to contribute to the Tibetan medical system, the heart-essence text of Tibetan medicine, the rGyu-shi, continues to be the principle textbook for all aspiring students and practising Tibetan doctors. The whole of the Tibetan medical system is contained within this precisely defined and brilliantly formulated volume.

The Tantras of the oral instruction of the science of healing are four in number:

1. *Tsa-gyud*   The Root Tantra.

2. *Shad-gyud*   The Explanatory Tantra.

3. *Mannag-gyud*   The Oral Tradition Tantra.

4. *Chima-gyud*   The Last Tantra.

The teachings contained within the rGyu-shi are mainly based on eight branches, namely:

The body in general.

Children's diseases.

Women's diseases.

Evil spirits' diseases.

Injuries from wounds.

Toxins, or poisons.

Rejuvenation for the elderly.

Aphrodisiacs and fertility.

1. *Tsa-gyud* – the Root Tantra

The first tantra is a short text and mainly presents a condensed outline of the whole of the medical teaching. It is accordingly said that:

A brilliant student can understand the essence of Tibetan
medicine from the six chapters contained in the Root
Tantra.

As the tantras go on they are further clarified. Therefore, it is said that an intelligent student can understand the essence of the teachings through the second tantra, a pretty good student through the third tantra and an average student understands the system through the fourth.

The first tantra consists of six chapters, and begins by considering the body in a state of health when all three humours are perfectly balanced. It is explained that the three humours can be found within all human beings, that when they are in balance they are supportive to the body, but out of balance immediately become afflictive. This is the dual function of the three humours, or *nyespas*, which, in harmony, promote and support good health, but in disharmony propel the body towards a state of disease, being the cause of a whole host of mental and physical disorders and disruptions.

In the second chapter of the first tantra, a question is raised about the reason why someone would want to study the healing science. The answer is given:

Those who want to lead a healthy life, to protect themselves
and others from diseases, and who desire to be respected by
society are welcome to study the healing science. The life of
a human being always depends on a doctor. Even a king
has to obey a doctor when he suffers from an illness.

The section on the healthy body presents each of the three humours, the five different types of each humour and their respective functions. This is a most important section for those wishing to understand Tibetan medicine. The tantra then goes on to explain the particular actions of each of the five types of *rLung*, the five types of *Tripa* and the five types of *Badkan* when, in an unbalanced state, they promote disease. In this way, the tantra enables one to differentiate between the body in a state of health and the body in a state of disease. The Root Tantra also gives an overview of the different diagnostic techniques and methods of treatment. It also briefly touches upon other topics which are presented in much more detail within the remaining three tantras.

2. *Shad-gyud* – the Explanatory Tantra

The second text, the Explanatory Tantra, is comprised of thirty-one chapters which are arranged in eleven divisions as follows:

Division of the summary chapter of the tantra: summary of the remaining chapters.

Division of the body: formation, similes, condition, type, etc.

Division of diseases: cause, secondary cause, entrances, characteristics, classification, etc.

Division of behaviour: in normal life, specific occasions, seasonal changes, etc.

Division of diet: dietetic rules and restrictions.

Division of medicine: tastes, inherent powers, compounding process, etc.

Division of surgical instruments and their uses, etc.

Division of the procedure for a healthy and rejuvenated life.

Division of diagnosis of the exact disordered humour on the basis of symptoms.

Division of the method of healing: by treatment for diseases in general and specific procedures.

Division of the physician: the physician, his qualities and responsibilities.

This second tantra begins with a description of how the embryo is formed and moves through the developmental stages of the foetus up to the point at which it is born, and so on, right up to the point of death. A discussion then follows on the five different types of each of the three humours, *rLung*, *Tripa* and *Badkan* together with a description of the general qualities of each humour. This section then moves on to discuss the whole process of death and its accompanying signs, whatever the cause.

The next section proceeds to reveal the various causes of disease. Surrounding such causes are certain conditions which then encourage the disease to manifest. What this emphasizes is that, even with the cause of a disease present within the human condition, without the particular conditions necessary for the arousal of a specific illness, it will remain dormant. This section goes on to detail all the classifications of diseases and culminates in a description of the particular characteristics of each of the different disease types.

There then follows a complex section listing the various ingredients of medicines, their respective tastes, potencies and effects upon manifesting disorders once the medicines have been digested. This is followed by a description of the actual way in which the different tastes and potencies work. The particular post-digestive potencies of the medicines are described, explaining how each healing substance has a particular effect when first taken into the body, as opposed to the different effects after digestion as the medicine is more fully assimilated.

The next section focuses on treatment and advice with regard to lifestyle and diet, emphasizing how this can facilitate better health and longer life. The topic of diet includes the way in which food should be ingested, how much food the body normally requires and what constitutes an abusive diet. Finally, this division looks at various patterns of behaviour, whether daily, temporary (for example, seasonal) or continuing patterns of behaviour.

The divisions detailing the procedure for a healthy and rejuvenated life tackle the issue of prevention through a maintenance of the humoural balance within the body, thus ensuring that disease cannot manifest. A discussion on the various means of curing different disorders and imbalances then follows.

The last section presents the strict ethical code to be followed at all times by practising Tibetan doctors. This includes the serious commitments they must make, the particular regard they should give to their patients and other similar codes of practice and behaviour.

3. *Mannag-gyud* – the Oral Tradition Tantra

The third text, the Oral Tradition Tantra, consists of ninety-two chapters arranged in the following fifteen sections:

Healing the three humours *rLung*, *Tripa* and *Badkan*.

Healing abdominal diseases such as indigestion, tumours, pallor, oedema, etc.

Healing fevers of general and specific types.

Healing diseases of the upper parts of the body such as the head, eyes, nose, ears, etc.

Healing diseases of the vital organs (heart, lungs, spleen, etc.) and hollow organs (stomach, intestines, colon, etc.)

Healing diseases of the secret organs such as the male and female genital organs.

Healing miscellaneous ailments such as hoarseness, thirst, hiccough, asthma, etc.

Healing physical eruptions such as growths (cancer), haemorrhoids, glands, fistula etc.

Healing children's diseases.

Healing women's diseases.

Healing the diseases caused by spirits.

Healing the injuries caused by weapons.

Healing poisoning.

Healing elderly people though rejuvenation processes.

Healing defective reproductive essence and infertility.

The *Mannag-gyud* Tantra goes into more detail on the topic of what constitutes a healthy, balanced condition and how it can become diseased, once again essentially focusing on the three humours and their different types. This section details forty-two types of *rLung* disorders, twenty-six types of *Tripa* disorders and thirty-three types of *Badkan* disorders, making a total of 101 different diseases linked to the three mental poisons through their respective humours. The causes and conditions of each of these diseases are presented together with their presenting signs and symptoms. This is accompanied by the respective therapies as far as dietary and behavioural advice is concerned together with appropriate medication, should the dietary and behavioural advice fail to bring about a cure. For cases where medication also fails, or needs to be supplemented by something else, there then follows a discussion of the various therapies useful for the alleviation of specific diseases.

The five *rLung* energies, five *Tripa* energies and five *Badkan* energies are like fifteen workers in a factory who work upon ten objects which are subsequently divided into two: the seven constituents and the three wastes. As workers, the fifteen manifestations of the three humours should satisfy the factory owner by making sure that everything in the body flows in the right way.

4. *Chima-gyud* – the Last Tantra

The last tantra contains twenty-five chapters which are explained in four sections:

Examination of pulse and urine for diagnosing diseases.

The process of compounding medicines.

Eliminative therapy for expelling diseases.

Mild, rough and forceful surgical operations.

The first section presents a fully detailed description of diagnosis through the medium of the pulse and examination of urine. A section then follows which explains how medicines are prepared. These medicines must be carefully processed in line with their content, nature and potency, and may take the form of pills, powders, syrups, pastes, liquids, etc. The third section details such medications as those which have the effect of forcefully expelling the disease by means of purging, enemas and emetics together with certain medications that will subdue or destroy the particular disease. Finally, there follows a section presenting certain therapies which can be used as a means of prevention, or in certain cases where other methods have failed, to cure the disease. They are either mild or severe in form and include bloodletting, fomentations, medicinal baths, surgery and the application of heat or fire, called *metsa*, involving the use of metals or a herb burned at particular points on the skin. However, with regard to these therapies, major surgery is no longer used and bloodletting is not practised in the West.

At the end of this tantra are two final chapters (making a total of twenty-seven) which complete the Four Tantras by way of a comprehensive summary of all that has gone before.

These Four Tantras, as sacred teachings, have always been essentially preserved within a carefully protected tradition which does not lightly disseminate the highly specific teachings to all and sundry, regardless of inner capacity. The Tibetan medical system considers the characteristics of both student and practising physician to be of supreme importance.

The Inner Qualities of a Tibetan Physician

The study of this Buddhist system demands a high degree of personal inner confrontation, for the key to understanding Tibetan medicine, as the Buddha has originally taught it, can be found within the following assertion, that:

'Within oneself deliverance must be sought.'

As has already been emphasized, the key to health is to achieve a perfect state of balance. Tibetan physicians therefore assess the patient's inner state, detecting where there may be imbalances, disorders or disruptions within the physical, mental, emotional and spiritual systems of the person in order to begin restoring health. However, if the physician's own inner state is out of balance, how can this doctor even begin to treat a patient? This kind of activity would be like viewing the world through distorted spectacles. All subsequent assertions and deductions about the world would of course also be distorted.

Therefore it is paramount that a Tibetan physician be completely free of disturbing emotions and distorted views in order to treat others. The medicine, prescribed by the Buddha in order to help us overcome our suffering, is the dharma (his teachings) or indisputable spiritual truth. The essence of this truth is to seek enlightenment through achieving freedom from the self-imposed prison of the mind and the disturbing passions and deranged views which arise within this prison. Buddhist teachings offer a key to unlock the prison gates and free oneself from the seemingly endless desires, hatred and anger, delusion and confusion which all inevitably lead us on to disease. Through its particular focus on the mind and its particular connection with emotions, Tibetan Buddhist medicine reveals a crucial gateway to a more enlightened, healthy state.

The physicians in Tibet built a whole philosophy upon the understanding of the close relationship between the process of thought and problems manifesting in the body, so naturally the life of the physician is attuned to this fundamental truth. There is accordingly a profound acceptance that it is our negative emotions that hinder our progress on the crucial road to health, and that the mind must be tamed and mastered. Conflict arises when we become the slave of the raw energy of emotion. When we use the mind as a route to relating positively to this energy, we begin to defuse the conflict and dilute the power of the emotion.

The focus of the mind for the Tibetan doctor is therefore all important in the approach to medical study and practice. Each Tibetan doctor at all times pays homage to the Medicine Buddha, who is considered to be the 'Unsurpassed Physician' and the 'Teacher of all Medicine'. By means of this powerful spiritual focus, recitation in the form of mantras and prayers, and devotional visualizations, one builds an inner protection from the lower emotions which cause so much suffering. Through this dedicated practice, the three mental poisons of desire, hatred and closed-mindedness can be steadily eliminated, thus protecting the body from the diseases of the three humours, *rLung*, *Tripa* and *Badkan*. So homage to the Medicine Buddha is an inner, natural outpouring from a place of peace and deep devotion within every Tibetan doctor.

Humility in everything is extremely important. For the Tibetan doctors there is no rush, no need to be the first, no glamour or great show, but only a life of sacrifice, devotion and compassion. This inner spiritual attitude is reflected in the fact that as a nation we revere Mount Kailash, yet forbid anyone to climb it and proclaim it to be conquered. Tibetans prefer to walk in devotion round the sacred base of this mountain, which is revered as the manifestation of Mount Meru, the cosmic centre of the universe. Tibetan aspirations, far from placing national flags upon the snow-capped peak and standing proudly looking down upon the world, are more towards the prostration of oneself from head to toe in a journey around its base, over sharp rocks and freezing streams in supplication to the Highest.

There are in fact three categories of physicians, the highest of which is the Medicine Buddha and the lowest of which is someone who becomes a doctor as a means of making a living, hoping to become rich and renowned. The latter is considered to be making a serious mistake, somewhat in the manner of an upstart or charlatan. Further to this, the Tibetan medical system declares that if a doctor proceeds to practice medicine without engaging in any accompanying spiritual practice, this will be a cause of great suffering, no different to the action of cutting out one's heart, yet assuming one can then continue to help others as if nothing has changed.

In fact, the modern approach of pharmaceutical big business which, in collaboration with the medical profession, may seek to develop extensive self-profit through the administration of drugs, is following a practice totally at odds with the Tibetan Buddhist medical system. For when individual profit and selfishness lie at the heart of one's practice, this is considered through the laws of cause and effect to have very serious consequences for one's future.

Returning to the three categories of physician, the middle category is the expert physician, who is defined as someone who is loving, is compassionate, who carries great integrity and who has developed the capacity to read the inner world of other sentient beings to such a degree that it could be called extrasensory perception. Such a doctor can become so attuned to every patient, that an accurate diagnosis can be reached without extensive recourse to the patient's own description of the disease. Then, whilst focusing inwardly upon the Unsurpassed Physician to whom all other doctors can only aspire and who, as the Medicine Buddha is the source of all healing, the practitioner seeks to restore balance to the patient's condition.

Tibetan doctors therefore understand a very different kind of process to most other medical systems. This process is akin to alchemy, for a doctor must attempt to undergo a vital inner transformation which allows it to be possible for him to effect cures. This is achieved by means of a perfect inner attitude which must be maintained throughout times of study, apprenticeship and daily practice as a qualified physician. He must at all times have regard for his own teacher and revere him like a Buddha. He must believe in what the teacher has to teach him with not even a shred of doubt appearing. His respect and reverence must naturally extend to all the medical texts. Unaffected sincerity towards and sympathy for every patient is essential. He must regard the medicine as a sacred offering from the Medicine Buddha. Wisdom and compassion should be generated daily in an effortless fashion. The ideal of the bodhisattva, a person who lives in the world for the sole purpose of assisting all sentient beings, is the ideal of all doctors from Tibet. The healing skills of a physician relate directly to his inner capacity, level and quality of aspiration, degree of compassion and selflessness and ability to practice the spiritual medical truths of the Buddha.

In the Tibetan medical system, medicines are termed as 'benefit' and the physician as 'benefactor'. Therefore a medical practitioner must be a person with a compassionate mind. I quote from our medical text:

> A physician should develop Bodhicitta by first seeing the suffering of the patient, developing compassion, helping with the healing knowledge, developing faith in the healing science, practising equanimity and treating all patients sincerely and equally by not thinking of whether the patient or the person is kind or cruel to you.

The physician must feel the suffering of the patients and develop compassion within his or her mind. To establish compassion in the physician's mind it is very important to see the sufferings of the ailing patient first. This approach towards the patients should be permeated with the same kind of love, care and affection as a mother has towards her children.

Disease is the intolerable suffering from pains and aches both in mind and body due to the disruption or imbalance of the body elements. Seeing such sufferings of ailments in the patients, a physician will experience a sense of compassion towards those patients. This establishing of compassion within the mind of the physician is the foundation of sincere treatment. By seeing the suffering and by developing compassion the physician can thoroughly diagnose the disease which can be correctly treated by food, lifestyle, medicine and therapy.

Finally, the patient can be set free from the sufferings of the disease. Any success is not self-acclaimed by the doctor, but directly connected with the unfailing Tibetan medical science, or *Sowa Rigpa*. The physician must develop deep faith in this science of healing, and happiness for the liberation of the patient from suffering.

If a physician is sincerely practising equanimity, then he will not think about the social and economic status of the patient and whether the patient is kind or cruel towards him. He will treat the patient as a patient only. This way of giving service to the ailing patient means that the physician is developing within himself the quality of *Bodhicitta*, an enlightened state of perfection in oneself for the sake of all other sentient beings in the world. A physician who is not greedy and deceptive and who dedicates himself to the service of the patient will definitely go to the place of Buddha, whose specific healing emanation is referred to within the medical text as *Sangye Menla*, the Medicine Buddha.

The inner qualities of all Tibetan doctors are therefore valued above everything else. Great knowledge and theoretical skill might well be acquired, but inner focus, inner wisdom and compassion must be generated daily through the act of devotion and surrender if the physician is to become successful in helping others. This belief, that it is the personal inner qualities of the healer that are important, is paramount when considering a study of the Tibetan medical system, its concepts and techniques.

In summary, there are six qualities required to be present in a Tibetan doctor:

1. Intelligence, having a broad, firm and observant mind.

2. Compassion, aspiring to obtain the mind of Bodhicitta.

3. Commitment. This takes the form of three pledges:

The first pledge has the following six aspects, called *Loshag Drug*, meaning six to be kept in mind:

- Consider your Guru as the real Buddha.

- Take your Guru's teachings as being those of the Great Sages.

- Consider your medical science as being the direct oral lineage teachings of Buddha.

- Consider your colleagues as your own brothers and sisters.

- Treat your patients as you would your own children.

- Without any loathsome feelings, consider the patients' issuing body fluids, such as blood and pus, as your pet dogs and pigs.

The second pledge has two aspects, or *Sunja Nyi*, meaning two to be held:

- Regard one who has the knowledge of Tibetan medicine as a Deity.

- Consider all medical instruments as being the instrumental ornaments of the Deity.

The third pledge reveals three important attitudes, called *Sheyja Sum*, meaning three to be known:

- Value all medicines as wish-fulfilling gems.

- Consider the medicine as disease-eliminating ambrosia.

- Consider the medicine as an offering made to one's Deity.

4. Talent, which means:

- To be talented through the body by being expert in the use of all medical instruments.

- To be talented in speech by being able to develop comfort and happiness in each patient through sharing sweet conversation.

- To be talented in mind by being intelligent and clear minded with no doubt or confusion arising in the mind.

5. Endeavour.

The endeavour required is both for one's own cause, aiming to become self-literate and qualified in medical science with no doubt or hesitation, and for the cause of others, whereby a medical practitioner should be physically, vocally and mentally dedicated to the service of patients without distraction.

6. Skilled in Worldly Dharma.

This means to be skilled in the ways of the world, according to the positive aspects of religion and culture.

How to Approach the Study of Tibetan Medicine

There are two particular teachers to whom I remain indebted as far as my own study of Tibetan medicine is concerned. Firstly, Professor Barshi Phuntsok Wangyal was a great scholar and a renowned master of Tibetan medicine and astrology. As one of my first teachers in 1968, he taught me the basics of the medical system. He always maintained a wonderful disposition, smiling and happy in his work, taking particular delight in the development and achievements of his students. I have never seen him looking tired, for teaching was such a great source of joy and energy to him, whether in a formal setting, or informally outside of normal teaching hours, when he would invite students to visit him with any doubts and problems, whatever the time of day or night. I remain indebted to him as a great guru, guide and constant source of inspiration.

Secondly, I must mention what for me became three golden years (from 1979) under the tutelage and guidance of the great physician, Dr Yeshi Dhonden, with whom I was invited to take an internship. Aside from practical therapies, I received the initiation of the Four Tantras and specific teachings on the Mannag-gyud, or Third Tantra, from him. He was always very kind and encouraging, and I learned an immense amount from him.

Tibetan medicine is not something you can study lightly. The key to every system lies within its natural language, which at times can be quite daunting to the unpractised reader. Without some familiarity with the culture, traditions, language and inner ethos of a particular nation one can at times be completely at a loss as to how one can ascertain the profound secrets lying within any of its ancient texts. Indeed, it is just as if we stand before an undissected body, with no knowledge of the language and the tools which can assist us in the case of anatomical dissection – within Tibetan tantric medicine there are many concepts and practices which may often seem irrational and alien to the Western mind.

Indeed, the Tibetan medical system is quite unique, even though there has traditionally been some cross-fertilization of ideas during its early development. I am occasionally asked to compare the Tibetan medical system with other systems, for instance the Chinese medical system. However, in the case of the latter, although there are some similarities, fundamentally the two systems are completely different. The Chinese system is dualistic – based on Yin and Yang – whilst Tibetan medicine is tripartite – based on the three humours. In this respect we share more similarities with the Indian Ayurvedic system, which is also tripartite, based on what are known as the three doshas, termed *Vata*, *Pitta* and *Kapha*. Nevertheless, in the end each system must be solely understood on its own terms.

As Tibetan doctors, from a very early age we have been steeped in a monastic environment where we have thoroughly studied this Buddhist medical system. From ancient times it has been recognized that it will take a period of at least thirteen years to truly study and internalize this system. Year after year, we absorb ourselves completely in devoted studies, following a precise tradition of learning the science of healing, which has been handed down over millennia. We always aspire to the very highest and dedicate our lives to following our vocation as doctors in the footsteps of the Buddha, who demonstrated a life of self-sacrifice upon the altar of compassion.

Many people from the West have a growing interest in Tibetan medicine, and many patients around the world are now depending upon Tibetan consultations and medicines. Yet Tibetan doctors never seek to advertise their wares or stoop to using any form of propaganda. Word of mouth is the cause for this dramatic rise in interest – word of mouth from those who have been healed. So, unsurprisingly, Tibetan physicians are now often called upon to lecture in different parts of the world, for people naturally are being drawn to hear more about this successful healing system.

Something of the essence of this system can be ingested simply through the reading of this book. These teachings were given by the Lord Buddha for the benefit of mankind, and our aim as physicians is to disseminate his teachings as widely as possible. Naturally, one can decide to go even more deeply into this system of medicine, and in the modern world our system is already much more accessible than in earlier centuries. Indeed, there are a number of doctors who give lectures and teachings in different languages. For those who wish to absorb even more of the system, the study and understanding of Tibetan Buddhism and its medicine can be greatly assisted when one begins to grasp a sense of the Tibetan mentality, inner point of view, standards and culture – which in these days when the world has become a global village is much easier to achieve.

In India it is a pleasure to discover that the younger generation are inspired to study Tibetan medicine. There are three particular colleges, Men-Tsee-Khang, Chagpori and the Institute of Higher Tibetan Studies based in Saranath. The latter has been deemed a university. In these colleges, students learn the rGyu-shi, the Four Tantras, for five years, and then complete an internship for one year before their practice can begin. In this way, after six years they can achieve a full degree called the Kachupa. It is marvellous to see Tibetan medicine so well preserved and clearly flourishing, thus offering its very rich rewards to human beings across the world.

I also encourage, wherever possible, a study of the Tibetan language as being of enormous benefit in a serious study of the medical system, for in order to come even closer to understanding

Tibetan medicine, it is important that the language is in some way understood. To this one could also add an understanding of Sanskrit. This is because there are so many texts of medicine in Sanskrit and Tibetan which reveal their treasured secrets to the discerning student. Also, the tantric text, the rGyu-shi is condensed to a prohibitive degree if there has not been some grasp of the language. In the same way, many commentaries on this most basic text are effectively lost. So if one really wants to enter a much deeper study of this medicine, an attempt to learn the language can be enormously beneficial.

Through the translation into other languages, we inevitably lose some of the deeper essences of medicine from Tibet. Many doctors with extensive, rich experience and unique knowledge can offer theory and practice to the student, but these doctors only write and speak Tibetan. With a common grasp of the language, one can also learn so much from the Tibetans as a people who have absorbed this ancient system, so are generally conversant with the three humours, for example, and can even offer remedies from home to treat and cure a known imbalance.

I am also concerned that the study of the system without knowledge of the language may contribute to a gradual dilution and degeneration of Tibetan medicine as a system. For within the basic texts it has been stated:

> Don't experiment with the lives of human beings – what
> you must do is study until you are completely confident.

It is a tried and tested science, dealing with the lives of people, human beings – therefore it is so important to apply oneself to study over five or six years with at least a basic understanding of the language.

Throughout the study of Tibetan medicine, it is always the Buddha who gives us our sense of true perspective. We continue to revere him above everything else, for it was he who taught the system in his form of the Medicine Buddha. Across thousands of years the

Tibetan science of healing has been deeply enriched by the tireless work of many great physicians. Yet such doctors have never sought worldly acclaim. Indeed, we consider ourselves only servants of Lord Buddha, as drops in the ocean of his wisdom who must flow as we are directed. We continue to re-work the texts, adding further commentaries and conducting research in collaboration with other medical systems, thus allowing Tibetan Buddhist medicine to be taken further into the modern medical arena for the benefit of all. Yet all physicians carry inwardly essential characteristics to ensure that this vital essence of healing remains pristine, pure and sublime, as a spiritual system which cannot ever be polluted.

For those who are enthusiastic to study Tibetan medicine, the following five points should be noted:

1. A person willing to live without sufferings and with a desire to heal the sufferings of others should study healing science.

2. One wishing to attain longevity of life should study healing science.

3. One with a desire to achieve Dharma (the Absolute Truth taught by Lord Buddha) the wealth of wisdom, and happiness should study healing science.

4. One wishing to liberate sentient beings from suffering illness should study healing science.

5. One desiring to practise as a respected physician should study healing science.

The Parable of the 'Three Defective Vessels'

A student who does not pay attention to the medical teachings is like a vessel turned upside down.

A vessel with a hole in it can be compared to a student who forgets everything he has learned.

A student with bad motivation is likened to a dirty vessel.

This parable, located within the medical text itself, indicates that motivation whilst studying the Four Tantras is of primary importance, for aspiring to be rich and famous is certainly a bad motivation for a Tibetan doctor, and no-one is ever likely to approach such a person for true healing, just as nobody would ever drink from a dirty glass.

But of course the parable is applicable to all human beings, whatever we focus upon, read, study or ingest. How often do we consider the quality of our motivation when we come to apply our attention to a particular subject, object or person? Are we seeking to get something when we do so? Or are we seeking to give something? Is what we idealize and act upon aimed at increasing suffering or reducing it?

It is helpful to ask ourselves these kinds of questions, whatever we choose to look upon and thereby take into our system. Our inner being is directly related to our focus upon the outside world, and our ability to ingest information is directly related to the exact nature of our motivation.

17

Diagnosis and Treatment According to Tibetan Medicine

*B*ODY CONCEPTS AND DISEASES are considerably different in the Tibetan medical system from general Western thought and Western science in particular. But it is not easy to proceed to make a comment on a system when one doesn't have full knowledge of it. For example, I never use a stethoscope nor have I Western instruments for checking the condition of the patients. Such instruments should remain with Western physicians, who clearly have better knowledge of the stethoscope and other measuring instruments, whilst I wish to adhere strictly to the system I have been trained in, as I feel it is important to preserve Tibetan medicine in its very purest form.

I never use a sphygmomanometer, the typical machine for

measuring blood pressure in the West. This is in line with my training for, according to Tibetan medicine, an imbalance in blood pressure pertains to an energy imbalance in the body, so as a Tibetan doctor I need firstly to present the question: 'Does the pressure come from an imbalance of the *rLung* energy, the *Tripa* or *Badkan* energy?'

Thus through a reading of the pulse the Tibetan physician can not only ascertain the pressure level in the blood, but also, vitally, can feel within the pulse if it is strong, weak, or empty. From the characteristics manifesting in the beating pulse a doctor can gain a clear idea about the nature of the illness. Many illnesses present very similar symptoms, thus symptoms by themselves should not be completely relied upon as guides to lead the doctor to the cause of the disease, just as we might see clouds in the sky, but they are not all indicative of rain.

To take a small example, a headache is often caused by the *Tripa* energy, for although this humour is located in the middle of the body, it can move into the head, because inherently the energy of *Tripa* rises upwards like a flame. But on the other hand, it is possible that imbalanced *rLung* has caused the headache by pushing the *Tripa* energy upwards. So the treatment of the headache will of course be rather different if the cause is really *rLung* and not the *Tripa* humour acting by itself. On top of this, our aches and pains alone are not the indicators of disease. When someone is suffering from a headache it does not necessarily mean the problem is located in the head. The pain is just another symptom and the root may lie within a different organ and in very different parts of the body.

Causes and Symptoms

I recall a man I once treated in New Delhi who had suffered for a long time from his headaches. He had consulted many doctors, but in vain. Upon an examination of the pulse, urine and symptoms mentioned, I reached a diagnosis that the cause of this man's headache was connected with his stomach. It was chronic indigestion, constipation, gas formation – all malfunctions of the stomach that had caused his long-term problem. After taking Tibetan medicine for a fortnight, he was cured almost miraculously. The stomach is very important when looking at the symptoms of a patient. Even certain problems with sight can be improved through a correction of the function of the stomach.

So it is really important to look carefully beneath presenting symptoms. In the case of a fever, this condition is typically due to an imbalance in the *Tripa* humour, yet the cause might in fact be due to another humoural disorder. The story of a very old lady in Dharamsala comes to mind. She was lying in her bed with cold towels upon her forehead in an effort to reduce her rising temperature. When the treatment was not working I was called for my opinion. As the pulse was weak and fast, and all the points upon the body that related to the rising of the *rLung* energy were very sensitive to touch, I quickly realized that this was an example of what is referred to as an 'empty fever' provoked by a *rLung* imbalance. After taking off the towels, then heating up a little butter for massage upon her palms and soles, her head and other *rLung* points, more blankets were put over her and finally some hot milk was given for her to drink. Ten minutes later she had completely recovered. Here the *rLung* energy had caused the problem, in the same way that a breath of wind (*rLung*), when blown upon a spark of fire (*Tripa*), will cause the fire to rise, and thus the heat will then increase. Because of this finely balanced, close relationship between the vital humours, caution is always advised in diagnosis so as to eliminate mistakes.

> *Neglecting the cause of a disease and struggling to merely*
> *treat the symptoms is like leaving the roots of a poisonous*
> *tree whilst cutting away the leaves, branches and twigs.*

This is the reason why Tibetan medicine is particularly good for diseases that are chronic in nature, for our holistic system constantly delves beneath the obvious surface of the symptoms, however serious they may be, in order to find the root of the problem. Symptoms are indeed important, but they are ultimately only a reflection of the deeper perturbations in the body. We can stir the surface ripples on the water whilst ignoring the inner currents located more deeply within. Tibetan medicine knows that giving treatment solely to the symptoms is more likely to suppress the real disease rather than cure it, so to find the cure we must search for the cause.

I have been practising for over thirty years, mainly in India but also in a lot of Western countries. Throughout this time, I have found Tibetan medicine to be very effective in curing a great variety of diseases. On the chronic side, specifically arthritis, asthma, diabetes, liver problems, rheumatism and illnesses related to the nervous system and digestive system can be treated most successfully by taking Tibetan medicine. In our medical texts it states that chronic diseases are as resistant as stone to remedies. Therefore, in such cases, prescribed dietary and lifestyle advice, medication and exercise therapy should be prolonged in order to ensure effective treatment. Such long-term medication can be efficacious, and without any side effects.

Most of the chronic diseases are called *gChong-nay* in the Tibetan medical system. Such lingering, long-lasting diseases ultimately decrease the life supporting elements in the body, have a negative effect on the digestive system and cause abdominal problems. With chronic diseases it is absolutely essential to understand the principle of cause and effect. There can be no effects without a cause, just as there can be no fruits without seeds. Treating the cause prevents undesirable effects.

The digestive system assumes a particular importance in the treatment of chronic diseases. For the digestive heat, or digestive *Tripa* must be maintained to prevent indigestion, as it is the undigested or semi-digested particles of various types of food which form impurities, poisons and toxins which are the cause of almost all the abdominal chronic diseases, called *gChong-nay*.

gChong-nay can come in the following forms:

1. *Drilwa* – 'rolled' in the form of growths and tumours.

2. *Sagpa* – 'leakage' in the forms of fluids, e.g. ascites, oedema and dropsy.

3. *Jerwa* – 'scattering' or spread of diseases such as poisons, herpes and leprosy.

4. *Gingwa* – 'a swirl' or storage in one particular place of toxins. These localized toxins result in spleen or liver enlargement or expansion with the accumulation of diseased blood in the affected organs.

Once the concept of *rChong-nay* and its different types is perfectly understood, the physician will initially concentrate the treatment on eradicating the primary cause, then as the disease subsides, include treatment of the secondary effects. Since chronic diseases are particularly difficult to treat, it is very important for the patient to continue taking the medication and to follow a proper diet and lifestyle as advised by the doctor.

There are also a range of rejuvenation medicines known as *bChulen* in the Tibetan medical system. Following the right instructions, which include particular preliminaries to ingestion of the medicines, the administration of *bChulen* can eliminate *rLung* diseases, promote physical strength, improve life span and generally maintain good health with quite dramatic results, rather like the effect of pouring fresh water on fading flowers.

Methods of Diagnosis

In the West, diagnosis generally refers to identification of the disease after it has manifested. In Tibetan medicine the concept of diagnosis implies a monitoring of the derangement of the balance of the three humours. Once the nature of the imbalance is understood, balance may be re-established through treatment.

The energies of *rLung*, *Tripa* and *Badkan* can be categorized into two types:

rLung and *Badkan* are cold in nature

Tripa and blood diseases are hot in nature.

A bird may fly very high, in any direction it wants to, soaring to any height it wishes, but wherever it flies it will always be contained within space. In the same way, there are many possible symptoms and diseases, but they all occur within the ten fundamental elements of the body, known as the seven constituents and the three wastes.

Tibetan medicine accepts that there are germs, parasites and these sorts of things. But still the disease can always be treated from the perspective of its hot or cold nature. We may live in a very clean room, but if we leave a dirty cloth in the corner, within two days the living bacteria will develop. If there is no such material, nothing will grow. Tibetan medicine takes the dirt away, whereas allopathic medicine goes for the virus and bacteria. But since both germs and dirt have the same characteristics, the main direction of the treatment is the same.

The medical texts say:

> *All diseases can be understood by using the three methods*
> *of visual examination, touch examination and questioning*
> *the patient.*

Tahwa, or visual examination

In this case, the eyes of the doctor identify the signs and symptoms of the body, the height, body structure, complexion, speech and behaviour, which indicate the ongoing imbalance, in particular through the observation of the tongue and urine.

Rekpa, or examination by touch

This method includes checking the temperature, external parts of the body, and skin texture in cases where there are bumps or growths, and in particular reading the state of the body by means of the pulse.

Driwa, or questioning

This is a form of diagnosis whereby the patient is first asked about the approximate past cause of the disease, then secondly the present signs and symptoms and its current location. The patient's responses to the suggested future treatment are also registered by the doctor.

Tongue Diagnosis

Although not a primary source of information for the physician, the tongue can be utilized alongside urinalysis and pulse examination as a means of establishing the nature of the disease, for example:

In a *rLung* disorder, the tongue may be red, dry and coarse, with small pimples.

In the case of *Tripa*, the tongue will normally have a yellow coating and there will be a bitter taste in the mouth.

As for *Badkan* diseases, it may be moist, pale, soft, thick and whitish. By thick, this means that the tongue is somewhat swollen and there will be excessive saliva in the mouth since *Badkan* is watery in nature.

Urine Examination

Over and above most forms of diagnosis, pulse-taking is considered the most definitive, so the checking of the urine is not so essential in the case of highly experienced practitioners. However, it is particularly important for less practised physicians to check the urine, because this clearly exposes the hot or cold nature of the disease.

There are certain preliminary conditions which should be followed by the patient for both urinalysis and pulse examination in order to ensure that the diagnosis is not masked by more recent, temporary influences. Ideally, during the forty-eight hours immediately prior to the consultation with the doctor, patients are asked not to take in over-heating food, such as spiced, peppery food, or over-cooling foods such as food taken straight from the fridge, salads, raw, uncooked food and potatoes. They should also not ingest any food that they do not normally eat.

Alcoholic drinks should be avoided, as should excessive drinking of any particular liquid. The patient should abstain from sexual intercourse and strong exercise, and should ensure plentiful sleep, otherwise the body will be disturbed and will make precise diagnosis much more difficult.

The perfect time to check urine is immediately after the first morning sun, and the urine container should be white or transparent. There are many different things to be checked in the urine, from when it is hot until it becomes cold. Colour, bubbles and sediments should be carefully observed. Urine can indicate a fatal disease and the presence of negative spirits, but I am going to comment on the three general types:

A *rLung* condition is demonstrated by urine that is watery, thin and clear. When you stir it with a stick big bubbles are formed.

The *Tripa* energy will manifest in the urine as a reddish-yellow colour, and when the urine is fresh it has steam and a bad odour. If stirred, small bubbles form which disappear immediately.

Badkan diseases result in the urine being whitish in colour, and when you stir it saliva-like bubbles form which do not disappear.

Reading the Pulse

Pulse-reading is extremely important in Tibetan medicine, for the pulse is like a messenger between the disease and the doctor. Tibetan doctors therefore study and apply themselves diligently over many years to acquire the skill of taking the pulse. It is a highly refined art, with limitless possibilities and is held up to be a supreme indicator of the state of health or disease within a person.

The same preliminary dietary and lifestyle conditions apply as when examining the urine. Such conditions naturally apply also to the physician in both urinalysis and pulse diagnosis. The perfect time to read the pulse is early in the morning. The medical texts state that when you wake up in the morning, the instant that it is light enough for you to see the lines on your palm, then that is the time the doctor should read the pulse. This is because at that time the solar and lunar powers are in balance. However, these days doctors read the pulse anywhere and at anytime. They do this when the patient is relaxed, bearing in mind the time of day and the effect it has on the pulse.

An experienced physician adjusts pulse-reading according to the prevailing conditions. The pulse is checked on the radial artery of the wrist, because it is neither too near nor too far from the heart, so the pulsation is more balanced than in other parts of the body. The middle three fingers are used in pulse-taking. The index finger is placed near the joint and it lightly touches the skin. The middle finger adds a little more pressure, as if wanting to reach the flesh. The ring finger applies even more pressure downwards to feel the bone. This is due to the pulse being somewhat like a radish. As it grows into the arm it moves deeper, the arm becoming much thicker towards the elbow.

There is nothing grossly physical of course in the artery. The force of the blood produces the phenomena of the pulse. In order to feel the pulse of a patient clearly, the physician's hands need to be soft, and neither hot nor cold, and the fingertips should not be calloused or rough, but perfectly smooth, sensitive and pliant.

There are three types of natural or constitutional pulses: male, female and bodhisattva, or neuter. These terms refer to the actual quality of the pulse and not the sex of the patient, for a man or woman can have any of these pulses. A male pulse has a bulky and coarse quality, the female pulse subtle and rapid, whilst the bodhisattva pulse is smooth with a gentle, continuous beat. There is no particular spiritual connotation implied with the bodhisattva pulse. These pulses are read in a person who is in a state of health to assess the person's natural constitution.

There are also seasonal pulses, since the seasons and the accompanying predominance of certain elements at different times of the year will influence our body. There is also a specific pulse called the death pulse which can indicate in severe cases how long the patient has left to live. For general life expectancy, a special pulse is taken on the ulnar artery instead of the radial position.

Seven very particular 'Amazing Pulses' can also be read. By way of example, in one of these the condition of a member of a family can be ascertained by taking the pulse of a healthy substitute member of the same family. Therefore, if the father is ill, the pulse of the son can be checked. If there is no son, then the wife's pulse can be checked. If the wife is ill, then the husband's pulse can be checked. If the daughter is ill, the mother's pulse can be checked to obtain a prognosis of the disease. The need for such pulse-taking was particularly applicable in cases of patients living in Tibet's mountainous areas who could not travel to see the doctor. The diagnostic approach is based on calculations relating to the five elements, but such pulse-reading can only be possible from a person who is absolutely healthy, and even then the preliminary conditions to be observed before taking the pulse assume much greater importance, and certain other specific conditions are required.

In general, taking into account the patient's constitutional pulse, the speed of the pulse is determined by measuring the number of pulse beats against the doctor's own breath cycle of two inhalations and exhalations with a short period in between the two. If the number of beats in one cycle is six or more, this indicates a hot disorder, whereas if it is four or less, the disorder is cold.

The physician can read the state of each organ within the body by means of the pulse. There are accordingly twelve points of reading of the pulse, each finger being split into two, the top half nearest the thumb and the bottom half nearest the little finger. All are interwoven carefully without confusion. In general, the index finger reads the state of health in the top part of the body, the middle finger relates to the centre of the body and the ring finger detects the condition of the lower part. If the doctor is feeling the pulse with his right three fingers placed upon the patient's left wrist, with the index finger he can feel the heart and small intestine; with the middle finger he feels the spleen and the stomach and with the ring finger he feels the reproductive organs and the left kidney. When the doctor's left hand takes the pulse on the patient's right wrist, with the index finger he feels the lungs and the large intestine; with the middle finger he feels the liver and gall bladder, and with the ring finger he feels the right kidney and the bladder.

There is only one discrepancy between the sexes with regard to the pulse, whereby the lung and the heart pulse swap positions. This is because, according to our system, the heart energy moves to the left side in a man and to the right side in a woman. A doctor always begins by taking the pulse of the heart, so firstly takes the left wrist pulse in a man and the right wrist pulse in a woman.

Pulse characteristics.

The *rLung* pulse beats strongly and superficially. The more one applies pressure, the more it disappears. It is what we call an empty pulse. It is like a balloon on the water. If you press down it sinks and if you let go, the balloon comes up again. Sometimes it has a missed beat.

The *Tripa* pulse beats thin, fast, rolling and tight.

The *Badkan* pulse beats slow, sunken and weak, like the step of a lazy person.

Naturally, the language of the pulse takes years to fully understand, so terms such as 'rolling' and 'tight' can only really be assimilated and understood in practice, with an accomplished physician to assist. Yet through the pulse, the body is sensed as a microcosm, a universe in itself obeying the same laws of physics as all matter and energy, an intricate web of interconnected energies, within which disease will always manifest as a particular energy imbalance in the system, which accordingly manifests as a particular sensation within the pulse.

The Art of Questioning

The physician concerned should examine every word uttered by the patient. For instance, the patient may tell the doctor the approximate cause of the sickness, mention the accompanying signs and symptoms, point to the site of the aches and pains, inform the doctor of the country where the patient had fallen sick, and state the duration of the illness, etc. All this is valuable information; for instance, the location of the problem may in itself point to the particular humoural imbalance, due to the doctor's knowledge of the typical location and pathways of the three humours.

The medical texts say: 'Ask a question before you touch the patient.' The physician should in this way attempt to pinpoint the cause of the illness on the basis of wrong diet, unwholesome behaviour, inclement weather, etc. Then, by adding questioning to the other means of diagnosis, the doctor is gradually able to narrow down all incoming information in order to ascertain the exact nature of the disease.

For example, in the case of a *rLung* disorder, upon questioning, it may be discovered that the patient is suffering from a light and delirious mind, restlessness, insomnia, humming and slight deafness in the ears, dizziness, yawning, frequent sighing, nonlocalized pain, stiffness in the body, chills, shivering and depression. The disease will worsen in the evening, before dawn and on an empty stomach. Conversely, patients will notice some relief when they eat oily or particularly nutritious food.

Symptoms of a *Tripa* disorder may be yellow in the whites of the eyes, a bitter taste in the mouth, hunger, headache, increase in the body temperature, diarrhoea, nausea, vomiting containing bile, itching, pain in the upper part of the body and a worsening of the condition when it is hot, during the middle of the day, at night and after digesting food. Such patients are benefited by any cool conditions, or cool food and drink.

Symptoms of a *Badkan* disorder may be excessive formation of phlegm, or mucus, dullness in the mind and body, discomfort in the kidney and waist region, loss of appetite, poor sense of taste, indigestion, vomiting, belching, weakness in body heat, lethargy and increase in weight. The condition will worsen during the morning and evening or immediately after eating. Warm places and warm food will noticeably benefit the *Badkan* condition.

Further to this, if the patient is relieved with cold remedies and worsens with hot treatments he will be suffering from a hot disease, and vice versa.

Taken altogether, the diagnostic procedure must be followed by the physician with the utmost care in order to ensure that an accurate diagnosis is reached. The doctor must be completely focused upon the patient to the exclusion of all other influences. In fact, the level of concentration required cannot be overestimated, for as one of my gurus, Dr Yeshi Dhonden has stated in relation to the degree of care needed to be exercized throughout a consultation:

> *Imagine that you must walk with a pot full of oil on your*
> *head over a plank that has been laid from the roof of one*
> *tall building to another. If just one drop spills from the pot,*
> *you will be executed on the spot.*

From *Healing from the Source* by Dr Yeshi Dhonden, P.115

As Tibetan physicians, we therefore attempt to completely surrender to the process of diagnosis in its entirety, placing the patient at the centre of our every breathing moment whilst we conduct a thorough and exacting consultation.

Treatment

The essence of the Tibetan medical treatment is always to re-establish and maintain the three humours, *rLung*, *Tripa* and *Badkan* in a state of harmony and balance. Ideally, as far as treatment is concerned, the doctor will solely give advice on lifestyle and diet in order to rectify the problem. This relatively inexpensive approach to restoring health is based on common sense. In all cases, wherever possible, the doctor will avoid any more radical approaches to treatment, for the intention is to allow the patient to be restored to a state of health in a natural way without threatening to unbalance any other areas of the human condition through introducing medication or sometimes harsh therapeutics into the situation.

All treatment is based on:

Choelam, or lifestyle.

Sae, or diet.

sMen, or medicines.

Chae, or therapies.

Choelam – Treatment through Lifestyle

There are certain guidelines for behaviour which can assist greatly in the case of a particular disturbance. Obviously there are permutations of these, according to the exact nature of the illness and possible mixture of humoural imbalances, but within the medical text, the following information is presented as a general rule:

Treatment for a *rLung* disturbance:

A person affected by *rLung* is advised to spend time with close, loving friends in a warm, calm and quiet place. He or she should be kept free from stress and tension, entertained with music, interesting stories or amicable conversation.

Treatment for a *Tripa* disturbance:

The patient should stay in a cool place, such as near a river, seashore or under a tree with cooling powers, such as sandalwood or neem, must relax both physically and mentally, and be kept free from anger.

Treatment for a *Badkan* disturbance:

A person with a *Badkan* disease should spend time in a warm place, do some physical exercise, and try to resist general lethargy, keeping the mind alert to counteract the dullness of mind that typically comes with a *Badkan* disease.

Sae – Treatment through Diet

Dietary advice is almost always given, whether or not medicines are prescribed. Naturally, failure to follow such advice will work against the action of any pills ingested, and will certainly help return the body to its former diseased condition once the pills are finished. For food will always directly affect the humours, and such daily ingestion has a very potent influence on the patient's constitution. Therefore if one understands one's natural disposition as far as the humours are concerned, then an appropriate diet will act as a preventative against illness.

Care with the digestive system is considered to be of absolute importance, for any disorder in the digestive process can be particularly serious and lead to many different illnesses. Overeating is a common cause of many problems. In this respect, the Buddha gave a specific teaching on the amount of food necessary for the body's health and clarity within the mind. The stomach should be two quarters filled with food, one quarter filled with liquid and one quarter kept empty. This allows the process of digestion to operate correctly, through the functions of the Decomposing *Badkan*, Digestive *Tripa* and Fire-Accompanying *rLung*.

By way of example of an approach to treatment through dietary advice, the following foods are prescribed when treating the respective humoural disease:

Dietary advice for a *rLung* disease:

Take food with rich and nutritious qualities, oil, butter, mutton with vegetables, soups, porridge, hot milk and a little alcohol.

Dietary advice for a *Tripa* disease:

Food with either an inherently cool and light power such as yoghurt, light cereal, goat's milk, fruit juices and meat from animals that live at a high altitude, which means their meat is cooling in nature.

Dietary advice for a *Badkan* disease:

Food with hot and light power, such as light peppers, spices, honey, fish and ginger tea.

sMen – Treatment through Medication

Tibetan medicine uses pills, powders, decoctions, medicinal wines and butters, etc.

Medicines are used for each type of humour on the basis of their respective tastes and qualities.

Tastes and qualities to relieve a *rLung* disease:

sweet, sour, salty taste
oily, heavy, smooth quality

Tastes and qualities to relieve a *Tripa* disease:

sweet, bitter, astringent taste
cool, liquid, blunt quality

Tastes and qualities to relieve a *Badkan* disease:

hot, sour, astringent taste
sharp, coarse, light quality

Examples of medicines used for the different humoural diseases are the following:

A *rLung* disease will benefit from:

Eaglewood, nutmeg, cloves, asafoetida, molasses.

A *Tripa* disease will benefit from:

Swertia Chirata, Iris Germanica, Tinospora Cordifolia, myrobalan and bitter melon.

A *Badkan* disease will benefit from:

Pomegranate seeds, peppers, ginger, garlic and minerals with a hot power, such as coal and limestone.

As far as *rLung* and *Badkan* are concerned, the substances mentioned are available within the West. *Tripa* diseases are assuaged by the bitter taste, which can be found in a bitter form of cucumber, bitter melon and plants as given by their Latin names. The bitter taste is not commonly found in vegetables in the West.

Physicians will normally give patients three different types of medication for use every day, for example one to be taken just prior to breakfast, one after lunch and one after the evening meal. Each medication is designed to work to bring the humours into balance. One pill may be addressing the primary humour in imbalance whilst two further pills ensure that the other humours are kept in tact and not unbalanced by the treatment for the main condition. This way of addressing disease of course contrasts with most Western medication, where a single drug is prescribed for a certain illness. In the latter case, the drug may well target the main problem, but side effects may also be experienced, because the drug is causing problems elsewhere in the body at the same time.

The pills themselves are typically a combination of several ingredients, as many as ten, twenty, thirty, forty, fifty – even as many as a hundred or more in certain cases. The approach to the combination of ingredients is highly complex and very subtle, ensuring that all aspects of a particular condition are targeted and that once again there are no possibilities of any side effects. Western patients tend to expect quick effects with medication, as the desire for a quick approach to some kind of relief is more typical in the West. However, there is an important concept lying behind the steady approach of

Tibetan medication.

For any medicine to be of complete and wholesome effect to the body, it must be assimilated by the entire digestive process, which takes a full six days. Tibetan medicine is designed with this in mind; therefore a period of six days is required before one can really begin to experience the full effect of the medication. If any drug has a quick effect, this is generally a sign that it is not being digested properly, in essence not so very different to a poison which can harm one within a matter of hours or sometimes minutes.

With regard to consideration of the strength of any medication, problems can arise when too strong a medication is used for minor diseases or too weak a medication for strong diseases. For instance, it is said that if a load that is supposed to be carried by a Yak (Tibetan ox) is put on a sheep, the sheep may break its legs, whereas if a Yak carries a sheep's load it just won't feel anything at all. Consequently a treatment to an imbalance of one of the three humours, if incorrect in strength, may be either too powerful, having a negative effect, or if too weak, will have very little effect on the problem, bringing no relief to the condition, yet nevertheless with the potential to cause an imbalance in one or both of the other two humours. For the forceful elimination of certain diseases in particularly serious cases, purgatives can be used, as can emetics and suppositories.

Chae – Treatment through Therapies

Therapies are normally used in the final analysis when other approaches have not yielded positive results. However, certain therapies such as massage and exercise can be useful additions to lifestyle and dietary advice, or to accompany medicines. Other examples include medicinal baths, specific oils for massage, *metsa* which is the application of heat or fire on specific points using metals or moxa (the herb Artemisia), surgical therapy such as spoon therapy (so called because the instrument used is spoon-shaped, although this form of surgical operation is hardly ever used now) and some forms of acupuncture, such as the Golden Needle Therapy where a golden needle can be inserted at different points of the body, most typically lightly inserted at the crown of the head.

There are also hot or cold fomentations which can be applied to various parts of the body. The hot fomentations are typically cloth soaked in hot butter or oil, sometimes with the addition of a herb such as garlic. Cold fomentations are created in a similar fashion, but with the use of cold water. Such water can be snow water, or water which has been left out under the stars overnight. The water is actually chilled by the effect of the stars. Cold fomentations help reduce inflammation and fever. In both cases the fomentations are applied to particular points known to be sensitive during a particular humoural imbalance. For instance in a *rLung* imbalance three particular points on the spine will be sensitive. When the head is bent forward, the vertebra which is level with the shoulders is the first point, and counting down from here, the sixth and seventh vertebrae will be sensitive, as will a point on the sternum midway between the nipples. Massaging, or placing hot fomentations upon these points can help to alleviate the *rLung* condition.

Although bloodletting continues to be practised in Tibet and India, it is not as yet practised in the West. This is because there are so many special conditions which accompany the practice of blood-letting, such as the preparation of medical decoctions, and the whole procedure takes many days. It is possible that in the future it will be practised in the West, as its correct application can be very effective in particular conditions.

The following are examples of the types of therapies suitable for particular conditions:

In the case of a *rLung* disturbance:

Massage with warm oil. This is particularly effective for worried, tired and old people. Oily, hot fomentations are placed on the *rLung* points, such as the sixth and seventh cervical vertebrae, and enemas may be helpful.

In the case of a *Tripa* disturbance:

Bloodletting, cold fomentation and induced perspiration.

In the case of a *Badkan* disturbance:

Moxa and exercise.

Morning Dietary Advice

As can be seen, there are many varied and particular medications, therapies and advice on diet and lifestyle to assist people in the cases of various conditions. Yet time after time, wherever possible we will return to the simplest forms of advice when helping others maintain a state of balance and health.

In fact, one of the most regularly healthy things we can do first thing every morning before we ingest any other food or drink and before we begin the day is to drink a cup of boiled water. The same can be done at evening time, just after dusk. There are a number of reasons for this and subsequent benefits. Firstly, morning and evening are times when the cold, *Badkan* energy rises. Therefore boiled water keeps the cold *Badkan* energy under control at a cold time of the day.

Boiled water in the morning helps to cleanse the body of accumulated mucus in the throat and lungs. It is also very good for digestion, for it supports the digestive fire and is very effective for someone with hiccoughs, breathing problems and *Badkan* diseases. It will act as a preventative for people who frequently suffer from cold and coughs and also helps prevent infectious diseases.

All this in a simple cup of boiled water! Yet it is said that the first disease ever to arise in the world was a problem with digestion and the first medication ever to be prescribed was boiled water.

Chapter 18

Maintaining Health through Tibetan Medicine

*I*N ORDER TO MAINTAIN good health and promote longevity of life, it is very important to treat the causes of disease and not just the symptoms. Excessive or abnormal seasonal changes, the misuse, disuse or overuse of our sensory organs, mind and speech, an imbalanced ingestion of the different tastes and inherent powers in substances are the cause of imbalance within the three humours, the seven constituents and three wastes. Yet one can enjoy health and long life if we always maintain some awareness of the link between effects and causes, or flowers to their roots, for as the medical texts say:

> *It is vital for health to keep the flowers freshly nourished in fertile soil in order to maintain healthy roots.*

Eyes are the flowers of the liver, therefore it is very important to keep the liver healthy. A problem in the liver will adversely affect the eyes, causing a yellowish colour to manifest, a sure indication of hepatitis or jaundice.

Ears are the flowers of the kidney, therefore it is vital to keep the kidneys healthy. Too much cold energy will affect the kidney adversely, leading to problems with the ears, such as tinnitus.

Nostrils are the flowers of the lungs, therefore a blockage in the nose is an external sign indicating irregularity in the lungs.

The lips are the flowers of the spleen, so if they are cracked, or covered with a coating, or changed in colour it is an indication of a spleen disorder.

The flower of the heart is the tongue. Dryness on the tongue or sometimes stammering can indicate a heart problem.

If *rLung*, *Tripa* and *Badkan* are maintained well by adequate food, healthy lifestyle and regular meditation, they will operate harmoniously in our body. Food will be digested properly. Such correct nutrition in turn produces and develops the seven constituents, which are to be emphasized in more detail within this chapter.

Unfortunately, when any of the three humours move out of balance a chain reaction manifests itself, upsetting the finely balanced energies *rLung*, *Tripa* and *Badkan*. The owner of the body should be equally kind to his three workers (*rLung*, *Tripa* and *Badkan*). For instance, if our lifestyle and food excessively lean towards the *rLung* energy, through indulging in such activities as sleeping little, fasting for too long and only eating foods with a coarse quality (such as foods with a bitter taste, lacking in protein, and strong tea), then the *rLung* energy becomes overly strong in our system. This in turn affects the *Tripa* and *Badkan* so that disturbances begin to arise. If we eat only greasy food then *Tripa* will certainly increase. The *Tripa* will then attack the *Badkan* and one ends up with a malfunction of *Badkan* caused by overactive *Tripa*.

Clearly the malfunction of any one of the three humours can have serious consequences, therefore a balancing of *rLung*, *Tripa* and *Badkan* is stressed in Tibetan medicine. For these three energies always remain connected to the illusion of the ego and the three mental poisons to the extent that even if we enjoy good health, the potential for them to become out of balance is always within us. For we generally remain in an unenlightened state of ignorance. In this unstable state we might blithely consider that we can continue to take pleasure in a healthy body and live in the lap of luxury, whereas in reality, the slightest oversight in lifestyle and diet will bring imbalance to the system, create disorder and progress the body towards illness.

Healing and Regeneration

Yet within the human being there is great potential and a tremendous source of energy, for every person has the capacity for self-healing and self-regeneration. Humanity can and does change just as the world around is constantly changing. Humanity's vision of the world also transforms in line with the evolution of consciousness and the development of human perception. Greater awareness and a search for inner and outer balance can only benefit mankind and the wider environment.

A healthy human body is a vessel for transformation and is formed and maintained by a stable diet, appropriate ingestion of the six tastes and thereby a balanced assimilation of the five elements. The nutrition from the food which the body needs for vitality and freedom from illness results from the transformative process of the seven constituents: nutritional essences, blood, flesh, fat, bone, marrow and reproductive essence, through the process of digestion. It is the *rLung* energy that is responsible for the transformation of the seven constituents, which takes place through breathing, thinking power, speaking, the flow of urine, movement of faeces and menstruation.

Imbalances within the elements of the inner body can lead to serious disturbances in mind and spirit. Such imbalances can be initiated and exacerbated by poisonous substances, stress, anxiety, mental strain, powerful emotions, particularly grief which can weaken a person very quickly, and negative energies arising from a suspicious mind. In such conditions, the *rLung* energy which transforms the elements of the body can also exert a strong pressure within the mind in the shape of a neurosis or obsession, if we neglect a positive attitude towards life. It is not uncommon to come across people who even find themselves on the verge of committing suicide under this pressure. In such a situation it is imperative to assist the person in regaining some sense of balance and perspective, for nobody really knows where our mind, our soul and our consciousness will go after a self-inflicted death. However, what one can be sure of is that it will not be to a place any better than our former life, even if we thought it was a particularly unpleasant one.

According to Buddhism, the human birth is regarded as an excellent birth to have, which should never be wasted. Here, the human being has the opportunity to experience the particular balance of pleasure and pain, happiness and suffering for the benefit of the soul's evolution. On this unique journey each individual has the capacity for reflection upon one's actions, and thereby the potential for an intelligent use of the free will in order to benefit oneself and others. The ultimate goal of enlightenment is always within one's grasp, through the extraordinary vessel of transformation given as a miracle of nature – the human body.

The potential for enlightenment, for growth into something miraculous and wonderful is there in each one of us as a blueprint, just as surely as the blueprint of the beautiful rose is there within its seed. No-one can predict with any certainty the definite outcome of this seed. There is no certainty of the magnificence to come, the exquisite unfolding of its mandala-like petals, its particular colour and subtle perfume. Indeed this seed of a rose, however carefully planted, may flourish or fail. However, we can be certain that nothing will ever emerge from the seed of a rose if it is kept in a bottle. If we wish to give the flower a chance to bloom, we must first plant the seed in the earth, then water it, and allow the light of the sun to reach it.

We are like the rose and should give ourselves the best chance in life. We should take care of the seeds of our future by ensuring the environment in which we place ourselves, the foods we ingest, the thoughts we allow into our minds and the emotions which emerge from our hearts are conducive to a healthy, balanced existence. For if favourable conditions prevail, then illness will not manifest. Favourable conditions include attention to one's diet, lifestyle, thinking state and appropriate seasonal adjustments.

When seeking conditions for a happy, healthy life, we must accept the law of call and echo, cause and effect, choice and response. For as creatures of choice, we must take account of what we respond to and thus claim as our possession. If we choose love, love chooses us. If we choose hate, then hate overwhelms us. If we claim evil, evil leaves its mark upon our heart. If we seek out the good, then the good will appear and surround us. If we look for the world and ignore the riches within, then our short-sightedness will bring us the trappings of transient wealth and lose us our deepest self, the inner gold of which alchemists dared to dream and to which they devoted their every energy.

In our search for the way in which we can maintain good health, we should also take account of our place and time upon this planet earth, for this will always have a profound effect upon the body condition.

The Impact of Time, Season, Location and Age on the Physical Body

It is a great mistake to assume that we are in some way completely separate from everyone and everything around us. This is the illusion of separation and isolation, fed by the desire of the little ego to be different from and indeed superior to everyone else. Such deception is a source of great pain and suffering, for this self-generated pulling away from our environment and the people who surround us works against the fundamental laws of nature.

In reality we are profoundly linked to all existence through the subtle energies in our physical bodies. Tibetan medicine recognizes this and can pinpoint the magnetic effects of the time of day, the seasons and the geological location on the physical body. For we are a tiny drop of life immersed in the universal ocean, stretching from the beginning of time into the distant future, intimately connected with all that has gone before, all that is and all that will be.

In this respect the ancient medical system of Tibet shares the vision of many modern theoretical physicists. Indeed, Einstein's 'field theories' have particular relevance in aiding a deeper understanding of how Tibetan medicine works. His theories reveal that the particles of which the fundamental universe, including the body universe, are constructed, are not separately suspended solid particles within a void, but are in fact concentrations of energy with fields which influence the space around them. The particles are actually charges rather than substances which produce an electric current by dint of their motion. In this way, Einstein demonstrated existence as a unified whole, completely interrelated through these particles, their fields, currents and surrounding space. At the level of the human body, the primary energy force responsible for the body's composition can transform into innumerable energy forms which are all interrelated and interdependent.

To this vision of countless electromagnetic fields in dynamic interrelationship with each other is added the issue of gravity and what is known as curved space. Electromagnetic fields are subject to the laws of attraction and repulsion, whereas in the case of gravitational fields they not only attract one body to another body but also curve space around themselves by attracting equally in all directions. However, it is in any case a condition of space that it is curved and cylindrical along its axis. Einstein therefore concluded that the geometrical properties of space are not independent, but depend upon the distribution of masses within it. This profound observation underpins the interdependent nature of all things, for all matter, fields and space are inextricably interconnected and interwoven as the vital fabric of existence. Taking this further then the whole of the universe has an effect upon any single point within it, whilst that same point has a real effect upon and contribution to make to the universe.

Applying this to the human body we can understand the body as a complex fabric of dynamic woven energy in motion. The physical body forms the centre of the various fields, around which the magnetic currents curve. Through its various fields, whether electric, magnetic or electromagnetic, the body is inevitably affecting and being affected by other bodies, objects and the environment as it moves through space and time.

From this point of view, it is understood as imperative for the Tibetan physician to take account of environmental factors, which include the exact season, time of day and geographical location when checking the pulse of an individual, or the diagnosis may prove wrong. With this in mind, the pulse cannot be taken anywhere, any place, any time without taking into account the exact time of day, season, location and age of a patient. The physician needs to allow for the acting magnetic forces operating at the time of consultation, and their influences on the pulse. For instance, if a physician does not allow for the fact that the pulse is being checked in the autumn, in the middle of the day and in a dry and hot region, when the *Tripa* energy is strong, then the strong *Tripa* pulse will be diagnosed as an illness. It is precisely for this reason that the humours are elaborately linked to the seasons, the time of day and location of the persons being treated.

Each of the three humours relates to a particular time of the day. The *rLung* rises within the body most typically in the evening and at dawn, whilst *Tripa* manifests at midday and midnight and *Badkan* manifests in the morning and at dusk. It is accordingly better to eat hot food at *Badkan* times, in the morning and evening, as *Badkan* is a cold energy. Raw or cold food may be taken at lunch time because this is right in the middle of the day's activity when the temperature is at its highest.

Each of the three humours relates to seasonal and temporal

factors. The *rLung* energy manifests in the rainy season; *Tripa* energies are at their optimum level in autumn and *Badkan* accumulates in spring. So for instance, if a doctor was practising in countries such as Scotland, Ireland and parts of Canada where it rains throughout the year, he would understand these to be '*rLung* places' due to the cooling nature of the rain in the air, and would adjust his diagnostic approach accordingly, expecting a general increase in the *rLung* energy within the people living in those areas.

Each particular region favours a predominance of a certain humour. Therefore an area that is windy and cold favours an increase of *rLung* in the people living there. Dry and hot areas naturally increase *Tripa* energy in the inhabitants of that area, whilst wet, humid, muddy and generally damp places, where the elements of earth and water pre-dominate, are regions where *Badkan* develops.

This point can of course be extended further to include the tendencies of a particular nation at that point in time, for the nature of the place and people where one lives favours the occurrence of a predominance of a certain humour. For instance, in a place where there is much torture and where malnutrition is rife, the children born into and growing up in that environment will tend to be *rLung*-type children for their body elements will be developed by a diet and lifestyle likely to increase *rLung*.

Finally, each humour is a natural condition at a particular age, for the older a person grows, the more that person is susceptible to *rLung*, when the energies of the body are diminished. *Tripa* is the natural condition of an adult when the body is well matured and at its peak, whilst children are prone to *Badkan* when the body energy is just developing.

Accordingly, if a person succumbs to the corresponding disease linked to their age, such an illness can be particularly severe. In general, energy decreases with age, so *rLung* is then easily developed. Those who keep on smiling will remain healthy. During the adult stage there is a lot of heat in the body, and since fully developed adults are prone to get into fights and feel strongly about things, this all increases *Tripa*. Children cry, wet beds, love sweets and live on milk. They are ignorant about the world and have to be taught everything. They are prone to *Badkan* diseases.

Perhaps the greatest consideration throughout the Tibetan medical approach is one of maintaining a precise balance in all things. This can be applied to all areas of body, mind and speech and is vital to the successful operation of the process of digestion, which in its successful operation is one of the greatest preventative systems as far as disease is concerned.

Tibetan Medicine – the Science of Equilibrium

All natural forms contain within them an inner geometry of exquisite perfection which is precisely balanced. These forms operate in harmony with their surroundings through a process of mutual exchange and interdependency. This inner precision is multiplied across the universe as a blueprint at both microcosmic and macro-cosmic levels. This is the magnificence of natural form, the absolute quality of both the inner and outer universe.

On an astronomical level, the planets represent the organs of the body of the universe, moving in relationship with each other through their respective planetary paths and all dependent upon the heart of the macrocosm – the sun. On an astrological level, these planetary relationships form a unique impression embedded within every human being's psyche at the very instant of their birth. On an anatomical level, the inner universe follows the age-old principle 'as above, so below', and the various organs and glands of the body relate to, exchange with, and are dependent upon each other through the various physical systems. They in turn are ultimately reliant on the driving force of the sun at the centre of us all – the heart.

In this way the perfection of form can be found within the fundamentals of everything in existence. Yet this grand manifestation of the higher workings of the universe can be at best veiled and at worst destroyed when our exchanges and interactions with our environment and those around us produce suffering, pain and conflict. Unfortunately, in this instant we become locked into a limited vision, a narrow perspective. It is as if, facing a jewel, we no longer see the diamond as a whole, only a tiny facet which soon becomes the whole picture. So all our tension, pain and suffering becomes completely overwhelming, trapping us in a blinkered vision along a self-perpet-uating path towards destruction in the form of various illnesses.

Yet if we could only raise our awareness above our painful self-obsession, we might at last understand that the experiences we perceive to be unfortunate are part of a process of growth and trans-formation, no different to the process of digestion within the body. Of course 'digesting' experiences is not an easy process, yet it can be eased by developing a holistic view of life in its entirety. It is a little like expanding one's view of a tiny thread twisted around the particular warp of a tapestry until one can view the whole picture in all its magnificence. Such a wider view of existence can enable us to withstand the inevitable ups and downs of daily life. If we can accept a certain degree of friction and tension as part of the process of becoming, of taking our place within an interdependent universe which has purpose and meaning, then we can truly enter the wheel of life and allow ourselves to be turned and transformed.

There is a profound link between the body universe and the macrocosmic universe, whereby each has a real effect upon the other. From the holistic viewpoint, the world has a digestive process whereby it attempts to separate nutrition from waste, or one might say the good from the evil. Every person, through their own individual, astrological stamp of the universe, has a unique part to play in this process and can make a real contribution to the future of mankind. Dr Carl Jung's idea that the world might be saved from annihilation by a number of individuals who are able to accept and contain the opposites of good and evil within themselves relates directly to this point. For on a day-to-day level, in any particular tense and fractious environment, pregnant with internal conflict, it will be the person who is able to maintain the wider vision of the whole, emanating a certain quality of stillness and calm rather than being swept up into the developing maelstrom, who will make a real difference.

Extending this idea further, one might be able to gain a better understanding of how those who meditate in complete stillness, deliberately retreating from the world at large, can have an enormously positive effect upon mankind at a distance. A consciousness which can embrace the entirety of the universe through a process of prayer and meditation can actually help to hold the various parts together in a state of equilibrium.

The Elements of Life

As Tibetan physicians, we are trained to maintain a holistic viewpoint of every patient we meet and to treat every person equally with compassion and understanding. We offer a perspective of the body in health and disease which was presented to the world through ancient Buddhist texts and which reveals the fundamental human problem to be ignorance, from which develops the three mental poisons, attachment, anger and closed-mindedness, manifesting in the body as the three humours, *rLung*, *Tripa* and *Badkan*. We attempt to engage and involve each person we treat in the healing process, so that they may truly participate in their personal path of development and transformation.

Each person is given a range of experiences, whether thought to be good or bad, which need, just like food, to go through a process of digestion, whereby the elements of all these experiences considered useful to the person are gradually transformed and assimilated into the psyche. This progression essentially takes some time, to allow further and further refinement of each experience into its essence, which at last may be absorbed into the heart and there embraced with love. Any elements of experience felt to be injurious can, once the process of assimilation and understanding has taken place, be discarded as waste.

This process of discarding unwanted elements of life is an extremely important one, just as the impure portion of food and drink has to be differentiated and expelled in order to purify the system. For if the impurities or waste products of the body were to be retained and assimilated as nutrients they would eventually poison the whole body. In the same way, our task in life is to attempt to rid ourselves of the three fundamental impurities, the mental poisons that so easily infect our condition, poison our lives and disrupt our peace of mind.

In this way, the process of digestion operates on a number of different levels as being of crucial importance to the body's health, and manifests on the physical level as the seven constituents and the three wastes. Here, these seven vital supporters of life are formed over a six-day period, during which a balanced, natural flow of the separation of nutrition from waste is needed, as a breakdown in the process would prove harmful to the body. As each constituent is developed from the one that precedes it in a process of increasing refinement of the essences extracted from the food, the body produces the three wastes of faeces, urine and perspiration, which are essential for the purification of the body. The presence of urine and faeces retains elements of the food in the body long enough to allow complete assimilation of the nutriments before the waste is expelled.

Just as we need time to truly understand and assimilate the various experiences in life, risking the build-up of an emotional or mental disorder if we attempt to gloss over something that we feel we cannot quite face and comprehend, so this six-day period of digestion must take its natural course. Digestion begins at the point when the food reaches the stomach to be decomposed by the Decomposing *Badkan*, given heat by the Digestive *Tripa*, and finally separated into two parts by the Fire-Accompanying *rLung*. This is the first day, whereby an initial separation of the nutritional essences of the food are extracted and transformed into blood, the life-giving fluid and moisturiser of the body, within the liver. The waste element of this process assists the development of the Decomposing *Badkan* in the stomach.

On the second day, the essence of blood transforms into flesh, which gives the body its form, and the waste part of this process becomes gall bile. On the third day, the essence of flesh transforms into fat, the body's lubricant, and the element of waste is excreted through such orifices of the body as the nose and mouth. Proceeding to the fourth day, the essence of fat is transformed into bone, the structural element of the body, and produces waste as the greasiness of the body and sweat.

Day five sees the essence of bone transforming into bone marrow, the body's source of vitality, and the waste matter forms the teeth, nails and pore hairs until on the last and sixth day, the essence of bone marrow transforms into the essential reproductive essence of the male semen and female ovum. The waste becomes skin, the faeces, body grease and discharge from the eyes. The reproductive essence becomes a vital super-essence residing in the heart, responsible for the strength and length of life, manifesting as a good complexion and general body glow.

This process of transformation of these seeds is an essential final stage in the whole process when even more refined elements of the reproductive seeds go up to the heart to form *mDang-chhog*, the most highly refined feature in the body. It is a vital essence which pervades the entire body by means of extremely subtle channels and which supports life. The brightness and radiance of the face is said to come from the super-essence of *mDang-chhog* in the heart, and it is responsible for physical and mental strength. When someone becomes overly worried and depressed, this energy decreases and the life might be in danger.

Therefore, in order to retain this super-essence in the heart it is so important to eat nutritious food and endeavour to be happy, refraining from mental tension and stress. This may seem difficult in a world which is facing so many problems and where there are many people suffering from sadness, anxiety and depression. Yet, as will be seen from the practice detailed at the end of this chapter, even the simple act of smiling can have a very real, direct effect upon this life supporting essence in the heart.

Tibetan medicine is a science of equilibrium, which understands the close relationship of our bodies to the universe as a form of cosmic embrace in the dance of existence. When we are in tune and at one with the universal forces, our body is in a state of health, but once we begin to fall out of step then disease is the result as the humours become unbalanced. As physicians we are therefore constantly seeking to restore balance within the body system and thereby a sense of balance in the person's condition in relation to outer experiences and events.

These are the essential points on Tibetan medicine, and I believe I have given you the best quality seeds. Compassion should be developed in this practice. When someone comes to see us, it doesn't matter who they are, whether they are important or not. The only thing that we should be concerned about is that they are suffering. If your interaction with a person, your experiences and relevant knowledge makes somebody smile, then you smile too.

Remember that in this life we may enjoy wealth, but in the final analysis it is only our accumulated merits that we can take with us when the time has come for us to leave this world.

The Practice of the Three Smiles

Throughout my medical consultations in India and all over the world, I always advise my patients to smile three times a day. This is a very easy yet inwardly powerful exercise that can help calm and ease the levels of stress in the body, which inevitably cause us harm and are linked to the increase of the *rLung* energy in the body, which can be so disruptive to our peace of mind. This exercise has a direct effect upon *mDang-chhog*, the super-essence which resides within the heart, and which from there pervades the whole body, maintaining longevity, and bringing a certain glow to the complexion. Certain people seem to naturally bring a positive glow into a room like a ray of sunshine which is particularly noticeable when they smile. This is a sign that the super-essence residing in that person's heart is in very good order.

This practice can be performed anywhere, and does not need any particular conditions in order to be performed correctly. In fact, it is arguably even more importantly conducted at times which are particularly stressful, for it will act as an antidote against the negative effects of stress. Putting it simply, it just requires you to smile three times a day, which will help to create the right conditions for an improvement in your body, mind and spirit.

Even flowers need certain conditions in order to bloom, such as the wind is needed to blow and develop the flower, water to moisten it and earth for its base. With these conditions we can enjoy looking at beautiful flowers. Otherwise the flower is simply a bud at first, just as firmly closed as the occasions when we shut off our heart and mind. If we recollect on our past, we will know that we have suffered from many illnesses, pain, aches, delirium, stress, anxiety and depression, so much so that sometimes we even seem to forget our true inner selves. This happens when the channels connecting our mind and body become either obstructed or disrupted by deranged energies in the body.

So it is very important to me to advise my patients to smile at least three times a day, whatever humoural disease they may be suffering. In very simple terms:

Be Happy!! Smile Three Times a Day!! – Recommendation for a *rLung* disease

Stay Cool!! Smile Three Times a Day!! – Recommendation for a *Tripa* illness

Warm up!! Smile Three Times a Day!! – Recommendation for a *Badkan* disorder

But by smiling, I mean smiling from the heart, not just on the surface, because if you cannot smile from the heart, life cannot be enjoyed. Even if you have every facility required for life, yet cannot produce a smile from the inner mind, you are not a happy person, and you cannot enjoy the wealth that you have.

So try smiling three times right now, and at the same time, just think that the first smile will eradicate anxiety, the second smile will eradicate stress and the third smile will eradicate depression.

Conclusion

W E LIVE IN A UNIVERSE into which we are inextricably embedded and intertwined, and into which we decide to be born. Like a spark from the sun, our soul spirals down through the heavens, bouncing across the cosmos, rushing headlong towards living, breathing life. Our soul is driven to enter the here and now on this planet which we call earth, for we have agreed to play our part in the vast cosmic whole, the interlaced fabric of existence that streams from time immemorial into the limitless beyond.

Our chosen birth holds the basis for all pleasure and pain, for suffering and happiness, for the vast richness of experience. For at birth we unavoidably enter the entire life process, the great wheel of transformation, the extraordinary journey from birth to death.

The mistake so many of us make is that we spend most of our lives missing the plot! We doggedly pursue our everyday lives, busily cramming every second with a trivial pursuit, when the greater journey remains so near, yet so far. Just as we are born into ignorance – so we die in ignorance. Such ignorance is not blissful, but a terrible waste of a great opportunity.

Birth plants us in the universal garden, where we are immediately connected to the forces of nature, the laws of physics, and the interconnections of creation. As we begin to grow, our sense of the interdependence of all that surrounds us is constantly expanding to encompass more and more forms of life, systems of energy and atmospheric forces out to the fringes of our solar system and beyond into the known and unknown universe. As particles within the ocean of existence, we are ceaselessly nourished by the matrix of energetic streams that enmesh humanity within the cosmic environment.

Just as the existence of a macrocosm implies the corresponding existence of a microcosm, so the outer universe will always lead us towards the inner universe, where we can find our particular blueprint, unique code and personal stamp. Here, a specific arrangement of the forces of existence determines our reason for being, our relationship to everything around us, our purpose in life. If we have the capacity to lift the veil and to truly and deeply look within, we may at last begin to intuit our basic reality, and in so doing may be given a glimpse of the tapestry of the gods, offering us a key to understanding the basic forces which we channel both consciously and unconsciously.

Every human being is a tiny, particularized facet in the universal jigsaw, born in answer to the question posed by the forces of existence at a split second in time. Tibetans refer to this as the workings of karma. Astrology charts this unique constellation of the planets at the moment of our first breath. Up to our last gasp we are answering a need of the times and potentially offering a solution to the problem. It may prove to be a lifetime's task to reach a vision of our part in the whole, yet it is a journey well worth making, and the brilliance of Tibetan medicine can assist us in shining a light upon a deeper understanding of ourselves.

In Tibetan medicine the world of the spirit is completely intertwined with the world of matter. The fundamental model for the body universe can be found within the balance of the three humours. This trinity of energies in every human being determines the nature of a person and defines to what extent he or she may be considered in sickness or in health. At its simplest level, if these energies are balanced and harmonious, then we may be blessed with health and happiness. But as soon as they are disturbed or unbalanced, sickness and unhappiness will inevitably result. A Tibetan physician aims to look within us, to weigh the balance of the three humours, and arrive at some form of diagnosis, so that a remedy may be prescribed.

Tibetan medicine is leading us towards the roots of our suffering

– our self-grasping, attachment and desire, our anger, arrogance and hatred, and our persistence in a state of ignorance whereby we close off our minds to anyone and anything else perceived to be a threat to the all-important 'I'. The Tibetans understand that the very instant that we chose to take human birth, we were propelled into a condition of sickness. This is the secret behind the three mental poisons. For even when we are in a state of perfect health, we are considered to be sick, because we have found ourselves in our human condition due to the negative emotions of desire, aggression and closed-mindedness.

The spark of the soul did not mutely allow itself to flutter down to earth – it wanted to be here. The very desire to be born required an act of force, an act of aggression to actually fight its way into life. Yet on the dense level of human existence we largely remain ignorant of our greater self, our inner spirit, our soul which is calling to us to achieve at least some insight into the nature of reality. For thereby we stand a chance of breaking the self-perpetuating process of birth, ignorance and death. To stand any chance of a decent view of the horizons within which we operate, we need to become more aware of the roots of our suffering, and look more carefully at our inner motivations. Tibetan medicine focuses immediately and most importantly on these roots. In this way, we are offered a route to healing, increased understanding, and greater personal awareness.

But how many of us dare to look inside ourselves to find the vital answer to our illness and our pain? We tend to feel we've been invaded, interrupted, or assaulted by an agent from the outside, like a virus, some affliction that we really don't deserve. We don't accept that in some way we might perhaps have played a part in every illness that befalls us. If we can take responsibility for health upon ourselves, we collaborate in what is a marvellous opportunity for growth and for development upon a personal level.

Tibetan medicine has achieved an unparalleled level of complexity and sophistication in a system that does not separate religion from medicine, and which looks upon the body as nature in miniature.

Through a very particular training that includes precisely defined spiritual practices, practitioners are able to achieve a high degree of extrasensory and supernatural powers. However, in response to those who perceive curing on the psychic and spiritual levels as some kind of hocus pocus, the doctor will always refer all medical skills and healing capacity back to the exact, proven science of the Four Tantras, and through these sacred teachings to the Medicine Buddha.

There is a powerful thread of alchemy running throughout Tibetan medicine, for it aims to transform the energies in the body by the use of various medicinal herbs and substances. All medicines and their prescriptions are imbued with and empowered by potent spiritual practices such as the use of mantras, prayers and recitations. Again, it is important to emphasize that such practices have been given to the physicians through an oral tradition traceable back to the Buddha. A Tibetan doctor is so attuned to the workings of the universal unconscious, that on occasions he or she may receive essential medical instructions by means of dreams and visions, which can subsequently be applied with supreme faith and diligence.

Historically, mercury, the base metal used in alchemy, was also used to great success within Tibetan medicine. Naturally this highly toxic substance was only used after it had been transformed and purified by an intense and exacting process. Because of its highly volatile nature, mercury had to be stabilized, but thereafter it proved to be highly effective in all cases of disease and generally improved the strength of the body. Purified metals and minerals such as mercury were used within special formulation pills, which could be used to support yogis who wished to retreat in meditation without normal food for long periods.

Somehow it seems that there is no limit to the wonders of Tibetan medicine. As has already been noted within this book, there is a particular and most profound synchronicity involved in the propelling of Tibet into exile, thereby facilitating a much wider dissemination of its teachings than ever before. Tibetan medicine was prepared thousands of years ago for the modern times and its particular diseases. The ancient texts refer to a period of 500 years, which is believed to have begun in the eighteenth century, and in which a total of eighteen modern microbial and infectious diseases will manifest. These are believed to include various forms of cancer, and AIDS, all of which Tibetan medicine is already helping to address. Increasingly, Western doctors are noticing this major contribution to humanity and are inviting physicians to participate in exchange and research in the shared aim of conquering modern diseases. So we would do well to hope and pray that the spread of Tibetan medicine will at least keep pace with, and hopefully overtake, the virulent spread of such modern diseases.

A particularly intense and profound impression of Tibetan medicine and its practitioners occurred when I accompanied a very great and deeply spiritual lady to consult Dr Pema Dorjee. Well over eighty years of age, she had been housebound for at least two years, suffering from an acute arthritic condition manifesting as severe pain in her legs. Although Tibetan medicine typically offers herbal pills to assist in healing the energy blocks within the body, on this occasion my friend insisted she did not want pills, but only a mantra, as she trusted Dr Dorjee's powers completely. I was privileged to witness Dr Dorjee silently reciting a healing mantra, after which we left his clinic. After three days my friend was completely cured of her arthritis.

Clearly there is a tantric way of healing with mantras, which my friend, a former traveller in India, must have understood. All energy is vibration, and this is naturally reflected in the body itself. Disease within the body will therefore manifest as dissonant, disordered vibrations. By reciting mantras, which carry within them a very powerful vibration of healing, the body can be refined and realigned as the discords within the body's vibrations are directly affected by the chanted mantras. In this sense the physician is somewhat similar to a piano tuner, for he is aiming to attune the body to a sense of 'perfect pitch', seeking to draw the body away from the density of pain and towards much more highly refined and healthier vibrations.

Clearly, through daily recitation, the same approach can be applied in order to purify the body's vibrations generally.

In Tibetan medicine, different mantras can be used for particular ailments, although there is an all-healing mantra of the Medicine Buddha which is very powerful. This mantra is an evocation of praise for the Supreme Healer, to whom all power is due, as follows:

> *Tadyatha Om Bhekhadze Bhekhadze Maha Bhekhadze Bhekhadze Raja Samudgate Svaha*

After witnessing the wonderful and seemingly miraculous healing of my friend, little did I know that ten years later I would enter the door of Dr Pema Dorjee myself – in a desperate state of post-traumatic shock, feeling completely vanquished.

As I sat beside Dr Dorjee I had expected some sort of pessimistic confirmation of serious ill health – instead he suddenly swung round and commanded me to look into his eyes. As I looked deep within the ocean of his vision, the storm within me subsided and peace enveloped me as I felt the inner shock move up through my body and out through the top of my head.

Whatever form of dharma medicine he used, I cannot begin to know. However, I experienced it as a miraculous blessing, when one ray of his compassion utterly transformed a feeling of crucial defeat into a sense of wonder and awe. This was reflected in his kindness and gentleness towards my feeling of being beaten down by the event that had caused the shock. Somehow, I understood that Dr Pema Dorjee had transferred the cosmic energy purity of the Medicine Buddha to me, when he said: "You're all right now. You still had a little bit of shock in the nervous system – now it will go away."

On reflection, it seems to me that this great doctor had summoned a very high healing power of light for a creative purpose. In fact, the visualization of light is a practice quite central to tantric healing. The visual training of physicians is very intense and particular, whereby they will meditate and focus upon precisely painted images of the Medicine Buddha, to the extent that they can produce this glorious scene in its entirety within the mind. This image within the mind is a living entity, to such an extent that the fully trained doctor has the power to visualize rays of light emanating from the Medicine Buddha, and entering the patient's body. These powerful rays of healing light, by means of a form of psycho-spiritual transference can penetrate the patient's body for the purpose of healing all forms of disease.

It seems that Tibetan medicine offers those who have ears to hear and eyes to see, an extraordinary catalogue of successful healing experiences – even in the face of potentially annihilating catastrophes. Dr Tenzin Choedrak has recounted the miraculous healing of some of the victims of the Chernobyl nuclear catastrophe after he prescribed some precious pills. Following a period of only twenty days, out of a total of twenty-two patients, only eight or nine remained in hospital, for the rest had been discharged:

> *I assembled all the doctors and asked them to have a look at the results of each patient. Symptoms like low blood pressure, swollen glands, palpitations and pains in the bones were eased and mitigated as if water had been poured over to soothe them.*
>
> **Knowledge of Healing, a film by Franz Reichle, Artificial Eye, Switzerland 1996.**

One of the first full-length films to deal extensively with Tibetan medicine, *Knowledge of Healing* explains the fundamental text of Tibetan medicine and demonstrates how it can bring relief to patients suffering from illnesses normally considered to be incurable in the West. There are a number of case studies, including a man with a heart condition from Switzerland. Clearly written off by conventional medicine, amazingly he is guided to a small but significant Tibetan herbal formula containing a number of different ingredients. It is the particular combination of many ingredients that provides the desired therapeutic effect. Tibetan doctors reportedly have over 1,000 natural substances from which they can compound medicine. The application of this particular formula ultimately saved this man's life.

After all the modern deliberations, analyses, examinations, tests and research, at the end of the day, it is a question of what works that is important. The Tibetan physicians remain humble in the face of such success, for their focus at all times remains upon the source of all healing power, the Medicine Buddha.

Tibetan medicine has not sought to sell itself, to advertise wild claims widely, to preach to the world its miracles – for after all, for the greater part of its centuries it was hidden within Tibet itself. Truly we are blessed to receive such ancient healing, and if anyone raises the question of proof, the following indisputable truism (from *Man: Known and Unknown* by John Langdon Davies) may be helpful:

> '*Medicine has one great advantage over other branches of knowledge: the only criterion of truth in medicine is that it should work.*'

Janet Jones

SHORT GLOSSARY OF TIBETAN AND BUDDHIST TERMS

Badkan – one of the Three *Nyespas*, or Humours, translated as phlegm, which is cool in nature, based on earth and water and represents all the fluids in the body.

Bardo – an intermediate state which represents the passage from one's death towards one's next life in the world.

Bodhicitta – an enlightened state of perfection in oneself for the sake of all other sentient beings in the world.

Bodhisattva – a person who lives in the world for the sole purpose of assisting all sentient beings.

Buddha – i) Buddha Shakyamuni; ii) completely enlightened person.

Buddha-field – a divine realm, or sacred place beyond the earthly plane of illusion.

Buddhahood – the stage of enlightenment where one becomes like a Buddha.

Buddha nature – literally the nature of the Buddha. Each physician aspires to realize the Buddha nature, specifically the Medicine Buddha nature within himself.

Buddha Shakyamuni, or Gautama Buddha – lived 563–483 BC, achieved perfect enlightenment and gave spiritual teachings known as the dharma.

Chakras – wheel-like psychic nerve centres which exist within the body, operating on the etheric level.

Dalai Lama – His Holiness the Fourteenth Dalai Lama, also known as Ocean of Wisdom and Wish Fulfilling Jewel, who is the spiritual and temporal leader of Tibet, and revered as an incarnation of the deity, Avalokiteshvara, the Buddha of Compassion, who has pledged to continue to incarnate into this world until all suffering has ceased.

Dharma – Teachings of the Buddha, or indisputable spiritual truth.

Emptiness – *Shunyata* in Sanskrit, a very high state of enlightenment, whereby everything is perceived and understood to be impermanent. This state also disperses the illusory feeling that we are separate from the people who surround us.

Enlightenment – spiritual liberation, or achievement of a high form of spiritual awareness.

Four Tantras – four medical texts known as the rGyu-shi (see below).

Guru – a teacher who has achieved a degree of realization.

rGyu-shi, or Four Tantras – the primary text of Tibetan medicine, held to be sacred as transmissions from the Lord Buddha, revelations from certain deities, and the result of research and development by various renowned Tibetan physicians. The version as referred to today was produced in the twelfth century by the physician, Yuthog Yonten Gonpo the Younger, who took all previous teachings and revelations and drew them together as the Four Tantras, called the *rGyu-shi*.

Ignorance – a blind and unenlightened state, where the mind is unaware of the nature of reality. This state leads to the arousal of what are termed the 'three mental poisons' of desire, anger and closed-mindedness.

Julai – another name for the Buddha Shakyamuni, meaning 'he who has gone likewise', or rather he who has followed in the steps of the great beings who have gone before him.

Karma – law of cause and effect, defining the present as the result of actions in the past, and the future as the result of actions in the present. An understanding of karma lies at the root of the Tibetan Buddhist's code of ethics.

Katak – traditional Tibetan white silk scarf, hung in monasteries and often offered to Lamas and Rinpoches by way of a request for a spiritual blessing.

Lama – literally 'la' means nobody is above this person in terms of spiritual experience, and 'ma' means someone whose compassion is like that of a mother – thus a spiritual practitioner of a very high calibre.

Lama Doctor – a Lama who also practises as a doctor.

rLung – one of the Three *Nyespas*, or Humours, translated as wind and responsible for all the different kinds of movement within the body.

Mandala – strongly symmetrical diagram, concentrated about a centre and generally divided into sections of equal size. In the centre, one typically finds the domain of the deity, around which is a circle, or a set of further circles, symbolizing all the phases of initiation and the different planes of consciousness. Mandalas are vehicles to concentrate the mind in meditation, and aids to visualization and initiation.

Mantra – a word or number of words, typically repeated, which have been potentized through spiritual practices and handed down orally, thus carrying within them a very powerful vibration, e.g. *Om*, *Ah* and *Hung* are visualized and recited during the Medicine Buddha empowerment ceremony.

Medicine Buddha, also known as the Blue-faced God, Great Physician, King of Aquamarine Light, King of Radiant Light, Sangye Menla, Teacher of all Medicine, Unsurpassed Physician, and Vaidurya – an emanation of Buddha Shakyamuni who manifested for the purpose of healing and giving medical teachings.

Menpa – Tibetan word for doctor.

Mount Meru – mythical mountain, regarded as the cosmic centre of the universe.

Mount Kailash – located in Tibet and believed to be a manifestation of Mount Meru.

Nirvana – a state of full enlightenment, enabling the person to experience freedom from the earthly cycle of existence.

Pandit – Indian term for a scholarly person.

Prana – termed as such in India as the energy of life, or consciousness, similar to one of the five types of *rLung*, known as Life-Sustaining *rLung*.

Reincarnation – Buddhist belief in rebirth, whereby humanity is continually reborn into this world until achieving enlightenment, which affords the possibility of liberation from the continuous cycle of existence.

Rinpoche – literally 'jewel' accorded typically to a lama, or lama doctor who is a recognized reincarnation of a previous lama, or lama doctor.

Sentient Beings – all beings with consciousness who have not attained Buddhahood.

Stupa – *Chorten* in Tibetan – a sacred monument which is a devotional symbol of the whole of creation throughout the cosmos.

Tanatuk – literally 'pleasing when looked upon' – a mountain plateau created by the Buddha Shakyamuni where he manifested as the Medicine Buddha.

Tantra – i) texts; ii) path to enlightenment, e.g. a Tibetan doctor understands the practice of medicine to be a spiritual path; iii) knowledge that protects the body.

The Ten Non-Virtuous Activities –
specific negative tendencies listed
according to the Buddhist system,
which are extremely harmful to others
and oneself. On the physical level these
are the act of killing, sexual misconduct
and stealing. As far as speech is
concerned they are slander, abuse, lying
and idle gossip. On the level of the
mind they are avarice, malice and
holding false views.

Terma – literally 'hidden treasures',
original teachings, typically directly
transmitted or falling from the divine
realms, which were subsequently buried
until the time was ripe for them to be
revealed and propagated, when they
would be revealed to a person with
supernatural knowledge, who was told
where to find the teachings.

Thangka – sacred Tibetan scroll
painting, used as a religious aid in ritual
actions, or visually in meditation. By
seeing the figures depicted,
concentrating on them, and identifying
with the central deity or personage, the
believer strives for 'liberation through
beholding'. Tibetan physicians use this
specifically to focus upon healing
deities, visualizing themselves as the
deity, e.g. the Medicine Buddha in order
to transmit divine healing to the patient.

The Three Mental Poisons – derived
from fundamental ignorance, these are
desire, anger and closed-mindedness,
respectively linked to the three humours
of *rLung*, *Tripa* and *Badkan*.

The Three *Nyespas* – three humours, or
three defects, or three harmers which
are three energies in the body, called
rLung, *Tripa* and *Badkan*. These
humours essentially need to be
balanced in order to maintain health.

Tonglen – a form of prayer whereby one
visualizes the act of taking into oneself
other people's pain and suffering, whilst
giving back in return an essence of
goodness.

Tripa – one of the Three *Nyespas*, or
Humours, translated as bile, and
corresponding to the element of fire,
responsible for the body's heat.

Vajrasattva – purifying deity, visualized
as part of the Medicine Buddha
empowerment ceremony.

Yoga – Sanskrit word meaning 'union',
which is a science of the body, mind,
consciousness and soul, aiming through
a range of postural and breathing
practices to promote control of the body
and mind to attain physical and
spiritual wellbeing, focusing the
individual on the true essence of reality.

Yogi, or Yogin – male practitioner of
yoga who has achieved a high level of
spiritual insight.

Yogini – female practitioner of yoga
who has achieved a high level of
spiritual insight.

BIBLIOGRAPHY

Avedon, John F. – *In Exile from the Land of Snows* – Wisdom Publications 1985

Baker/Shrestha – *The Tibetan Art of Healing* – Thames and Hudson 1997

Choedrak, Tenzin, Dr – *The Rainbow Palace* – Bantam Books 2000

Clark, Barry, Dr – *The Quintessance Tantras of Tibetan Medicine* – Snow Lion 1995

Clifford, Terry – *Tibetan Buddhist Medicine and Psychiatry – the Diamond Healing* – Aquarian Press 1984

Crow, David – *In Search of the Medicine Buddha* – Tarcher/Putnam 2000

Dalai Lama, the – *A Human Approach to World Peace* – Wisdom Publications 1984

Dalai Lama, the – *Stages of Meditation* – Rider 2001

Dhonden, Yeshi, Dr – *Healing From the Source* – Snow Lion 2000

Dhonden, Yeshi, Dr – *Health Through Balance* – Snow Lion 1986

Dorjee, Dr Pema with Richards, Elizabeth – 'Cures and Concepts of Tibetan Medicine' – Tibetan Medicine, Library of Tibetan Works and Archives, Series 2, 1981

Einstein, Albert – *Relativity: the Special and General Theory* – Crown Publications 1995

Evans-Wentz, W.Y. – *Tibetan Yoga and Secret Doctrines* – Oxford University Press 1958

Finckh, Elizabeth – *Foundations of Tibetan Medicine I* – Watkins 1978

Finckh, Elizabeth – *Foundations of Tibetan Medicine II* – Element 1988

Gonpo, Yuthog Yonten – *Chalak Chogye* – Men-Tsee-Khang Library (original ancient text, commentaries on the rGuy-shi)

Gyalpo, Sukar Lodoe – *Mepoi Shelung* – Men-Tsee-Khang Library (original ancient text, commentaries on the rGuy-shi)

Gyatso, Gyalwa Gendun, the second Dalai Lama – 'Extracting the Essence' – Tibetan Medicine, Library of Tibetan Works and Archives, Series 5, 1982

Gyatso, Sangay – *Bedurnyonpo* – Men-Tsee-Khang Library (original ancient text, commentaries on the rGuy-shi)

I-Ching – Richard Wilhelm translation – Arkana 1989

Jung, C.G. – *The Collected Works* – Routledge & Kegan Paul 1979

Men-Tsee-Khang – *Fundamentals of Tibetan Medicine* – Men-Tsee-Khang 1995

Norbu, Namkhai, Prof. – *On Birth and Life* – Tipografia Commerciale Venezia 1983

Pawo, Lopon – *Yenlak Gyepa* – Men-Tsee-Khang Library (original ancient text, commentaries on the rGuy-shi)

Rechung Rinpoche – *Tibetan Medicine* – Wellcome Institute 1973

Thrangu, Khenchen Rinpoche – *Medicine Buddha Teachings* – Snow Lion 2004

Tibetan Book of the Dead, The – translation by Fremantle & Trungpa – Shambhala 1975

Tibetan Medical Paintings – Plates and Text – Serindia 1992

Tibetan Medicine – Series of Annual Journals – Library of Tibetan Works and Archives

Trungpa, Chogyam – *Cutting Through Spiritual Materialism* – Shambhala 1973

Various – *The Buddha's Art of Healing* – Rizzoli, NY 1998

Wangyal, Lobsang, Dr – *Based on the Prophecy of Lord Buddha, a Brief Life Story of His Holiness the Dalai Lama and Related Events* – Men-Tsee-Khang 2000

Whitton, Joel L. & Fisher, Joe – *Life Between Life* – Warner 1988

Winder, Marianne – *Catalogue of Tibetan Manuscripts, Xylographs and Thangkas in the Wellcome Institute Library* – Wellcome Institute for the History of Medicine 1989

RESOURCES

Alpha Centre
E-mail: info@alphacentre.org.uk
Website: www.alphacentre.org.uk

Central Institute of Higher Tibetan
Studies (Deemed University)
Saranath, Varanasi, 221007, U.P. India
Tel: 0091 5422 586337
E-mail:ngawang_samten@yahoo.com
Website: www.smith.edu/cihts

Chagpori Tibetan Medical Institute
Trogawa House, North Point
Darjeeling 734104, West Bengal, India
Tel/Fax: 0091 3542 270266
E-mail: chagpori@satyam.net.in

Drepung Loseling Institute
2531 Briarcliffe Road, Suite 101
Atlanta, Georgia 30329, USA
Tel: 404 982 0051
Fax: 770 938 9505
E-mail: institute@drepung.org
Website: www.drepung.org

Drukpa Trust
114 Harvist Road
London NW6 6HJ, UK
Tel: 0208 964 2337
E-mail: london@drukpa.org.uk
Website: www.drukpa.org.uk

Kailash Centre of Oriental Medicine
7 Newcourt Street
London NW8 7AA, UK
Tel: (+44) 0207 722 3939
Fax: (+44) 0207 586 1642
E-mail: info@kailash.fsnet.co.uk
Website: www.orientalhealing.co.uk

Medicine Buddha Healing Center
6593 Clyde Road
Spring Green, W1 53588 USA

Tel: (608) 583-5311
Fax: (606) 583-4243
E-mail: mail@globalview-intl.com

Men-Tsee-Khang
Tibetan Medical & Astrological Institute
of H.H. the Dalai Lama
Gangchen Kyishong
Dharamsala – 176215, H.P., India
Tel: 0091 1892 222618
Fax: 0091 1892 224116
E-mail: tmai@men-tsee-khang.org /
tmai@vsnl.com
Website: www.men-tsee-khang.org

Rigpa
330 Caledonian Road
London N1 1BB, UK
Tel: (+44) 0207 700 0185
E-mail: enquiries@rigpa.org.uk
Website: www.rigpa.org.uk

Tibet Foundation
1 St. James' Market
London SW1Y 4SB, UK
Tel: (+44) 0207 930 6001
Fax: (+44) 0207 930 6002
E-mail: enquiries@tibet-
foundation.org.uk
Website: www.tibet-foundation.org.uk

Tibet House
1 Culworth Street
London NW8 7AF, UK
Tel: (+44) 0207 722 5378
Fax: (+44) 0207 722 0362
E-mail: secretary@tibet-house-
trust.co.uk
Website: www.tibet.com

Tibet Med
e-mail: info@tibetmed.org

INDEX

goat's milk 262
golden needle therapy 265
gossip, idle 194
grains 187
grapefruit 219
gravity 183
green pepper 219
grief 270
growths 151, 153, 251, 252
    see also cancer; tumours
Gyalwa Gendun Gyatso, the Second
    Dalai Lama 54

haemorrhoids 231
hair 179
    see also body hair; pore hair
hallucination 151, 163, 168
hands 101, 162
hatred xx, 140, 148, 149, 174, 194,
    207, 209, 235, 285
head 101, 167, 184, 198, 231
    crown of 109, 113, 170, 265
    needle inserted in 265
headache 180, 181, 211
    causes of 37, 248
    New Delhi example 248–9
healing, self healing 269–71
health
    healthy body 208
    negative 205
    positive 205
heart 37, 128, 129, 162, 180, 210, 211,
    231, 256, 257, 275
    pain 185–6
    problems 195, 201, 268, 289–90
heart attack 167
heat, application of (Tib. *metsa*) 233,
    264
    see also moxa
hepatitis 195, 268
herbs 7, 201
    harvest of 59–60
herpes 251
hiccoughs 166, 168, 231, 266
hidden meanings *see terma*

hidden treasures *see terma*
Hinduism 85
hips 162, 170, 210
hoarseness 189, 231
honey 262
hot
    energy 164
    powers 220
humility 42, 111, 235
humours, the three (Tib. *nyespas*) xx,
    35–6, 38–9, 58, 92, 98, 125,
    129–30, 147–50,
    150–3, 208, 209, 228, 284
    energies categorized into two types
    251–2
    firewood simile 148
    interactions with each other 150,
    212–13
    like fifteen workers 232
    like three brothers 164–5
    linked to seasons 213, 273–4
    linked to specific countries, or
    nations 213
    linked to specific regions 273
    linked to the five elements 85,
    153–4, 197–8
    location 210–11
    origins of 148
    pathways 211–12
    seesaw simile 212
    superficial understanding of 123
    table of characteristics and qualities
    218
    as a Trinity 85
Hung, letter 112, 114
hunger 149, 174, 258
hysteria 151, 168

ignorance xx, 35, 75, 124, 136–7, 138,
    140, 144, 148, 209, 277, 283, 285
illness 131, 133, 139
    beginning of 164–5
    experienced as an invasion 285
    see also disease
illusion 138, 176, 269, 271
impatience 222

prana 167
prayer 11, 25, 61, 78, 130, 143, 226, 235, 277
precious pills *see under* pills
pregnancy 42, 103
pride 138, 175, 180
profit 236
propaganda 87, 242
prostrations 191, 235
psyche 30, 80, 223, 275, 277
psychiatry 91, 93
psychic epidemics 135, 140
psychic reality 134
psychology 124, 140
psycho-spiritual transference 289
pulmonary 178
pulse 37–9, 56–7, 123, 248, 252, 254–7
    allowance for magnetic forces 273
    the art of taking the pulse 34, 39, 254
    Badkan 257
    bodhisattva 255
    condition of physician's hands and fingertips for reading 255
    conditions for reading 255
    correct position for taking 38
    death 255–6
    diagnosis 36, 37–8, 43
    discrepancy between sexes 257
    environmental factors affecting 273
    female 255
    fingers used 255
    like a messenger 37
    like a radish 255
    male 255
    measurement of beats 256
    radial 256
    rLung 257
    seasonal 255
    specific organs read 256–7
    and three humours 38–9
    time to read 254–5
    Tripa 257
    ulnar 256

see also Seven Amazing Pulses
purgatives 264
purging 152, 233
purification 108–10

qualities 165–6
    absorbent 166
    coarse 166
    cold 166
    hard 166
    light 166
    mobile 166
    to relieve a *Badkan* disease 218
    to relieve a *rLung* disease 218
    to relieve a *Tripa* disease 218
    the seventeen 216–20
    subtle 166
questioning, examination by (Tib. *driwa*) 253, 258–9

radial artery 38, 255
radishes 187
rage 209
rainbow 3–4, 99, 114
rainbow body 97
rains, torrential 213
rectum 170
red pepper 219
redness, in the face 176
reincarnation 93
rejuvenation 227, 232
    medicines for (Tib. *bChulen*) 251
relaxation 145, 184
religion 71, 72, 94
    as spiritual power 142
reproductive seeds (Tib. *khuwa*) 149, 186, 269, 279
    healing defective 232
    linked to life years 158
    reproductive essences 156, 158
    see also semen
restlessness 167, 258
rGyushi see Four Tantras, the
rheumatism 250
rhythms